Sir Laurence Olivier
1907 —

Property of DR. F. J. DONEVAN COLLEGIATE		
NAME	FORM	YEAR
Scott Pullen	4SK	88/89
David Brown	4AL	90/91
Tullis Rose.	4HW	91/92
Filip Swinski	4BA	92/93
Tracey Foshay	4PH	93/94
John Patterson	4KE	94
Melissa Hawley	4CA	97
Adrian Logan	5TM	97
CLAYTON CHURCHER	5EB	98
Stacey Jin	5EB	99
Long Nguyen	5KE	/00

HAMLET

THE FALCON

SHAKESPEARE

. . . and for his crest or cognizance a falcoun, his wings displayed argent, standing on a wreath of his colours, supporting a speare gould steeled as aforesaid. . . .

So in part reads the confirmation of the Grant of Arms made by the Herald's office to John Shakespeare in 1599 as described by Garter King of Arms.

Edited by BETTY BEALEY

HARCOURT BRACE JOVANOVICH, CANADA

HAMLET

by William Shakespeare

© 1963 BY ACADEMIC PRESS CANADA
COPYRIGHT© 1987 BY HARCOURT BRACE JOVANOVICH CANADA INC.,

15 16   88

ISBN 0-7747-1028-4

For my father
ERNEST RICHARD BEALEY

Words, words, words!

CONTENTS

SHAKESPEARE'S GREATNESS: A CAPSULE

> A thousand poets pried at life,
> But only one amid the strife
> Rose to be Shakespeare.
>
> *Robert Browning*

IN AN oversimplified analysis of the genius of Shakespeare, it may be said that he was a great poet, a great playwright, a great patriot, and a psychologist who had an unerring insight into human nature.

As a poet, he used words with unforgettable magic; the felicity of his phrases echoes all the way from Macbeth's:

> I have liv'd long enough: my way of life
> Is fall'n into the sear, the yellow leaf,

to Horatio's:

> Good night, sweet prince,
> And flights of angels sing thee to thy rest.

It ranges from Antony's "I am dying, Egypt dying" to Prospero's

> We are such stuff
> As dreams are made on; and our little life
> Is rounded with a sleep.

It extends from lyric sweetness to tragic splendour.

As a playwright, Shakespeare was a master of his art; he understood and practised with consummate success all the theatrical devices required for low comedy and high tragedy. Memorable scenes spring to mind: the quarrel of Brutus and Cassius in *Julius Caesar*, the blinding of Gloucester in *King Lear*, the trial in *The Merchant of Venice*, the play extempore in *Henry IV, Part I*, the scene of Duncan's murder and its sequel in *Macbeth*.

Shakespeare was a great patriot; his love for England shines through the lines of "time-honour'd Lancaster" in *Richard II:*

> This blessed plot, this earth, this realm, this England,
> This land of such dear souls, this dear dear land.

It speaks in the proud words of Philip Faulconbridge at the end of *King John:*

> This England never did, nor never shall,
> Lie at the proud foot of a conqueror.

But Shakespeare's chief glory lies in the creation of characters. Although Hamlet is the supreme example, on his heels tread Falstaff, Lear, Macbeth, Shylock, Rosalind, and a host of others. Browning's comment does indeed go to the heart of the matter.

BIOGRAPHY OF SHAKESPEARE

(This sketch does not pretend to be a definitive life; it is inserted only as a guide to the Multiple Choice Quiz, p. 284, which presents some miscellaneous facts about Shakespeare's life.)

Birth, Parents, Education

With regard to Shakespeare's birth, we know only that the baptismal register for the parish church of the Holy Trinity, Stratford, bears the following entry for April 26, 1564: *Gulielmus, filius Johannes Shakespeare.* The house on Henley Street is assumed to have been the place of his birth. Neither Shakespeare's father nor his mother could write; the former, a man of civic importance who later fell on evil days, signed documents with his mark, a pair of glovers' compasses. Shakespeare's mother, born Mary Arden, used a running horse as her "signature". Ben Jonson said of his friend Will that he had "little Latin and less Greek", but others have brushed aside his lack of a classical education by saying that he was "naturally learned". His knowledge of the work of the poet Ovid is evident in his writings. It is probable that he left the Stratford Grammar School at the age of thirteen; later in his youth, he may have been a schoolmaster in the country, according to a tradition reported by John Aubrey.

Family

Married at eighteen to Anne Hathaway, who was eight years older than he, Shakespeare was the father of three children: Susanna, and the twins, Hamnet and Judith, the latter named after a young couple who were friends of the Shakespeares. One of the great tragedies of Shakespeare's life was the death of his son in 1596 at the age of eleven. It has been suggested that the many precocious small boys in his plays owe their existence to Shakespeare's memories of Hamnet. Although both his daughters married, Shakespeare's own family became extinct with the death of his granddaughter Elizabeth in 1670. The three sons of his daughter Judith (Mrs. Thomas Quiney) died young: one in infancy, the other two in 1639.

The Years Between

A tradition, which cannot be substantiated, states that Shakespeare left Stratford in the late 1580's because he had been accused of poaching on the estate of Sir Thomas Lucy. For a number of years, we lose sight of him. Some critics maintain that he must have been a soldier in the Low Countries; others that he was a sailor. These convictions are based on his sound knowledge of both these occupations, the military and the sea-faring. Another tradition has it that he first made a living holding horses at the playhouse door. In 1592, however, a jealous playwright referred to him as "this upstart crow, beautified with our feathers". Shakespeare was already on the high road to fame and fortune.

Later Years

In 1596, Shakespeare's father applied for and in 1599 received a coat of arms: "Gould on a bend sable, a speare of the first, the point steeled proper" with the proud motto *Non sans droit*. In the year 1597, Shakespeare purchased the largest dwelling in Stratford, New Place, for the sum of sixty pounds; it was described as "a pretty house of brick and timber" with two barns and two gardens. A mulberry tree, reputed to have been planted by Shakespeare in his garden, was cut down in 1758. Shakespeare died at New Place on April 23, 1616, and was buried in the chancel of the parish church; he lies there still, since no one has apparently been bold enough to invoke the curse mentioned in his epitaph. In an elaborate will, which contained bequests to the poor of Stratford and to his friends for the purchase of "mourning rings", Shakespeare provided carefully for his family, leaving his wife specific items of furniture.

Achievements and Interests

In a period of about twenty years, Shakespeare wrote 37 plays, 154 sonnets, and 2 long poems: a record that indicates matchless energy and inspired industry. The great majority of his plays were acted at the Globe Theatre, which burned down in 1613 during a performance of what may have been Shakespeare's final play, *Henry VIII*. About half of his plays were published separately during his lifetime in quarto form, including the longest one, *Hamlet*. The shortest of the tragedies, *Macbeth,* was first published in the Folio of 1623.

Shakespeare's interests must have been wide and varied; it appears that he was keenly interested in sports, particularly bowling. He must have read widely, though the only book that we know he owned was a copy of Florio's translation of the writings of Montaigne, the French essayist. (Even the authenticity of his signature in it has been challenged.)

Certain American scholars have tried to discredit Shakespeare as the author of the plays, maintaining that Francis Bacon (or perhaps Christopher Marlowe) wrote them. The most distinguished and eminent critics, however, have no doubt that William Shakespeare wrote the mighty works attributed to him. "Any other assumption about the authorship of these works shows a wanton and reckless disregard of unimpeachable evidence" (Wilfred J. Osborne).

THE SOURCES OF HAMLET

The story of *Hamlet* is based on an old Norse legend found in a history of the Danes by Saxo Grammaticus, which was written towards the end of the twelfth century. In this tale, Feng and his brother Horwendil are rulers of Jutland under the overlordship of the King of Denmark. After slaying the King of Norway, Horwendil marries Gerutha, daughter of the Danish King. A son, Amleth, is born to them. Feng slays his brother in jealousy and marries the widow. Amleth, planning vengeance, pretends to be an idiot and confuses those about him by his oddly significant nonsense. In order to test his sanity, his enemies place his foster-sister in his way, but he is warned by his foster-brother and avoids the peril. One of King Feng's friends acts as a spy in an interview between Amleth and his mother, but Amleth discovers him and stabs him. Amleth convinces his mother of his sanity, tells her of his plan for revenge, and wins her over to his side. Feng sends Amleth to Britain with two companions who bear a letter containing a request to the British King to slay Amleth on his arrival. The Prince alters the document and sends the bearers to their deaths instead. Amleth returns, slays his uncle, and is named the successor to the throne. After many deeds of craft and daring, Amleth is killed in battle.

This story was translated by Belleforest into French (*Histoires Tragiques,* 1570); an English translation appeared in 1608. Since it is believed that Shakespeare's *Hamlet* was written between 1598 and 1602, it appears unlikely that he knew the Belleforest translation.

It is generally believed that Shakespeare's *Hamlet* was based on an earlier popular play on the subject by Thomas Kyd, author of the famous *Spanish Tragedy.*

THE TEXT

Editors today make use of three texts: the Bad Quarto (Q1) of 1603, an incomplete pirated version; the Second Quarto (Q2), which was probably printed from Shakespeare's own manuscript in 1604-5, by someone who had difficulty interpreting the playwright's handwriting; and the First Folio (F) which differs from Q2 (the most complete version) by the omission of 200 lines and the addition of 85. (The present text is based on Q2 with some of the more familiar phrases from F and accepted emendations by reputable editors.)

The terms "folio" and "quarto" refer to the sizes of sheets of paper. A folio is a sheet of paper folded once, producing a page approximately twelve by eight inches.[1] The Shakespearian folios

[1]William Shakespeare, *King Lear, A Facsimile of the First Folio Text,* Intr. by J. Dover Wilson (London, Faber & Faber Limited).

are made up of pages this size. The First Folio, containing thirty-six of the plays, was published in 1623; a single copy cost £1. In 1955, a copy of this Folio changed hands for £17,000. This edition was reprinted three times, the Fourth Folio appearing in 1685.

A quarto, on the other hand, is a sheet of paper folded twice, producing a page approximately five inches by seven inches.[1] About half of Shakespeare's plays are known to have been published in these six-penny pamphlets during his lifetime.

Below is given a section from the Introduction to the First Folio, by John Heming and Henry Condell.

It had bene a thing, we confesse, worthie to have been wished, that the Author himselfe had liv'd to have set forth, and overseen his owne writings. But since it hath bin ordain'd otherwise, and he by death departed from that right, we pray you do not envie his Friends, the office of their care, and paine, to have collected and publish'd them; and so to have publish'd them, as where (before) you were abus'd with diverse stolne, and surreptitious copies, maimed and deformed by the frauds and stealthes of injurious impostors, that expos'd them: even those, are now offer'd to your view cur'd, and perfect of their limbes; and all the rest, absolute in their numbers, as he conceived them. Who, as he was a happie imitator of Nature, was a most gentle expresser of it. His mind and hand went together: And what he thought, he uttered with the easinesse, that wee have scarse received from him a blot in his papers. But it is not our province, who onely gather his works, and give them you, to praise him. It is yours that reade him. And there we hope, to your divers capacities, you will finde enough, both to draw, and hold you: for his wit can no more lie hid, then it could be lost. Reade him, therefore; and againe, and againe. . . .

---

[1]William Shakespeare, *Hamlet, First Quarto, 1603, Shakespeare Quarto Facsimiles No. 7*, Intr. by W. W. Greg (London, Oxford University Press).

Structure of Hamlet, *Incorporating the
Main Incidents of Importance*

1 Revenge Plot
2 Norwegian Subplot
3 Romantic Subplot

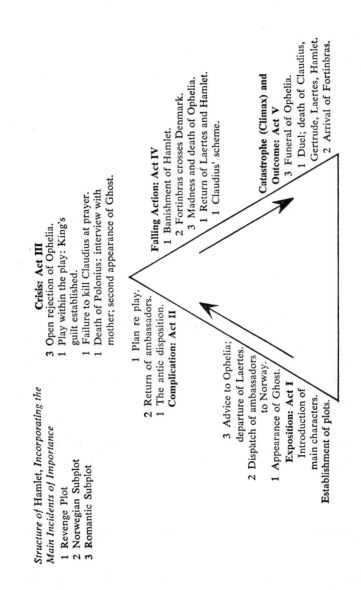

Crisis: Act III
3 Open rejection of Ophelia.
1 Play within the play: King's
  guilt established.
1 Failure to kill Claudius at prayer.
1 Death of Polonius: interview with
  mother; second appearance of Ghost.

Falling Action: Act IV
1 Banishment of Hamlet.
2 Fortinbras crosses Denmark.
3 Madness and death of Ophelia.
1 Return of Laertes and Hamlet.
1 Claudius' scheme.

**Catastrophe (Climax) and
Outcome: Act V**
3 Funeral of Ophelia.
1 Duel; death of Claudius,
  Gertrude, Laertes, Hamlet.
2 Arrival of Fortinbras.

1 Plan re play.
2 Return of ambassadors.
1 The antic disposition.
Complication: Act II

3 Advice to Ophelia;
  departure of Laertes.
2 Dispatch of ambassadors
  to Norway.
1 Appearance of Ghost.
Exposition: Act I
  Introduction of
  main characters.
Establishment of plots.

The Revenge Plot

Main Characters

Hamlet
Claudius
Gertrude
Ghost
Polonius
Laertes
Horatio

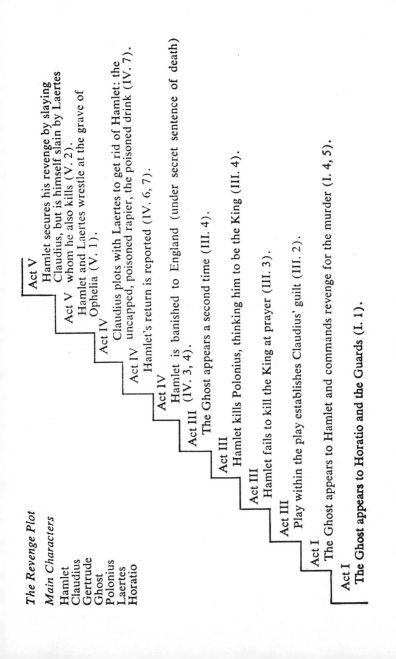

Act V
Hamlet secures his revenge by slaying Claudius, but is himself slain by Laertes whom he also kills (V. 2).

Act V
Hamlet and Laertes wrestle at the grave of Ophelia (V. 1).

Act IV
Claudius plots with Laertes to get rid of Hamlet: the uncapped, poisoned rapier, the poisoned drink (IV. 7).

Act IV
Hamlet's return is reported (IV. 6, 7).

Act IV
Hamlet is banished to England (under secret sentence of death) (IV. 3, 4).

Act III
The Ghost appears a second time (III. 4).

Act III
Hamlet kills Polonius, thinking him to be the King (III. 4).

Act III
Hamlet fails to kill the King at prayer (III. 3).

Act III
Play within the play establishes Claudius' guilt (III. 2).

Act I
The Ghost appears to Hamlet and commands revenge for the murder (I. 4, 5).

Act I
The Ghost appears to Horatio and the Guards (I. 1).

The *Norwegian Episode or Fortinbras Subplot*

Main Characters

Claudius
Ambassadors
Fortinbras
Hamlet
Horatio

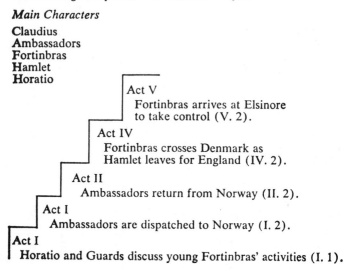

Act V
Fortinbras arrives at Elsinore
to take control (V. 2).

Act IV
Fortinbras crosses Denmark as
Hamlet leaves for England (IV. 2).

Act II
Ambassadors return from Norway (II. 2).

Act I
Ambassadors are dispatched to Norway (I. 2).

Act I
Horatio and Guards discuss young Fortinbras' activities (I. 1).

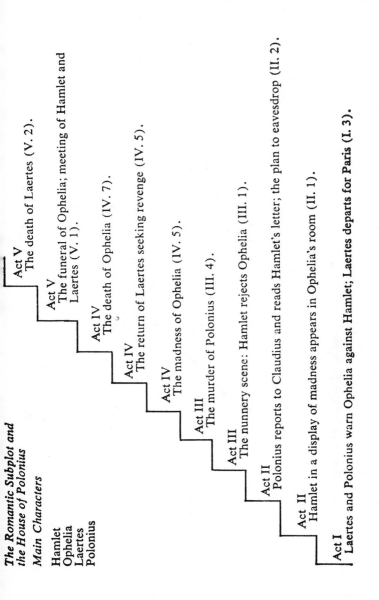

The Romantic Subplot and the House of Polonius

Main Characters

Hamlet
Ophelia
Laertes
Polonius

Act V
The death of Laertes (V. 2).

Act V
The funeral of Ophelia; meeting of Hamlet and Laertes (V. 1).

Act IV
The death of Ophelia (IV. 7).

Act IV
The return of Laertes seeking revenge (IV. 5).

Act IV
The madness of Ophelia (IV. 5).

Act III
The murder of Polonius (III. 4).

Act III
The nunnery scene: Hamlet rejects Ophelia (III. 1).

Act II
Polonius reports to Claudius and reads Hamlet's letter; the plan to eavesdrop (II. 2).

Act II
Hamlet in a display of madness appears in Ophelia's room (II. 1).

Act I
Laertes and Polonius warn Ophelia against Hamlet; Laertes departs for Paris (I. 3).

Show how the diagram below illustrates the various triangular relationships in the play.

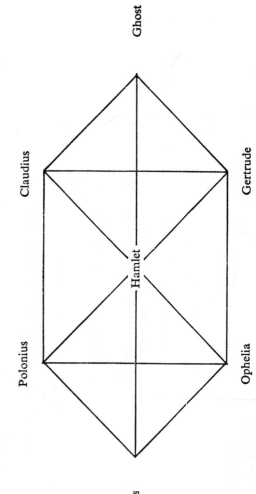

SOME NOTES ON THE CHARACTERS

Hamlet

"It is we who are Hamlet", wrote Hazlitt and in this statement we see the reason for the universal appeal of Shakespeare's most absorbing character. It also hints at the mystery of Hamlet, for who among us really knows himself? Thus the Prince of Denmark is an enigma, but a fascinating one. It is odd that many words beginning with the letter "i" can be used to describe his character. He is *intellectual* and *introspective* as shown in the probings of the soliloquies and in the restless, *inquiring* mind that plays with ideas and words. Professor Bradley[1] emphasizes this aspect of Hamlet's character; his intellectual genius "shows itself . . . as unusual quickness of perception, great agility in shifting the mental attitude, and a striking rapidity and fertility in resource".

Hamlet is both *impulsive* and *irresolute,* strange contradictions that emphasize the complexity of his character. He can murder Polonius without a moment's hesitation, and yet it would seem that the murder of Claudius is at last thrust upon him. He cries in the last soliloquy "I do not know/Why yet I live to say 'this thing's to do'." His poetic *imagination* reveals itself in the beauty of his words in praise of earth and its "majestical roof fretted with golden fire". His sense of humour shows itself in a fondness for the *ironic* and the satirical, and he can at times be supremely cynical. These aspects can be seen in his attitude towards Polonius and later towards Osric. A strain of cruelty is sometimes visible also. Even Horatio is moved to exclaim "Why, what a king is this!" when Hamlet tells how he deliberately sent Rosencrantz and Guildenstern to their deaths. His treatment of

---

[1]A. C. Bradley, *Shakespearean Tragedy,* (London, Macmillan & Co., Ltd., 1904), p. 113.

Ophelia in the nunnery scene also illustrates this quality. And yet he could be *idealistic;* even his enemy, Claudius, remarks "he, being remiss,/Most generous, and free from all contriving,/ Will not peruse the foils." Hamlet's apology to Laertes shows a winning generosity.

It has been stated that Hamlet is the only one of Shakespeare's characters who could have written the plays of his creator. His interest in the Players and his arrangements for *The Murder of Gonzago* illustrate this, but there is a histrionic vein in him as well, as we see when he plays the madman. (There are times when his excitable, hysterical behaviour makes us believe that he is perilously close to being truly insane.) That he is melancholy, in an almost pathological way, there is no doubt; his first soliloquy illustrates this in marked fashion.

Professor G. B. Harrison[1] emphasizes the qualities of Hamlet as a man of action: "The last thought in *Hamlet,* thrice stressed, is that he was a soldier; and the soldierly virtues are courage, intelligence, quick determination, ruthlessness." This echoes Fortinbras'

> Let four captains
> Bear Hamlet like a soldier to the stage,
> For he was likely, had he been put on,
> To have proved most royal.

Hamlet's loyalty to Horatio and his admiration for his friend's stability and good judgement reveal qualities that the Prince admired and wished he had:

> Give me that man
> That is not passion's slave, and I will wear him
> In my heart's core, ay, in my heart of heart,
> As I do thee.

Professor Dover Wilson[2] presents the theory that Hamlet is

[1]G. B. Harrison, *Shakespeare's Tragedies* (London, Routledge & Kegan Paul, Ltd., 1951), p. 109.
[2]J. Dover Wilson, *The Essential Shakespeare* (Cambridge, Cambridge University Press, 1952), pp. 104-7.

Shakespeare's effort to understand the brilliant, enigmatic, ill-starred Earl of Essex. He suggests that Essex, like Hamlet, possessed the following qualities: courtesy, kindness to inferiors, intellectual virtues, a passion for drama, an interest in spiritualism, an open and free nature, nobility of bearing, piety, bravery, a genius for friendship, brilliant wit, a love of field sports, hawking, and horsemanship; on the other side, moods of profound melancholy, a touch of insanity, dangerous impetuosity, frequent talk of suicide, coarseness, brutality and callousness to women, ruthlessness to those he hated, theatricality, and above all, complete inability to think out a continuous line of action.

No analysis of Hamlet's character would be complete without a reference to his disgust at sensual excesses. He speaks bitterly of the King's drinking habits and the "heavy-headed revel" that cause Denmark to be "traduc'd and tax'd of other nations". His mother's behaviour in posting "with such dexterity to incestuous sheets" fills him with loathing; it is this that prompts the misogyny to which he falls victim, and it is this that causes him to speak words of coarse brutality to Ophelia.

Actually, Ophelia's analysis is a very sound one; she refers specifically to Hamlet's "noble mind" and sums up his qualities in the following lines:

> The courtier's, soldier's, scholar's eye, tongue, sword,
> The expectancy and rose of the fair state,
> The glass of fashion, and the mould of form,
> The observ'd of all observers.

Perhaps the last words on the subject should be those of Horatio, intense in their simplicity: "Now cracks a noble heart."

Claudius

The character of Claudius is brought out in his one major soliloquy, in a few revealing remarks, and through the comments of Hamlet and the Ghost.

When first we meet him, he is shown to be a capable monarch, discreet and smooth. He deals skilfully and diplomatically with the Norwegian problem and with Laertes' request. Nevertheless, this is the man to whom the Ghost, his own brother, refers as "that incestuous, that adulterate beast" who won Gertrude with "witchcraft of his wit". That he is pleasant and plausible is brought out by Hamlet who refers to him as a "smiling, damned villain", one who "drains his draughts of Rhenish down" in the coarse and sensual indulgence of a corrupt court. And yet this man is not without remorse as shown in his aside "How smart a lash that speech doth give my conscience!" (In such lines and in his one soliloquy, Claudius seems father to Macbeth.) He is decisive in his dealings with Hamlet as he resolves, after the play within the play, to dispatch that dangerous young man to England. His plans for Hamlet's execution on arrival reveal his unscrupulous nature, but later he is not without courage in facing Laertes and the roused citizenry. His crafty nature is also revealed in the plans for Hamlet's murder, and we note too the clever way in which he takes advantage of Laertes and uses that young man to further his own designs. His predilection for poisoning as a method of ridding himself of those in his way suggests a treacherous, underhand nature. Although he is ambitious and hypocritical, his love for Gertrude is sincere and deep, but not deep enough to prevent her drinking from the poisoned cup. Hamlet, however, describes him contemptuously as "a mildew'd ear" who "from a shelf the precious diadem stole/ And put it in his pocket! . . . A king of shreds and patches." Granville-Barker sums him up as "a consummate hypocrite".

Gertrude

"Frailty, thy name is woman!" cries Hamlet. The Queen is weak, unfaithful, shallow, and sensuous. It is difficult to understand Hamlet's devotion to her, Claudius' love for her, or the affectionate tenderness of her first husband. Bradley compares her to a sheep in the sun. Only in the scene where Hamlet lashes out at her do we see any depth of emotion. She does remain loyal to her son from this point on, though she does not appear to break with Claudius. She shows affection for Ophelia, a desire to protect the King from the mob, and concern for Hamlet in his duel with Laertes. It may be that as she dies, she sees with dreadful clarity what kind of person Claudius is.

Polonius

According to Dr. Johnson[1], "Polonius is a man bred in courts, exercised in business, stored with observations, confident in his knowledge, proud of his eloquence, and declining into dotage." Polonius had been in his day a competent adviser, but his weaknesses appear to be sharpened and exaggerated by age. Dover Wilson sees in him a caricature of Elizabeth's minister, Burleigh. The old man's vanity is evident:

> Hath there been a time, I'ld fain know that,
> That I have positively said " 'tis so",
> When it prov'd otherwise?

His eloquence has degenerated into garrulousness and an old man's forgetfulness: "And then sir, does he this—he does—what was I about to say?"

His statesmanlike cunning has developed into a mania for spying and eavesdropping; his method has always been "by indirections" to "find directions out". His sententious moralizings are now a source of humour, and Hamlet dismisses him scornfully: "These tedious old fools!" His treatment of Ophelia shows a lack of both understanding and affection. Although Gertrude refers to him as the "good old man", we feel that as a meddlesome busybody, he was at least partly to blame for his own death. His epitaph is spoken somewhat bitterly by Hamlet:

> Thou wretched, rash, intruding fool, farewell; . . .
> Thou find'st to be too busy is some danger.

Laertes

Laertes is as different from Hamlet as night is from day. They

---

[1]*Samuel Johnson on Shakespeare,* W. K. Wimsatt, Jr., ed. (A Dramabook; New York, Hill and Wang, Inc., 1960), p. 110.

share only one quality: love for Ophelia. It is she who responds to her brother's advice in a quiet, meaningful way:

> Do not as some ungracious pastors do,
> Show me the steep and thorny way to heaven,
> Whiles like a puff'd and reckless libertine,
> Himself the primrose path of dalliance treads,
> And recks not his own rede.

Laertes' dissipated life in Paris is the object of his father's curiosity; however, on his return after the murder of Polonius, he shows impetuous determination to avenge his father's death. His unscrupulous nature is brought out in his willingness to accede to Claudius' dastardly scheme; indeed he goes him one better. In his desire to secure revenge on Hamlet, he is prepared "to cut his throat i' the church", should this be necessary. We feel that it is family pride, rather than love, that prompts him in this matter, but he does show genuine grief at his sister's death. He also shows some qualms of conscience in the duel with Hamlet, and we sense a sincerity in his desire to be forgiven as he dies. Hamlet in his own generosity had referred to Laertes as "a very noble youth".

Ophelia

Ophelia has been harshly criticized for being weak and ineffectual, and yet she deserves our pity and sympathy. Child-like and inexperienced, she turns naturally to her father for advice and is eventually caught (in a moment of crisis) between him and the man she loves. In trying to save her father from Hamlet, whom she believes to be insane, she tells a lie that many of us would feel to be justified. This conflict of loyalties, followed by the murder of Polonius at the hands of Hamlet, understandably makes her lose her mind. Her madness is tinged with pathos: "pray you, love, remember", and even in death she is associated with flowers: "And from her fair and unpolluted flesh/May violets spring."

Horatio

Horatio appears in the first scene of the play as a sceptic and a scholar, but it is his stability and sound judgement that make him memorable. Hamlet's admiration and affection for his friend are based on the integrity of Horatio's character; he is one who has taken "fortune's buffets and rewards" with equanimity and stoic courage. His heart and brain act together; this combination makes him a trusted, valued friend, the only one on whom Hamlet can rely. Nor is he afraid to tell Hamlet the truth. His loyalty to the Prince is so great that at Hamlet's death, he is on the point of committing suicide in order to join his friend. Only Hamlet's urgent request that Horatio live on to tell the true story prevents him from playing the "antique Roman".

Fortinbras

The very name of Fortinbras seems to symbolize the strong arm of the soldier. We hear of him first as a wild, immature youth "of unimproved metal, hot and full" who has "shark'd up a list of landless resolutes" for a raid against Denmark; soon, however, we learn that he has settled down and become a responsible commander, and when he leads his troops across Danish territory in an attack on Poland, he shows himself to be calm and competent. At the end of the play, he once more gives an impression of strength and determination as he takes hold of the situation and issues the necessary orders. He stands in sharp contrast to both Hamlet and Laertes as a strong-minded and single-minded man of action, an uncomplicated, ambitious pragmatist.

DRAMATIC DEVICES IN *HAMLET*

A STRUCTURAL DEVICES

1. *Establishment of the main plot and subplots:* apparent in Act I and in the skilful interweaving of these plots throughout the play.

2. *Conflict:* the clash of opposing forces without which there is no drama:
   a) man vs. man: Hamlet vs. Claudius and Hamlet vs. Laertes.
   b) man vs. himself: Hamlet's inner struggle.

3. *Crisis:* the turning point in the play. (In a Shakespearian play it usually occurs in the third act.) In *Hamlet,* most critics consider that the Prince's failure to kill the King at prayer is the turning point.

4. *Catastrophe:* the destruction (or failure) of the leading character (the protagonist). Hamlet's death might be considered the catastrophe, whereas the *climax* would be the fact that he kills Claudius and achieves his long-sought revenge. The arrival of Fortinbras, with the return to normality, marks the *outcome* of the play.

B DEVICES THAT ADD INTEREST

1. *Suspense:* a state of anxious uncertainty. In *Hamlet,* suspense rises and falls in a pattern of waves. Examples are numerous: whether the Ghost will appear to Hamlet, whether Hamlet will kill Claudius at prayer, whether Hamlet will secure his revenge in the final scene of the play.

2. *Surprise:* the occurrence of the unexpected; *e.g.,* Hamlet's return to Denmark after being banished to England.

3. *Coincidence:* the occurrence of events without apparent causal connection; *e.g.,* the arrival of the Players just when Hamlet can make most use of them.

4. *Contrast:* the juxtaposition of opposites; *e.g.,* within the character of Hamlet himself; between characters; *e.g.,* Hamlet and Laertes; in atmosphere; *e.g.,* between the grave-diggers' scene and the funeral of Ophelia.

5. *Parallelism:* here, the fact that two characters find themselves in similar situations; *e.g.,* Hamlet and Laertes.

6. *Nemesis:* the principle of retributive justice; *e.g.,* the death of Claudius.

7. *Foreshadowing of events:* a premonitory warning of what may happen; *e.g.,* Hamlet says "Thou wouldst not think how ill all's here about my heart."

8. *Irony:* the juxtaposition of incongruous elements; *e.g.,* that Laertes should be slain with the sword that he had uncapped and poisoned to bring about Hamlet's death.

9. *Dramatic irony:* the effect produced when a speech or situation has one meaning for the actor and an inner or opposite one for the audience. In *Hamlet,* there is dramatic irony in the fact that Hamlet is unaware of the uncapped, poisoned rapier, but the audience, Laertes, and Claudius are aware.

10. *Pathos:* that which excites pity; *e.g.,* the madness of Ophelia.

11. *Supernatural:* an agency above or outside the forces of nature; *e.g.,* the Ghost of Hamlet's father.

12. *Humour:* a) word play; *e.g.,* the grave-digger's pun on "arms" (V. i. 34 ff.).

    b) nimble repartee; *e.g.,* exchanges with Rosencrantz and Guildenstern (II. ii. 220 ff.).

    c) abuse of words; *e.g.,* the grave-digger's coinage of "argal".

    d) euphuism (artificial or affected style); *e.g.,* Osric's speeches (V. 2).

e) satire (the use of irony or ridicule to expose or discourage vice or folly); *e.g.*, Hamlet makes fun of Polonius (II. ii. 197 ff.). (The whole character of Polonius seems to be a satire on the undesirable characteristics of a meddlesome busybody.)

IMAGERY

Imagery has been defined by Laurence Perrine[1] as "the representation through language of sense experience". An image is therefore a sense impression.

In Caroline Spurgeon's *Shakespeare's Imagery*, the author uses the term, not to refer to descriptive details, but rather as synonymous with the terms simile and metaphor. Using this definition as her criterion, she finds 279 images in *Hamlet*. The dominant image is one involving rottenness, disease, and corruption. Claudius makes reference to "the quick o' the ulcer"; Hamlet urges Gertrude not to assume that his madness rather than her trespass speaks: "It will but skin and film the ulcerous place." The idea of a hidden tumour, mining all within, seems symbolic of the Danish court.

Because Shakespeare was a countryman, the play contains many images connected with nature, especially gardening. In Hamlet's first soliloquy, we find a reference to "an unweeded garden/That grows to seed". When speaking to his mother, he urges her not to "spread the compost on the weeds/To make them ranker". References to birds and animals abound: pelican, dove, chough, lapwing, hawk, porcupine, ape, tiger.

[1]Laurence Perrine, *Sound and Sense* (New York, Harcourt, Brace & World, Inc., 1956), p. 40.

Shakespeare's interest in games and sports is revealed in the various images connected with archery, hunting, fishing, and bowling. The last named was one of his favourite sports; he was fascinated by the "assays of bias" used by a player in directing the bowl to its target. Polonius refers to his political methods in this metaphor. A second bowling metaphor "ay, there's the rub" has become a proverbial phrase to describe an obstacle.

References to sleep are not as dominant as in *Macbeth,* but the "To be, or not to be" soliloquy contains a reference to the "sleep of death" and the dreams it may bring with it.

Shakespeare makes frequent references to the classical myths. Hamlet likens his mother to "Niobe all tears"; his father to Hyperion, Mercury, Mars, Jove; his uncle to a satyr. He contrasts himself with Hercules and tells Horatio that his (Hamlet's) imaginations may be "as foul/As Vulcan's stithy".

The mirror image too runs through the play. Hamlet uses it in his advice to the Players and in his chastisement of Gertrude. Ophelia calls him "the glass of fashion".

In addition, there are a number of images connected with the law, music, and the theatre. The last named is one of Shakespeare's favourites: "Each toy seems *prologue* to some great amiss"; "a *Vice* of kings"; "Bear Hamlet like a soldier to the *stage*"; "You . . . That are but mutes or *audience* to this *act*".

The most vivid and arresting images take the form of personifications. One of the most beautiful describes the coming of day, always a favourite topic with Shakespeare; it presents an unforgettable picture:

> But look, the morn in russet mantle clad
> Walks o'er the dew of yon high eastward hill.

The comparison of the stars to "wonder-wounded hearers" is a striking figure, and it is easy to picture "peace" with her "wheaten garland".

Shakespeare's fertile imagination is unmistakably evident in his use of images, drawn from a variety of sources and expressed in magic, memorable phrases.

THE SOLILOQUIES

A soliloquy is a speech made by an actor when he is alone on the stage. (It has been defined as a "thought projection".) The soliloquy has a threefold purpose: to reveal character, to advance the plot, and to create atmosphere. (In *Hamlet,* one soliloquy is delivered by Hamlet while the King kneels at prayer, but Claudius is not supposed to be aware of the Prince's presence.) Sir Laurence Olivier in his film *Hamlet* created the illusion of thought by having certain parts of the soliloquies recorded on the sound track, although on the screen his lips did not move.

Of the 4,000 lines in *Hamlet,* about 40 per cent are delivered by Hamlet himself, and of these, his seven soliloquies make up 210 lines. These soliloquies may be compared to seven pillars that hold up the arches of the play. It is significant that there is no soliloquy in the last act.

The first soliloquy (I. ii. 129-59) strikes a note of despair and shows us a Hamlet restrained from suicide only by the "canon of the Everlasting". His sorrow at his father's death is interwoven with his disgust at his mother's remarriage. The tone is one of anguish. Of this soliloquy, Sir John Gielgud[1] writes, "I find this the most exciting of the soliloquies to speak partly because it seems to set the character once and for all in the actor's and the audience's minds, and partly for its extraordinary, forthright presentation of information as to the whole plot, matched unerringly in the march of the words and the punctuation of the sentences."

In I.v.92-112, Hamlet is left alone on the stage after the departure of the Ghost and swears an oath of vengeance. In these lines, his course of action is determined; his feelings towards his father, "poor ghost"; towards his mother, "O most

[1] *John Gielgud's "Hamlet"*, Rosamond Gilder, ed. (New York, Oxford University Press, 1937), p. 38.

pernicious woman"; and towards his uncle, "smiling damned villain", are sharply indicated.

As Act II ends, Hamlet delivers his longest soliloquy, "O what a rogue and peasant slave am I" (II. ii. 549-607). In this speech, which is inspired by the First Player's lines about the fate of Priam and the plight of Hecuba, he accuses himself of cowardice for failing to achieve his revenge and works himself up into a violent paroxysm of frustrated fury. Following this emotional explosion, his intellect asserts itself, and he makes plans to insert a speech into *The Murder of Gonzago* and thereby test the King's guilt. The soliloquy ends on a note of triumphant anticipation: "the play's the thing/Wherein I'll catch the conscience of the king."

The most famous of the soliloquies, "To be, or not to be", occurs in III. i. 56-88. Here the emphasis is on the philosopher-prince, and the speech does nothing to advance the plot. As in his first soliloquy, Hamlet considers the problem of suicide and once more, for different reasons this time, abandons the idea of seeking his own death. The tone of this soliloquy is searching and meditative; it has a universal and timeless quality that suggests a core of stillness at the very heart of the play. (It occurs in the ninth of the twenty scenes into which the play is conventionally divided.) It is this soliloquy that, more than any other, creates the image of "the melancholy Dane".

Prior to his interview with the Queen, after the success of *The Mousetrap,* Hamlet delivers another soliloquy, the shortest in the play (III. ii. 380-92). Here he gives an indication of the way in which he proposes to treat his mother: "I will speak daggers to her, but use none."

On his way to his mother's closet, Hamlet finds Claudius at prayer (III. iii. 73-96) and makes the momentous decision not to kill him. Many critics regard this speech as the turning point of the play; certainly, many significant actions stem from it. Dr. Johnson found these lines "too horrible to be read or uttered".

Hamlet's final soliloquy (IV. iv. 32-66) is inspired by the appearance of Fortinbras and his army, who are crossing Denmark on their way to Poland. This speech is not found in F and is sometimes sacrificed in the interest of a shorter production of the play; yet it is intensely important for the analysis Hamlet gives of himself in it. He subjects his character and his behaviour to a searching examination and at the end speaks with determination: "O, from this time forth/My thoughts be bloody or be nothing worth!" The speech illustrates sharply the contrast between Hamlet and Fortinbras.

The soliloquies of Hamlet, expressed in phrases that form part of the vocabulary of every educated person, are undoubtedly one of the chief glories of the play.

WHY DID HAMLET DELAY?

Theories purporting to explain why Hamlet delayed in carrying out the Ghost's command to avenge his father's death range all the way from the position that there was no delay to the unsatisfactory explanation that had he murdered Claudius at once there would have been no play.

That there was delay seems apparent. The Ghost appears a second time "to whet thy (Hamlet's) almost blunted purpose". Hamlet himself in his final soliloquy implies as much: "How all occasions do inform against me,/And spur my dull revenge!"

Professor Harrison[1], nevertheless, states emphatically: "*Hamlet* is usually considered a play of problems; and the problem which has chiefly exercised the critics is why did he delay? To which

[1]Harrison, *op. cit.*, p. 109.

the answer is that in the play which Shakespeare wrote there was no delay."

Other critics and other readers are equally certain that there was delay. Some maintain that the difficulties were external, that Hamlet delayed because he wished to make sure that Claudius was done to death in such a way and at such a time that his guilt would be recognized by all; Hamlet would then be seen as having acted as the instrument of justice.

The view expounded by Goethe is no longer fashionable. He saw in the problem "a great deed laid upon a soul unequal to the performance of it. . . . A beautiful, pure, most moral nature, without the strength of nerve which makes the hero, sinks beneath a burden which it can neither bear nor throw off." Could such a man have sent Rosencrantz and Guildenstern remorselessly to their deaths?

Coleridge's theory has its supporters. "We see a great, an almost enormous intellectual activity, and a proportionate aversion to real action consequent upon it. Hamlet . . . loses the power of action in the energy of resolve." Hamlet, it is true, does refer to "some craven scruple/Of thinking too precisely on the event" as possibly being the cause of his delay. This is the theory adopted by those who believe in the tragic flaw, "the stamp of one defect" referred to in "the dram of eale" speech (I. iv. 31). Sidney Lee calls Hamlet "a study of the reflective temperament in excess".

Professor Bradley's explanation is that Hamlet was the victim of an almost pathological melancholy that paralysed action.

Bernard Shaw[1] maintains that Hamlet lived in a society that supported the vindictive idea of vengeance as an eye for an eye and a tooth for a tooth; Hamlet had instead evolved the doctrine of the futility and wickedness of revenge. (It is this theme that Shaw develops in *Caesar and Cleopatra*.) Shaw's explanation of the delay does not, as he admits, account for the fact that Hamlet

---

[1]*Shaw on Shakespeare,* Edwin Wilson, ed. (A Dutton Paperback; New York, E. P. Dutton & Co., Inc., 1961), p. 80.

sends Rosencrantz and Guildenstern to their deaths without a tremor.

A modern psycho-analytic interpretation is that put forward by Dr. Ernest Jones[1] in *Hamlet and Oedipus*. Of Hamlet's insoluble inner conflict he says, "The call of duty to kill his stepfather cannot be obeyed because it links itself with the unconscious call of his nature to kill his mother's husband, whether this is the first or the second; the absolute 'repression' of the former impulse involves the inner prohibition of the latter also."

There is no final and definitive explanation; the heart of the mystery eludes us, as it eluded Hamlet himself:

> I do not know
> Why yet I live to say 'this thing's to do,'
> Sith I have cause and will and strength and means
> To do't.

CRITICS' COMMENTS

General Observation. If the dramas of Shakespeare were to be characterized each by the particular excellence which distinguishes it from the rest, we must allow to the tragedy of *Hamlet* the praise of variety. The incidents are so numerous that the argument of the play would make a long tale. The scenes are interchangeably diversified with merriment and solemnity; with

[1]Ernest Jones, *Hamlet and Oedipus* (A Doubleday Anchor Book; Garden City, Doubleday & Company, Inc., 1949), p. 102.

merriment that includes judicious and instructive observations, and solemnity not strained by poetical violence above the natural sentiments of man. New characters appear from time to time in continual succession, exhibiting various forms of life and particular modes of conversation. The pretended madness of Hamlet causes much mirth, the mournful distraction of Ophelia fills the heart with tenderness, and every personage produces the effect intended, from the apparition that in the first act chills the blood with horror to the fop in the last that exposes affectation to just contempt.[1]

Hamlet belongs to the same category of drama as *The Spanish Tragedy*: Shakespeare deals with a son avenging his father, instead of a father avenging his son. He borrowed other details, including a ghost, and a play within the play. But the revenge material is transformed so as to bring out the maximum of significance in the theme. Most revenge plays operate in a moral vacuum; Shakespeare revitalized the genre (we may suppose) by imagining a sensitive and civilized person, such as himself, in the role of the avenger. Hamlet is contrasted with the more conventional avenger, Laertes, who is bloody, bold, and resolute. He avenges his father, and acts in a way that many critics, including even Coleridge, suppose that Hamlet should have done. But he is put in the play precisely for the purpose of showing us what a Hamlet who unhesitatingly carried out his father's wishes would be. When Hamlet, in the duel scene, cries 'I'll be your foil, Laertes' the words are true in an ironical sense.

The function of Fortinbras is similar. Although Hamlet contrasts his own inactivity with the restless ambition of his rival, with some admixture of envy and shame, we are not really meant to admire wholeheartedly the

delicate and tender prince,
Whose spirit with divine ambition puffed,
Makes mouths at the invisible event.

[1]*Samuel Johnson on Shakespeare*, W. K. Wimsatt, Jr., ed. (A Dramabook; New York, Hill & Wang, Inc., 1960), p. 110.

At first sight there might seem to be more reason for believing that Horatio was intended to show up Hamlet's weaknesses. The stoical friend, who is never passion's slave, is contrasted (we are assured) with the neurotic and hysterical prince. . . . Although Horatio is a foil to Hamlet, Hamlet's weaknesses are the maladjustments of an extraordinary man, of one who suffers, as Lascelles Abercrombie put it, from 'the heroism of moral vacillation'.[1]

The problem presented by the tragedy of "Hamlet" is one of peculiar interest in at least two respects. In the first place, the play is almost universally considered to be the chief masterpiece of one of the greatest minds the world has known. It probably expresses the core of Shakespeare's philosophy and outlook on life as no other work of his does. Bradley[2] writes, for instance: "Hamlet is the most fascinating character, and the most inexhaustible, in all imaginative literature. What else should he be, if the world's greatest poet, who was able to give almost the reality of nature to creations totally unlike himself, put his own soul straight into this creation, and when he wrote Hamlet's speeches wrote down his own heart?" Figgis[3] calls Hamlet "Shakespeare's completest declaration of himself." Taine's[4] opinion also was that "Hamlet is Shakespeare, and at the close of a gallery of portraits, which have all some features of his own, Shakespeare has painted himself in the most striking of them all." It may be expected, therefore, that anything which will give us the key to the inner meaning of the tragedy will necessarily provide a clue to much of the deeper workings of Shakespeare's mind.

---

[1] Kenneth Muir, *Shakespeare and the Tragic Pattern,* Proceedings of the British Academy, Vol. XLIV (London, Oxford University Press, 1958), pp. 149-50.
[2] Bradley: *Oxford Lectures on Poetry,* 1909, p. 357.
[3] Darrell Figgis: *Shakespeare: A Study,* 1911, p. 320.
[4] Taine: *Histoire de la Littérature Anglaise,* 1866, t. 11, p. 254.

In the second place, the intrinsic interest of the play itself is exceedingly great. Already in 1711 the then Lord Shaftesbury[1] could describe it as "that piece which appears to have most affected English hearts and has perhaps been oftenest acted of any which have come upon our stage." Since then, of course, its fame has become world-wide, and it has moved countless millions. This universal appeal shows that its inmost theme must contain something to which the heart of mankind in general reverberates, and there is little doubt that this resides in the personality of the hero. Bradby[2] truly calls him "a central figure of surpassing interest and genius, which has gripped the imagination of the learned and the unlearned in all ages and which will continue to fascinate so long as the mind of man is haunted by the mystery of life and death." Dover Wilson[3] gives as his opinion that the understanding of Shakespeare's "Hamlet" is the greatest of all literary problems. Of the hero he says[4] that "to spectators in the theatre he is more convincingly lifelike than any other character in literature."[5]

I do not believe that Shakespeare intended us to pluck out the heart of Hamlet's mystery, since the play is concerned partly with the mystery of human personality. But I think it could be shown that Hamlet is placed in a corrupt society and faced with a moral problem for which there is no ideal solution. He has to work out his own salvation in fear and trembling; he has to make a moral decision, in a complex situation where he cannot rely on cut-and-dried moral principles, or on the conventional code of the society in which he lives; and on his choice depend

---

[1]Quoted by Stoll: *Shakespeare and other Masters*, 1940.
[2]C. F. Bradby: *The Problems of Hamlet*, 1928, p. 60.
[3]J. Dover Wilson: *Hamlet*, 2nd Edition, 1936, Introduction, p. xi.
[4]Idem: *What Happens in "Hamlet,"* 1925, p. 219.
[5]Ernest Jones, *Hamlet and Oedipus* (A Doubleday Anchor Book; Garden City, Doubleday & Company, Inc., 1949), pp. 23-25.

the fate of the people he loves and the fate of the kingdom to which he is the rightful heir.[1]

This, it would appear, is the way of Hamlet's tragedy. His supreme gift for philosophic thought allows him to know the universe better than the little world of which he is bodily a part. But his acts must be in this physical world: and his mind has distorted for him the particular objects of his actual environment. So he cannot act properly within it: or rather, towards those parts of it which the stress of his feeling and the heat of his imagination have made especially liable to intellectual distortion, he cannot oppose the right response. He can kill a Rosencrantz, but not his villainous uncle.[2]

In *Hamlet,* Shakespeare draws a complete character, not for the comparatively barren purpose of 'creating' a Hamlet for our admiration, but in order to show how he, like the others, is inevitably engulfed by the evil that has been set in motion, and how he himself becomes the cause of further ruin. The conception which unites these eight persons in one coherent catastrophe may be said to be this: evil, once started on its course, will so work as to attack and overthrow impartially the good and bad; and if the dramatist makes us feel, as he does, that a Providence is ordinant in all this, that, as with the Greeks, is his way of universalizing the particular event.[3]

Hamlet was not a single consistent character: like most men he was half a dozen characters rolled into one. There can be no questions, in the face of the text and the action of the play, that

[1]Muir, *op. cit.,* p. 154.

[2]H. B. Charlton, *Shakespearian Tragedy* (Cambridge, Cambridge University Press, 1948), pp. 102-3.

[3]H. D. F. Kitto, *Form and Meaning in Drama* (London, Methuen & Co., Ltd., 1956), p. 330.

Hamlet was greatly puzzled by the fact that he wanted neither the crown nor his revenge badly enough to kill the king, or even to shove him out of his way. He can kill him in a moment of excitement (his killing of Polonius is in intention a killing of the king); but when he is in his normal state, he simply reflects and criticizes. He is amazed at his own futility from the point of view of Fortinbras, the man of action. He watches Fortinbras' men "going to their graves like beds" about a scrap of land "that is not tomb enough and continent to hide the slain"; and yet, though he has ten times as much cause for action, he finds somehow that a crown, for which his uncle committed fratricide, does not interest him as much as the players, and that revenge is not worth the mess the king's blood would make on the floor. He asks himself whether he is a coward, pigeon livered and lacking gall to make oppression bitter.

All this is quite natural. Men who are superior to vulgar cupidities and ambitions, and to vulgar rancours, always do seem weak and cowardly to men who act on them. Sometimes they seem so to themselves. There is no contradiction or inconsistency in Hamlet to anyone who understands this.[1]

Hamlet, the student and thinker, is much alive to the import of words. His very first utterance is a bitter pun.[2] And the speech that follows, with its ". . . inky cloak . . . windy suspiration of forc'd breath . . . fruitful river in the eye," shows him nice in his choice of them, for sound and sense combined. He is speaking in public, of course; deliberately and for effect.

Yet words come easily to him, and he takes an artistic pleasure in them. Imagination finds them for him quicker than thought will; there is delight in that. And, stirred by passion, he will pile them up, phrase upon phrase, until he seems possessed

[1]*Shaw on Shakespeare,* Edwin Wilson, ed. (A Dutton Paperback; New York, E. P. Dutton & Co., Inc., 1961), pp. 82-83.
[2]A pun with Shakespeare, needless to say, was not necessarily a comic thing at all.

by words—and he despises the futile satisfaction of it. For words themselves he distrusts; they also are things which "seem," "the trappings and the suits" of reality, tricking the speaker as often as the hearer; and they are a weak man's weapon. Hamlet, in fact, despises in himself one of his chief abilities, and this is a part of the discord which disables him.[1]

In the first soliloquy, 'O, that this too too solid flesh', Hamlet is not so much actively contemplating suicide as passively longing to be dead. And the respect which makes it unthinkable to resort to self-slaughter is that the Everlasting has set his canon against it. In a way there is something of a pose in Hamlet's gesture: as if a young poet peering into the waters of a pool should long for the eternal quiet of its depths, but should be kept to the bank for fear that the water might be too cold. How much deeper in human nature are the constraints which withhold the Hamlet of the 'To be, or not to be' soliloquy! No merely intellectual recognition of a theological injunction, but a primitive fear of the unknown after-world. 'What dreams may come when we have shuffled off this mortal coil.' The first speech is that of a sensitive soul in spiritual discomfort, the second is that of a man in profound despair. The discovery of the murder of his father by his uncle, of an act of uttermost human sacrilege, drives him to abysses of grief deeper than those occasioned by his mother's frailty. Something more human, more overt and intelligible than the Freudian hypothesis is the main stress of Hamlet's tragic incapacitation.[2]

Shakespeare does not try to keep the play at poetic pitch throughout; he has for long seen the dramatic unwisdom of that.

---

[1] H. Granville-Barker, *Preface to Hamlet* (A Dramabook; New York, Hill & Wang, Inc.), p. 203.
[2] Charlton, *op. cit.*, p. 92.

But he has also passed beyond any simple mechanical division into poetry and prose; poetry for heroics and sentiment, prose for buffoonery. He has learned how to modulate his verse with ease to the expressing of many moods; his prose too; and to run the gamut, if he will, from the sublime to the commonplace without a break.

Verse prevails, of course. Not only is it by convention the dominant medium for such a play, but he needs, for his subject, its compelling and illusive power. Convention dictates prose for the Grave-diggers, and convenience its use for commentary upon the versified *Murder of Gonzago*. For the rest, Shakespeare will always have, seemingly, a specifically dramatic reason for employing it.

The longest stretch of prose begins when Polonius "boards" Hamlet, continues through the Rosencrantz and Guildenstern examination in lunacy, the reception of the Players (Æneas' tale to Dido relieving it), and is suddenly, violently broken and ended by the outburst of

O, what a rogue and peasant slave am I! . . .

The reason for its use here is obvious enough. The action is at a standstill; the impulse of verse would be wasted on it. Hamlet himself is adrift upon the slack water of doubt and impotence, no pulsing emotion left in him, nothing for poetry to express. The detached, sceptical mind—

What a piece of work is a man! how noble in reason! . . . and yet, to me, what is this quintessence of dust? . . .

—inevitably speaks in prose.

We have prose for the quiet pessimism of the graveyard. What else is possible? How fatally verse would compromise the gentle gravity, the limpid clarity of

Alas! poor Yorick. I knew him, Horatio; a fellow of infinite jest, of most excellent fancy. . . .

As well try to put the eighteenth chapter of St. Luke into verse!

We have prose for the scene with Osric and the anonymous Lord; a dry prelude to the high-colored drama of the final scene. The encounters with Rosencrantz and Guildenstern and with Claudius after the play-scene are all cast in prose; this, I think, is to throw the harsh mask of Hamlet's eccentricities here into contrast with the soliloquies hereabouts and the scene with Gertrude (all cast in verse), in which we see his true visage. And he is made to break suddenly into prose in the scene with Ophelia, to shatter the delicate melody of her tendering back his gifts, her

> Take these again; for to the noble mind
> Rich gifts wax poor when givers prove unkind,

with the strident

> Ha, ha! are you honest? . . . Are you fair? . . . That if you be honest and fair, your honesty should admit no discourse to your beauty. . . .

—and so, seemingly, to shatter the last of the harmony between them and of the beauty of his love for her. As if for a reversal of the process, the prose of the graveyard-scene shifts, with the arrival of the sorry little procession, to verse, stiff in cadence at first:

> The Queen, the courtiers: who is that they follow?
> And with such maimed rites? This doth betoken
> The corse they follow did with desperate hand
> Fordo its own life. . . .

But kindling to the anguish of

> I lov'd Ophelia; forty thousand brothers
> Could not, with all their quantity of love,
> Make up my sum. . . .

for which prose would never do.

We may say that, in the main, the prose Hamlet is never the innermost man. For the expression of that—of the combination of thought and feeling, instinct and impulse, and of the twilight travail of the spirit which has place there—only poetry will serve.[1]

In a letter of July 27, 1897, to Ellen Terry, Shaw hinted at what he would do with a Hamlet *production as opposed to what Henry Irving had done and what he assumed Forbes Robertson would do in his forthcoming production.*

. . . I am certain I could make Hamlet a success by having it played as Shakespear meant it. H. I. [Henry Irving] makes it a sentimental affair of his own; and this generation has consequently never seen the real thing. However, I am afraid F.R. [Forbes Robertson] will do the usual dreary business in the old way, and play the bass clarinet for four hours on end, with disastrous results. Lord! how I could make that play jump along at the Lyceum if I were manager. I'd make short work of that everlasting "room in the castle." You should have the most beautiful old English garden to go mad in, with the flowers to pluck fresh from the bushes, and a trout stream of the streamiest and ripplingest to drown yourself in. I'd make such a scene of "How all occasions do inform against me!"—Hamlet in his traveling furs on a heath like a polar desert, and Fortinbras and his men "going to their graves like beds"—as should never be forgotten. I'd make lightning and thunder (comedy and tragedy) of the second and third acts: the people should say they had never seen such a play before. I'd—but no matter.[2]

[1]Granville-Barker, *op. cit.*, pp. 191-3.
[2]*Shaw on Shakespeare,* Edwin Wilson, ed. (A Dutton Paperback; New York, E. P. Dutton & Co., Inc., 1961), p. 84.

HAMLET, PRINCE OF DENMARK

DRAMATIS PERSONAE

CLAUDIUS, *king of Denmark.*
HAMLET, *son to the late, and nephew to the present king.*
POLONIUS, *lord chamberlain.*
HORATIO, *friend to Hamlet.*
LAERTES, *son to Polonius.*
VOLTIMAND,
CORNELIUS,
ROSENCRANTZ,
GUILDENSTERN, *courtiers.*
OSRIC,
A Gentleman,
A Priest.
MARCELLUS,
BARNARDO, *officers.*
FRANCISCO, *a soldier.*
REYNALDO, *servant to Polonius.*
Players.
Two clowns, *grave-diggers.*
FORTINBRAS, *prince of Norway.*
A Captain.
English Ambassadors.
GERTRUDE, *queen of Denmark, and mother to Hamlet.*
OPHELIA, *daughter to Polonius.*

Lords, Ladies, Officers, Soldiers, Sailors, Messengers, and other
Attendants.

Ghost of Hamlet's Father.

SCENE: *Denmark.*

1   The introductory question creates tension at the outset.

2   **me:** The emphasis is on this word because normally the sentinel on guard would challenge the newcomer; **unfold:** disclose, identify.

3   **Long live the king:** the password for the night. Note the irony.

6   **carefully:** punctually.

7-9   Note the references to the time, the weather, and the mood of the speaker; **For this . . . thanks:** a now familiar quotation. Why? **sick at heart:** This phrase "gives us a grim first impression of a Denmark demoralized and in danger, its tried leader gone" (Granville-Barker).

10   Perhaps Barnardo pauses before the phrase "quiet guard".

13   **rivals:** partners; **bid them make haste:** Why?

15   **the Dane:** the King of Denmark.

16   **Give you good night:** God give you, etc.

19   **a piece of him:** a somewhat flippant reply, in contrast to the nervous uneasiness of the others. It may be a reference to the cold.

ACT I

Scene 1

ELSINORE. A PLATFORM BEFORE
THE CASTLE.

Francisco at his post. Enter to him Barnardo.

Barnardo.   Who's there?

Francisco.   Nay, answer me: stand and unfold yourself.

Barnardo.   Long live the king!

Francisco.   Barnardo?

Barnardo.   He.   5

Francisco.   You come most carefully upon your hour.

Barnardo.   'Tis now struck twelve; get thee to bed, Francisco.

Francisco.   For this relief much thanks, 'tis bitter cold,
   And I am sick at heart.

Barnardo.   Have you had quiet guard?

Francisco.   Not a mouse stirring.   10

Barnardo.   Well, good night.
   If you do meet Horatio and Marcellus,
   The rivals of my watch, bid them make haste.

Francisco.   I think I hear them; Stand ho, who is there?

   Enter Horatio and Marcellus.

Horatio.   Friends to this ground.

Marcellus.   And liegemen to the Dane.   15

Francisco.   Give you good night.

Marcellus.   O, farewell, honest soldier,
   Who hath reliev'd you?

Francisco.   Barnardo hath my place;
   Give you good night.   *Exit.*

Marcellus.   Holla, Barnardo!

Barnardo.   Say,
   What, is Horatio there?

Horatio.   A piece of him.

20 Note Shakespeare's method of introducing characters to the audience.

21 Note the effect created by the phrase "this thing".

23 **fantasy:** imagination.

29 **approve our eyes:** corroborate what we have seen.

30 Note Horatio's easy confidence. Why is this stressed?

31 **assail your ears:** force you to listen.

33 **two nights:** "The play opens on the eve of the coronation and marriage of Claudius; and the Ghost begins to walk three days before the ceremony" (Dover Wilson).

35 **last night of all:** last night; *nights* is understood after "all"

36 **yond:** yon (yonder); **star:** probably a planet, since it is referred to as having a "course"; **pole:** pole-star.

37 **his:** its; the possessive neuter singular is found nine times in F; however, the editors or printers may be responsible for its occurrence. Milton uses *its* only three times, and there are no examples of its usage in the King James version of the Bible. *It* was sometimes used for *its*. See *King Lear* (I. iv. 235-6): "The hedge sparrow fed the cuckoo so long/That it had it head bit off by it young."

39 **S.D. Enter Ghost:** Shakespeare himself is said to have played this part, a fact that suggests that he intended the audience to see the Ghost. (Shakespeare is also known to have played the part of Adam in *As You Like It*.)

42 **Thou art a scholar:** Being educated, Horatio could use the proper Latin formulae to exorcize the spirit if it proved to be an evil one. It was also believed that a ghost could not speak unless it was first addressed by a mortal.

44 **horrors:** terrifies.

45 **It would . . . to:** It wants to be spoken to. (Ghosts could not speak until spoken to.)

46-49 **What art . . . march:** Who are you that have unlawfully appeared at this time of night and have illegally put on the noble and soldierly form (in which the late King of Denmark formerly went to war)? **sometimes:** formerly.

50 **stalks:** strides. What is implied about the Ghost's way of walking and about its mood?

Barnardo.   Welcome Horatio, welcome good Marcellus.   20
Horatio.   What, has this thing appear'd again to-night?
Barnardo.   I have seen nothing.
Marcellus.   Horatio says 'tis but our fantasy,
  And will not let belief take hold of him,
  Touching this dreaded sight twice seen of us;   25
  Therefore I have entreated him along,
  With us to watch the minutes of this night,
  That if again this apparition come,
  He may approve our eyes and speak to it.
Horatio.   Tush, tush, 'twill not appear.
Barnardo.   Sit down a while,   30
  And let us once again assail your ears,
  That are so fortified against our story,
  What we have two nights seen.
Horatio.   Well, sit we down,
  And let us hear Barnardo speak of this.
Barnardo.   Last night of all,   35
  When yond same star that's westward from the pole
  Had made his course to illume that part of heaven
  Where now it burns, Marcellus and myself,
  The bell then beating one,—
      Enter Ghost.
Marcellus.   Peace, break thee off, look, where it comes again!   40
Barnardo.   In the same figure like the king that's dead.
Marcellus.   Thou art a scholar, speak to it, Horatio.
Barnardo.   Looks it not like the king? mark it, Horatio.
Horatio.   Most like; it horrors me with fear and wonder.
Barnardo.   It would be spoke to.
Marcellus.   Speak to it, Horatio.   45
Horatio.   What art thou that usurp'st this time of night,
  Together with that fair and warlike form,
  In which the majesty of buried Denmark
  Did sometimes march? by heaven I charge thee speak!
Marcellus.   It is offended.
Barnardo.   See, it stalks away.   50

51 How is Horatio's sense of urgency brought out?

53 **tremble and look pale:** an example of Shakespeare's "indirect stage directions" and evidence that he visualized the action on the stage in his mind's eye.

56 **might:** could.

57-58 **sensible and . . . eyes:** reliable witness of my sense of sight. Contrast Horatio's manner before he sees the Ghost with his attitude after he sees it.

61 **Norway:** the King of Norway, the country being used often by Shakespeare to refer to the monarch. See "Denmark" above (I. i. 48).

62 **parle:** parley. The incident and the late King's expression must have made a deep impression on Horatio.

63 **the sledded Polacks:** Poles on sledges (a famous crux or disputed passage). F reads *sledded Pollax;* Q1 and Q2 read *sleaded pollax;* another reading is *sledded poleaxe;* that is, a leaded (heavy) battle-axe (Harrison).

65 **jump:** exactly.

66 **martial stalk:** The warlike appearance and behaviour of the King are significant.

67 **in what . . . work:** with what specific intentions?

68 **gross and scope:** general range.

69 **bodes some . . . state:** implies that some unnatural disturbance is in store for Denmark.

70 **Good now, sit down:** Be so good as to sit down now.

71-72 **why this . . . land:** why the soldiers of the guard, so meticulous and alert, force the people of the land to labour night after night (in the shipyards and munition works of the period); **subject:** collective singular for the plural.

73 **cast:** casting.

74 **foreign mart:** purchasing in foreign countries.

75 **impress:** forced service.

77 **toward:** in the wind (round the clock, seven days a week).

71-78 The picture is one of feverish preparation for war.

83 **prick'd:** spurred; **emulate:** jealous.

Horatio.   Stay, speak, speak, I charge thee speak! *Exit Ghost.*
Marcellus.   'Tis gone, and will not answer.
Barnardo.   How now, Horatio? you tremble and look pale:
   Is not this something more than fantasy?
   What think you on't?   55
Horatio.   Before my God I might not this believe,
   Without the sensible and true avouch
   Of mine own eyes.
Marcellus.   Is it not like the king?
Horatio.   As thou art to thyself.
   Such was the very armour he had on,   60
   When he the ambitious Norway combated;
   So frown'd he once, when, in an angry parle,
   He smote the sledded Polacks on the ice.
   'Tis strange.
Marcellus.   Thus twice before, and jump at this dead hour,   65
   With martial stalk hath he gone by our watch.
Horatio.   In what particular thought to work I know not,
   But in the gross and scope of my opinion,
   This bodes some strange eruption to our state.
Marcellus.   Good now, sit down, and tell me, he that knows, 70
   Why this same strict and most observant watch
   So nightly toils the subject of the land,
   And why such daily cast of brazen cannon,
   And foreign mart for implements of war,
   Why such impress of shipwrights, whose sore task   75
   Does not divide the Sunday from the week;
   What might be toward, that this sweaty haste
   Doth make the night joint-labourer with the day:
   Who is't that can inform me?
Horatio.   That can I.
   At least the whisper goes so; our last king,   80
   Whose image even but now appear'd to us,
   Was, as you know, by Fortinbras of Norway,
   Thereto prick'd on by a most emulate pride,
   Dar'd to the combat; in which our valiant **Hamlet**

86 **seal'd compact:** formal agreement.

87 **heraldry:** The College of Heralds had the power to arrange formal combats and to enforce its own rules of procedure.

89 **stood seiz'd of:** possessed (a legal term).

90 **a moiety competent:** an equivalent portion.

91 **gaged:** pledged; **had return'd:** would have returned.

94 **carriage of . . . design'd:** intention of the clause as drawn up.

96 **unimproved metal:** undisciplined, unschooled spirit.

97 **skirts:** outlying districts.

98 **shark'd up:** picked up as a scavenger shark would do, collected haphazardly; **landless resolutes:** desperate adventurers with no property. (Another reading is *lawless.*)

100 **stomach:** spice of danger; hence, requiring courage.

101 **state:** statesman.

103 **terms compulsatory:** conditions forced upon us.

106 **head:** source (as of a river).

107 **romage:** hurly-burly (bustle, commotion).

109 **sort:** suit (**well may it sort:** that is, perhaps it is appropriate); **portentous:** ominous.

112 **moth:** mote, speck of dust (such a particle in the eye can be very unpleasant; similarly, the appearance of the Ghost disturbs the mind).

113 **state:** community; another meaning is *condition.*

114 **Julius:** There are more references to Julius Caesar in Shakespeare's plays than to any other historical character. How may this be explained?

115-16 **the sheeted . . . gibber:** Corpses in shrouds (winding sheets) uttered shrill, meaningless noises. Note the imitative harmony. Why is it effective? Compare this passage with the corresponding lines in *Julius Caesar* (II. ii. 24).

116 The following line is apparently omitted; it probably contained a reference to prodigies, such as comets, in the sky.

118-19 **disasters in the sun:** eclipses, thought to be of evil omen; possibly, sun-spots; **the moist . . . stands:** the moon, which controls the tides.

(For so this side of our known world esteem'd him)   85
Did slay this Fortinbras; who by a seal'd compact,
Well ratified by law and heraldry,
Did forfeit, with his life, all those his lands
Which he stood seiz'd of, to the conqueror:
Against the which a moiety competent   90
Was gaged by our king, which had return'd
To the inheritance of Fortinbras,
Had he been vanquisher; as, by the same cov'nant
And carriage of the article design'd,
His fell to Hamlet; now sir, young Fortinbras   95
Of unimproved metal, hot and full,
Hath in the skirts of Norway here and there
Shark'd up a list of landless resolutes,
For food and diet, to some enterprise
That hath a stomach in't, which is no other   100
(As it doth well appear unto our state)
But to recover of us by strong hand
And terms compulsatory, those foresaid lands
So by his father lost; and this, I take it,
Is the main motive of our preparations,   105
The source of this our watch, and the chief head
Of this post-haste and romage in the land.
Barnardo.   I think it be no other, but e'en so;
    Well may it sort that this portentous figure
    Comes armed through our watch so like the king   110
    That was and is the question of these wars.
Horatio.   A moth it is to trouble the mind's eye:
    In the most high and palmy state of Rome,
    A little ere the mightiest Julius fell,
    The graves stood tenantless, and the sheeted dead   115
    Did squeak and gibber in the Roman streets:
    .   .   .   .   .   .

Pathetic fallacy

As stars with trains of fire, and dews of blood,
Disasters in the sun; and the moist star,
Upon whose influence Neptune's empire stands,

120 **almost to doomsday:** almost as if it were doomsday, when a great darkness would supposedly cover the earth. Total eclipses of the moon had occurred twice in 1598, much to the alarm of the superstitious.

121 **precurse:** forerunners.

122 **harbingers:** officials sent ahead to make preparations when the court went on a progress or on state journeys; hence, as here, forerunners; **still:** always.

123 **prologue to . . . on:** forecast of the approaching calamity. Shakespeare often uses terms from drama metaphorically.

125 **climatures:** climate, country (Harrison). Why does Shakespeare have the Ghost appear again?

109-25 These lines are omitted in F, which may have been printed from an acting edition; they are found in Q2. Account for their omission in the later volume. What purpose does their inclusion serve?

127 **cross:** make the sign of the cross. In some productions of the play, Horatio here holds up his sword hilt; **blast:** destroy, strike with withering power. It was believed that evil spirits were powerless against this sign. It has been suggested that the meaning is *cross its path,* a dangerous procedure; **illusion:** spirit.

129 Lines 129, 132, and 135 betray the speaker's agitation.

133 **art privy to:** hast secret knowledge of.

134-8 **happily:** haply, perchance. Note the reasons suggested by Horatio for the fact that the Ghost is walking.

140 **partisan:** long-handled battle-axe, spear with cutting blade.

141 What action would take place on the stage?

145 What further hint is given here with regard to the behaviour of the Ghost? Why do they feel ashamed?

147 The crowing of the cock betokened the approach of dawn; at daybreak, spirits from the other world returned to their places of abode.

148-9 **and then . . . summons:** The picture is that of a guilty creature, conscience-troubled, who has long been fearing an arrest that has finally come about. In Shakespeare, the start or involuntary movement is an indication of a guilty conscience. Banquo's remark to Macbeth (I. iii. 51-52) supports this: "Good sir, why do you start, and seem to fear/Things that do sound so fair?"

150 **trumpet:** The metaphor suggests that the rooster is the herald of the dawn, just as the trumpet announces the arrival of an important personage.

151 **lofty:** of sound, *high.*

Was sick almost to doomsday with eclipse: 120
And even the like precurse of fear'd events,
As harbingers preceding still the fates
And prologue to the omen coming on,
Have heaven and earth together demonstrated
Unto our climatures and countrymen.   125
      Re-enter Ghost.
But soft, behold, lo where it comes again!
I'll cross it though it blast me; stay, illusion;
If thou hast any sound or use of voice,
Speak to me,
If there be any good thing to be done   130
That may to thee do ease, and grace to me,
Speak to me,
If thou art privy to thy country's fate,
(Which happily foreknowing may avoid)
O, speak!   135
Or if thou hast uphoarded in thy life
Extorted treasure in the womb of earth,
For which, they say, you spirits oft walk in death,
Speak of it, stay and speak! (*The cock crows.*) Stop it,
    Marcellus.
Marcellus.   Shall I strike at it with my partisan?   140
Horatio.   Do, if it will not stand.
Barnardo.   'Tis here!
Horatio.   'Tis here!
Marcellus.   'Tis gone!   *Exit Ghost.*
    We do it wrong, being so majestical,
    To offer it the show of violence;
    For it is as the air, invulnerable,   145
    And our vain blows malicious mockery.
Barnardo.   It was about to speak when the cock crew.
Horatio.   And then it started like a guilty thing,
    Upon a fearful summons; I have heard,
    The cock that is the trumpet to the morn   150
    Doth with his lofty and shrill-sounding throat

152 **god of day:** Apollo; although the religious imagery of the play is predominantly Christian, there are references to the deities of classical mythology.

153 **sea or . . . air:** the four elements of which all matter was composed; according to the belief of the times, there were demons (attendant spirits) associated with each element.

154 **extravagant:** wandering beyond its appointed bounds; **erring:** roaming as in *knight errant*.

156 **probation:** proof.

157 **faded:** Consider the effectiveness of this verb as opposed to *vanished*.

158 **'gainst:** against, in preparation for (the coming of that season).

160 Note the musical quality of this lyrical line. *The Bird of Dawning* is the title of a novel by John Masefield. Give examples of other books that derive their titles from Shakespeare's works.

162 **strike:** blast; the planets (including the moon) were believed to have a harmful influence.

163 **takes:** bewitches. Compare *The Winter's Tale* (IV. iv. 118-20): "daffodils,/That come before the swallow dares, and take/The winds of March with beauty."

165 Note Horatio's scepticism, as befitting a scholar; see also I. i. 148-9.

166-7 **the morn . . . hill:** Some texts print *eastern*. Consider the difference. This is one of the loveliest metaphors in Shakespeare. "Russet" may mean reddish-brown or grey. Either colour could suggest the beginning of daylight; the former is more colourful, perhaps suggesting brown autumn leaves (" 'tis bitter cold"); the latter may refer to the first pale light. Compare *Romeo and Juliet* (III. v. 9-10): "Night's candles are burnt out, and jocund day/Stands tiptoe on the misty mountain tops."

170 Note the skill with which Hamlet's name is brought into the play for the first time.

See also p. 249.

2 **green:** fresh.

Awake the god of day, and at his warning,
Whether in sea or fire, in earth or air,
The extravagant and erring spirit hies
To his confine; and of the truth herein   155
This present object made probation.
Marcellus.   It faded on the crowing of the cock.
Some say that ever 'gainst that season comes
Wherein our Saviour's birth is celebrated,
The bird of dawning singeth all night long,   160
And then they say no spirit dare stir abroad,
The nights are wholesome, then no planets strike,
No fairy takes, nor witch hath power to charm,
So hallow'd, and so gracious is that time.
Horatio.   So have I heard and do in part believe it.   165
But look, the morn in russet mantle clad
Walks o'er the dew of yon high eastward hill:
Break we our watch up; and by my advice
Let us impart what we have seen to-night
Unto young Hamlet, for upon my life   170
This spirit, dumb to us, will speak to him:
Do you consent we shall acquaint him with it,
As needful in our loves, fitting our duty?
Marcellus.   Let's do't, I pray; and I this morning know
Where we shall find him most convenient.   175

Exeunt.

Scene 2

A ROOM OF STATE IN THE CASTLE.

Flourish. Enter the King, Queen, Polonius, Laertes,
Voltimand, Cornelius, Lords, Attendants, and Hamlet.

King.   Though yet of Hamlet our dear brother's death
The memory be green, and that it us befitted
To bear our hearts in grief, and our whole kingdom

4   **contracted in . . . woe:** drawn into an expression of grief.

5   **discretion:** prudence; **nature:** feeling.

8   **sometime:** former.

9   **jointress:** partner.

10   **defeated joy:** Note this and other expressions that imply compromise. The King handles the situation expertly; **defeated:** marred.

11   **auspicious:** full of gladness; **dropping:** tearful.

13   **dole:** grief.

14   **barr'd:** excluded.

15-16   **gone with . . . along:** approved of.

18   **holding a . . . worth:** underestimating our true value.

20   **out of frame:** out of gear.

21   **colleagued:** coupled; **his advantage:** advancing himself.

23   **importing:** concerning.

27   **we have here writ:** What stage business would accompany these words?

29   **impotent:** powerless.

31   **gait:** course.

32   **proportions:** required numbers for the task force.

38   **delated:** conveyed to you; **allow:** The verb has been attracted by the plural noun that precedes it.

39   **commend:** be evidence of.

To be contracted in one brow of woe.
Yet so far hath discretion fought with nature   5
That we with wisest sorrow think on him
Together with remembrance of ourselves:
Therefore our sometime sister, now our queen,
The imperial jointress to this warlike state,
Have we, as 'twere with a defeated joy,   10
With an auspicious and a dropping eye,
With mirth in funeral, and with dirge in marriage,
In equal scale weighing delight and dole,
Taken to wife: nor have we herein barr'd
Your better wisdoms, which have freely gone   15
With this affair along. For all, our thanks.
Now follows that you know; young Fortinbras,
Holding a weak supposal of our worth,
Or thinking by our late dear brother's death
Our state to be disjoint, and out of frame,   20
Colleagued with this dream of his advantage,
He hath not fail'd to pester us with message
Importing the surrender of those lands
Lost by his father, with all bands of law,
To our most valiant brother; so much for him.   25
Now for ourself, and for this time of meeting,
Thus much the business is; we have here writ
To Norway, uncle of young Fortinbras,
Who, impotent and bed-rid, scarcely hears
Of this his nephew's purpose, to suppress   30
His further gait herein, in that the levies,
The lists and full proportions, are all made
Out of his subject; and we here dispatch
You good Cornelius, and you Voltimand,
For bearers of this greeting to old Norway,   35
Giving to you no further personal power
To business with the king, more than the scope
Of these delated articles allow:
Farewell, and let your haste commend your duty.

41 **nothing:** not at all.

43 **suit:** request.

44 **speak of reason:** make any reasonable request.

45 **lose your voice:** be denied.

47-49 **native:** akin; what is the King's purpose in this reference to Polonius?

42-50 Note the repetition of Laertes' name, as if the King cannot do enough for him.

52 **from whence:** actually redundant since "whence" means *from where.*

56 **pardon:** permission.

60 **will:** That Polonius is playing with words is shown by his use of the word "seal'd", which suggests a document.

62 **Take thy fair hour:** Go when conditions are favourable.

63 **and thy . . . will:** May you spend your time happily and becomingly.

64 **cousin:** kinsman (here, nephew).

65 Throughout the scene, we have been poignantly aware of the brooding figure of Hamlet, his face pale, his traditional black a sombre contrast to the gay colours of the King and his court. His first cryptic words arrest our attention; **a little more than kin, and less than kind:** "It is oddly appropriate that Hamlet's first words should be a word-play on which the commentators are equally divergent and indecisive" (Ridley). Professor G. B. Harrison explains the line as follows: "too near a relation (uncle-father) but far from dear". The terse, venomous comment speaks volumes. Claudius, if he hears it, pretends to ignore it.

66 **clouds:** of grief.

67 **too much in the sun:** a remark typical of Hamlet. The pun implies a) in the harsh bright light of the court and b) in the relation of a son.

68 **nighted colour:** mourning black. Hamlet's sombre attire is in marked contrast to the brilliance of the court.

69 **Denmark:** the King.

70 **vailed:** lowered. Compare *The Merchant of Venice* (I. i. 28-29): "Vailing her high top lower than her ribs/To kiss her burial."

Cornelius. } In that and all things will we show our duty. **40**
Voltimand. }
King.   We doubt it nothing, heartily farewell.
                    Exeunt Voltimand and Cornelius.
  And now, Laertes, what's the news with you?
  You told us of some suit, what is't, Laertes?
  You cannot speak of reason to the Dane
  And lose your voice: what wouldst thou beg, Laertes, **45**
  That shall not be my offer, not thy asking?
  The head is not more native to the heart,
  The hand more instrumental to the mouth,
  Than is the throne of Denmark to thy father.
  What wouldst thou have, Laertes?
Laertes.   My dread lord, **50**
  Your leave and favour to return to France,
  From whence, though willingly I came to Denmark,
  To show my duty in your coronation,
  Yet now, I must confess, that duty done,
  My thoughts and wishes bend again toward France **55**
  And bow them to your gracious leave and pardon.
King.   Have you your father's leave? What says Polonius?
Polonius.   He hath, my lord, wrung from me my slow leave
  By laboursome petition, and at last
  Upon his will I seal'd my hard consent: **60**
  I do beseech you give him leave to go.
King.   Take thy fair hour, Laertes; time be thine,
  And thy best graces spend it at thy will!
  But now, my cousin Hamlet, and my son,—
Hamlet (aside).   A little more than kin, and less than kind. **65**
King.   How is it that the clouds still hang on you?
Hamlet.   Not so, my lord; I am too much in the sun.
Queen.   Good Hamlet, cast thy nighted colour off,
  And let thine eye look like a friend on Denmark;
  Do not for ever with thy vailed lids **70**
  Seek for thy noble father in the dust;
  Thou know'st 'tis common, all that lives must die,

68-73 How does the Queen's opening speech illustrate her callousness? To what extent is "realism" a better word to describe this characteristic? **nature:** earthly life.

74 **Ay, madam, it is common:** Explain the bitter irony of this remark.

75 **particular:** special.

76 After his carefully controlled remarks, Hamlet lashes out in self-defence.

79 **windy suspiration of forc'd breath:** sighs; the circumlocution may suggest contempt for artificial grief. Note its imitative quality.

81 **dejected haviour . . . visage:** gloomy facial expression.

86 **trappings:** clothing worn for show.

76-86 What are the implications of this outburst? What contrast in Hamlet is implied? What does it reveal about Hamlet's state of mind?

90 **bound:** was bound.

92 **obsequious:** mourning, having to do with *obsequies* (funeral rites); **persever:** persevere, persist.

93 **condolement:** lamentation.

98-99 **as common . . . sense:** (death is) one of the commonest of commonplace sense experiences.

101 **Fie:** Shame!

104 **still:** always.

107 **unprevailing:** unavailing, useless.

Passing through nature to eternity.
Hamlet.   Ay, madam, it is common.
Queen.   If it be,
  Why seems it so particular with thee?   75
Hamlet.   "Seems," madam? nay, it is, I know not "seems."
  'Tis not alone my inky cloak, good mother,
  Nor customary suits of solemn black,
  Nor windy suspiration of forc'd breath,
  No, nor the fruitful river in the eye,   80
  Nor the dejected haviour of the visage,
  Together with all forms, moods, shapes of grief,
  That can denote me truly; these indeed seem,
  For they are actions that a man might play,
  But I have that within which passes show,   85
  These but the trappings and the suits of woe.
King.   'Tis sweet and commendable in your nature, Hamlet,
  To give these mourning duties to your father:
  But you must know your father lost a father,
  That father lost, lost his, and the survivor bound   90
  In filial obligation for some term
  To do obsequious sorrow; but to persever
  In obstinate condolement is a course
  Of impious stubbornness, 'tis unmanly grief,
  It shows a will most incorrect to heaven,   95
  A heart unfortified, a mind impatient,
  An understanding simple and unschool'd:
  For what we know must be and is as common
  As any the most vulgar thing to sense,
  Why should we in our peevish opposition   100
  Take it to heart? Fie! 'tis a fault to heaven,
  A fault against the dead, a fault to nature,
  To reason most absurd, whose common theme
  Is death of fathers, and who still hath cried,
  From the first corse, till he that died to-day,   105
  "This must be so." We pray you throw to earth
  This unprevailing woe, and think of us

108 Hamlet darts a look of contemptuous scorn at Claudius.
109 **most immediate:** next in line. (The King makes no mention of the fact that the Danish monarchy was elective.)
112 **do I impart:** am I disposed.
113 **in going . . . Wittenberg:** that is, to study as a graduate student. What is the significance of "back"? **Wittenberg:** a renowned university founded in 1502 and located about fifty miles south of Berlin. In 1517, Luther nailed his famous theses to the door of the church in Wittenberg. (The reference is an anachronism.) Why would Hamlet wish to return to his studies? Of what significance is his attendance at this university?
114 **retrograde:** contrary. Why would Claudius wish Hamlet to remain at court?
115 **bend:** The word has almost the force of a command. Show that Claudius' speech is both clever and hypocritical.
120 **you:** This word is emphasized. Why?
124 **sits smiling to:** delights.   125 **jocund:** joyful.
126 **the great cannon:** Contemporary accounts imply that this was a well-known Danish custom.
127 **rouse:** carouse, from *drinking deep* (Scandinavian); **bruit:** echo.
121-8 The King ignores Hamlet's pointed remark and speaks with jovial heartiness (which by this time is somewhat strained).
129-59 This is the first of Hamlet's mighty soliloquies, the speeches that seem to provide the arches that support the play. In this one, the note of dejection is struck and the death wish is uttered as he expresses his deep grief over his father's death and his disillusionment regarding his mother.
129 **sullied:** smirched. Q1 and Q2 read "sullied"; F has *solid*, but "sullied" seems to accord with Hamlet's mood. It also fits in better with "melt", "thaw", and "resolve". Why would he consider that his flesh was "sullied"?
132 **canon:** law; the reference is to the Sixth Commandment.
134 **all the uses:** the daily routine. In his melancholy, Hamlet makes sweeping statements.
135-6 **an unweeded . . . seed:** To Shakespeare, a countryman at heart, the well-tended garden was a symbol of the norm (Levin); **rank and gross:** These adjectives suggest coarse sensuality.
137 **merely:** utterly and completely.
140 **Hyperion:** a Titan, father of Helios; loosely, the sun-god. Note the combination of Christian and classical references; **satyr:** in Greek mythology, a creature half-man and half-goat noted for its lewd propensities; hence, Hamlet's contempt. The contrast is between the godlike and the bestial.

As of a father: for let the world take note,
You are the most immediate to our throne,
And with no less nobility of love 110
Than that which dearest father bears his son
Do I impart toward you. For your intent
In going back to school in Wittenberg,
It is most retrograde to our desire,
And we beseech you, bend you to remain 115
Here in the cheer and comfort of our eye,
Our chiefest courtier, cousin, and our son.
Queen. Let not thy mother lose her prayers, Hamlet:
I pray thee, stay with us; go not to Wittenberg.
Hamlet. I shall in all my best obey you, madam. 120
King. Why, 'tis a loving and a fair reply:
Be as ourself in Denmark. Madam, come;
This gentle and unforc'd accord of Hamlet
Sits smiling to my heart, in grace whereof,
No jocund health that Denmark drinks to-day, 125
But the great cannon to the clouds shall tell,
And the king's rouse the heaven shall bruit again,
Re-speaking earthly thunder. Come away.
> *Flourish. Exeunt all but Hamlet.*
Hamlet. O that this too too sullied flesh would melt,
Thaw and resolve itself into a dew, 130
Or that the Everlasting had not fix'd
His canon 'gainst self-slaughter! O God, God,
How weary, stale, flat, and unprofitable
Seem to me all the uses of this world!
Fie on't, ah fie! 'tis an unweeded garden 135
That grows to seed; things rank and gross in nature
Possess it merely. That it should come to this!
But two months dead, nay, not so much, not two;
So excellent a king, that was to this
Hyperion to a satyr, so loving to my mother, 140
That he might not beteem the winds of heaven
Visit her face too roughly; heaven and earth,

141-5   **beteem:** permit; Hamlet tortures himself with the memory of his father's gentle devotion to Gertrude and his mother's apparent devotion to the elder Hamlet. He has "a sensitive reverence for the beautiful and good" (Granville-Barker).

146   **frailty, thy . . . woman:** A memorable line in which Hamlet attributes to all women the shortcomings of his mother; this misogyny is dominant throughout the play.

147   **or ere:** before; **or ere . . . old:** a vivid concrete detail that underlines the brevity of the interval.

149   **Niobe:** a symbol of a mother's grief. In her pride, Niobe, Queen of Thebes, boasted that because of her fourteen sons and daughters, she was greater than Latona (Leto), mother of only two children. Latona's offspring, Apollo and Diana, avenged the insult by destroying all Niobe's children; the queen wept bitterly, and Zeus ultimately turned her into a stone.

150   **wants discourse of reason:** lacks power of speech.

153   **Hercules:** a Greek hero renowned for physical strength and the performance of the twelve labours. Why does Hamlet use this contrast?

154-5   **ere yet . . . eyes:** before the redness caused by weeping hypocritical tears had left her eyes. The emphasis is on the speed with which she turned from funeral to wedding.

156-7   **to post . . . sheets:** Hamlet regards marriage with a deceased brother's wife as being within the forbidden degrees of consanguinity. His mother's behaviour fills him with loathing; he has found that his idol has feet of clay.

158   Shakespeare not infrequently makes use of the double negative.

160   Hamlet speaks absent-mindedly; then, he suddenly and joyfully realizes who it is.

163   **change that name:** exchange the name of friend. Hamlet's unfailing courtesy prompts him to treat all men as his equals provided that they do not play false with him.

164   **make:** do.

168   evidence that Horatio is a scholar.

175   **for to drink:** Another reading is *to drink deep.*

Must I remember? why, she would hang on him,
As if increase of appetite had grown
By what it fed on, and yet within a month— 145
Let me not think on't; frailty, thy name is woman!
A little month, or ere those shoes were old
With which she follow'd my poor father's body,
Like Niobe, all tears:—why she, even she,—
O God, a beast that wants discourse of reason 150
Would have mourn'd longer,—married with my uncle,
My father's brother, but no more like my father
Than I to Hercules: within a month,
Ere yet the salt of most unrighteous tears
Had left the flushing in her galled eyes, 155
She married; O most wicked speed, to post
With such dexterity to incestuous sheets!
It is not, nor it cannot come to good;
But break my heart, for I must hold my tongue!
            Enter Horatio, Marcellus, and Barnardo.
Horatio.   Hail to your lordship!
Hamlet.   I am glad to see you well: 160
   Horatio, or I do forget myself.
Horatio.   The same, my lord, and your poor servant ever.
Hamlet.   Sir, my good friend; I'll change that name with
      you;
   And what make you from Wittenberg, Horatio?
   Marcellus.   165
Marcellus.   My good lord.
Hamlet.   I am very glad to see you. (*to Bar.*) Good even, sir.
   (*to Hor.*) But what, in faith, make you from Wittenberg?
Horatio.   A truant disposition, good my lord.
Hamlet.   I would not hear your enemy say so, 170
   Nor shall you do my ear that violence
   To make it truster of your own report
   Against yourself: I know you are no truant:
   But what is your affair in Elsinore?
   We'll teach you for to drink ere you depart. 175

180-1 **thrift, thrift . . . tables:** As an economy measure, the left-over refreshments from the first ceremony were used cold in the next; Hamlet exaggerates, but there is a grain of truth in what he so bitterly says.

182 **dearest:** worst.

183 **or ever:** before.

185 What does Horatio think Hamlet means?

186 A pause before "once" implies that Horatio was on the verge of telling Hamlet. What effect does this create?

187-8 a noble epitaph; account for its effectiveness.

192 **season your admiration:** moderate your wonder.

198 **waste:** So in F and Q2; modern editors prefer *vast*, a silent, desolate time (Q1).

200 **armed at point:** in readiness, fully armed. (F has *armed at all points*); **cap-à-pé:** from head to foot.

204 **truncheon:** baton; **distill'd:** melted.

205 **act:** operation.

Horatio.   My lord, I came to see your father's funeral.

Hamlet.   I prithee, do not mock me, fellow-student;
   I think it was to see my mother's wedding.

Horatio.   Indeed, my lord, it follow'd hard upon.

Hamlet.   Thrift, thrift, Horatio; the funeral bak'd-meats   180
   Did coldly furnish forth the marriage tables.
   Would I had met my dearest foe in heaven
   Or ever I had seen that day, Horatio!
   My father, methinks I see my father.

Horatio.   Where, my lord?

Hamlet.   In my mind's eye, Horatio.   185

Horatio.   I saw him once; he was a goodly king.

Hamlet.   He was a man, take him for all in all,
   I shall not look upon his like again.

Horatio.   My lord, I think I saw him yesternight.

Hamlet.   Saw? who?   190

Horatio.   My lord, the king your father.

Hamlet.   The king my father?

Horatio.   Season your admiration for a while
   With an attent ear, till I may deliver,
   Upon the witness of these gentlemen,
   This marvel to you.

Hamlet.   For God's love, let me hear.   195

Horatio.   Two nights together had these gentlemen,
   Marcellus and Barnardo, on their watch,
   In the dead waste and middle of the night,
   Been thus encounter'd. A figure like your father,
   Armed at point exactly, cap-à-pé,   200
   Appears before them, and with solemn march
   Goes slow and stately by them: thrice he walk'd
   By their oppress'd and fear-surprised eyes,
   Within his truncheon's length; whilst they distill'd
   Almost to jelly, with the act of fear   205
   Stand dumb, and speak not to him. This to me
   In dreadful secrecy impart they did,
   And I with them the third night kept the watch:

209 **deliver'd:** reported.
212 **these hands . . . like:** Horatio says that his left hand resembles his right hand as the Ghost resembled Hamlet's father.
213 **platform:** ramparts where cannon were mounted.
216 **it head:** See note on I. i. 37.
228 **Then saw . . . face:** F has a question mark; Q2 has a period. Which is preferable?
229 **beaver:** visor of a helmet.
234 **constantly:** fixedly.

Where, as they had deliver'd, both in time,
Form of the thing, each word made true and good,   210
The apparition comes: I knew your father,
These hands are not more like.
Hamlet.   But where was this?
Marcellus.   My lord, upon the platform where we watch.
Hamlet.   Did you not speak to it?
Horatio.   My lord, I did.
But answer made it none; yet once methought   215
It lifted up it head and did address
Itself to motion, like as it would speak:
But even then the morning cock crew loud,
And at the sound it shrunk in haste away
And vanish'd from our sight.
Hamlet.   'Tis very strange.   220
Horatio.   As I do live my honour'd lord 'tis true,
And we did think it writ down in our duty
To let you know of it.
Hamlet.   Indeed, indeed, sirs, but this troubles me.
Hold you the watch to-night?
Marcellus. }
Barnardo. }   We do, my lord.   225
Hamlet.   Arm'd, say you?
Marcellus. }
Barnardo. }   Arm'd, my lord.
Hamlet.   From top to toe?
Marcellus. }
Barnardo. } My lord, from head to foot.
Hamlet.   Then saw you not his face.
Horatio.   O yes, my lord; he wore his beaver up.
Hamlet.   What, look'd he frowningly?   230
Horatio.   A countenance more in sorrow than in anger.
Hamlet.   Pale, or red?
Horatio.   Nay, very pale.
Hamlet.   And fix'd his eyes upon you?
Horatio.   Most constantly.

235 **amaz'd:** astounded (stronger than it is today).

237 **tell:** count.

239 **grizzled:** grey, pepper-and-salt.

224-40 Hamlet's alertness of mind and intellectual quickness appear to advantage in this sharp cross-questioning.

241 **a sable silver'd:** black streaked with grey. How does this expression differ from "grizzled"?

244 **gape:** yawn.

247 **tenable:** retained; **Let it . . . still:** Say not a word about it.

250 **requite your loves:** recompense you for the trouble you are taking.

255 **doubt:** suspect.

254-7 What is the importance of Hamlet's postscript? The rhyming couplet concluding the scene has the effect of finality and is commonly used in Shakespeare to mark the end of a scene.

See also p. 250.

Hamlet.   I would I had been there.
Horatio. It would have much amaz'd you.   235
Hamlet. Very like, very like. Stay'd it long?
Horatio. While one with moderate haste might tell a hundred.
Marcellus. ⎫
Barnardo. ⎬ Longer, longer.
Horatio. Not when I saw't.
Hamlet.   His beard was grizzled, no?
Horatio. It was as I have seen it in his life,   240
  A sable silver'd.
Hamlet.   I will watch to-night;
  Perchance 'twill walk again.
Horatio.   I warrant it will.
Hamlet. If it assume my noble father's person,
  I'll speak to it, though hell itself should gape
  And bid me hold my peace; I pray you all,   245
  If you have hitherto conceal'd this sight,
  Let it be tenable in your silence still,
  And whatsoever else shall hap to-night,
  Give it an understanding, but no tongue:
  I will requite your loves; so fare you well: 250
  Upon the platform, 'twixt eleven and twelve,
  I'll visit you.
All.   Our duty to your honour.
Hamlet. Your loves, as mine to you: farewell.
                         Exeunt all but Hamlet.
  My father's spirit——in arms? all is not well;
  I doubt some foul play; would the night were come!   255
  Till then sit still, my soul: foul deeds will rise,
  Though all the earth o'erwhelm them, to men's eyes.
                              Exit.

1-2 Notice how Shakespeare creates the impression of a sea voyage.

3 **convoy is assistant:** means of sending a letter is available.

6 **a fashion:** the popular thing to do, or a mere mood; **a toy in blood:** a trifling impulse.

7 **in the . . . nature:** in the springtime.

9 **perfume and . . . minute:** momentary fragrance and pleasure.

5-10 Laertes judges Hamlet by his own sophisticated standards. Ophelia's rejoinder combines pathos and disbelief.

11 **crescent:** growing, waxing (as of the moon).

12 **thews and bulk:** sinews and size; **this temple:** the physical body.

14 **withal:** as well.

15-16 **no soil . . . will:** No stain or deceit mars his intention to do what is right.

17 **his greatness weigh'd:** when you consider his position.

19 **unvalued:** unimportant.

20 **carve:** choose.

21 **safety:** So Q2; F, *sanctity.*

23 **yielding:** consent.

26-27 **as he . . . deed:** as he is able to fulfil his promise.

Scene 3

A ROOM IN POLONIUS' HOUSE.

Enter Laertes and Ophelia.

Laertes.   My necessaries are embark'd: farewell:
 And, sister, as the winds give benefit
 And convoy is assistant, do not sleep,
 But let me hear from you.
Ophelia.   Do you doubt that?
Laertes.   For Hamlet, and the trifling of his favour,   5
 Hold it a fashion, and a toy in blood,
 A violet in the youth of primy nature,
 Forward, not permanent, sweet, not lasting,
 The perfume and suppliance of a minute;
 No more.
Ophelia.   No more but so?
Laertes.   Think it no more: 10
 For nature crescent does not grow alone
 In thews and bulk, but, as this temple waxes,
 The inward service of the mind and soul
 Grows wide withal; perhaps he loves you now,
 And now no soil nor cautel doth besmirch   15
 The virtue of his will: but you must fear,
 His greatness weigh'd, his will is not his own;
 For he himself is subject to his birth:
 He may not, as unvalued persons do,
 Carve for himself, for on his choice depends   20
 The safety and health of this whole state,
 And therefore must his choice be circumscrib'd
 Unto the voice and yielding of that body
 Whereof he is the head. Then if he says he loves you,
 It fits your wisdom so far to believe it   25
 As he in his particular act and place
 May give his saying deed, which is no further

30 **credent:** credulous.
31 **chaste treasure:** virginity.
32 **unmaster'd importunity:** undisciplined insistence.
34 **keep you . . . affection:** Do not let your emotions overpower your judgement.
36 **chariest:** most prudent, most virtuous.
37 **to the moon:** (let alone anyone else).
38 **calumnious strokes:** attacks of slander.
39-40 **The canker . . . disclos'd:** The canker-worm (maggot) mars early blossoms too frequently before the buds open. The metaphor, drawn from gardening as so many of Shakespeare's are, implies that Ophelia may destroy her future by being too indiscreet in the present.
41-42 **And in . . . imminent:** Just as the dark mists of morning cause destructive blights, so susceptible youth is likely to be the victim of violent emotions; **contagious:** destructive.
44 **Youth to . . . near:** So rebellious is youth that it revolts against self-discipline even though no one else is near (to be rebelled against). Laertes' tirade suggests much about his own character and behaviour.
45 **effect:** gist.
47 **ungracious:** without grace.
49 **puff'd:** bloated; **libertine:** one given to licentious living and over-indulgence in the pleasures of the senses.
50 **primrose path of dalliance:** the delightful life of worldly pleasure; a most engaging description. Shakespeare equated primroses with gay, empty delights. Compare the Porter's speech in *Macbeth* (II. iii. 20-21): "the primrose way to the everlasting bonfire".
51 **and recks . . . rede:** pays no heed to his own advice; **fear me not:** Don't worry about me.
47-51 In her quiet way, Ophelia shows that she is well aware of the type of life her brother leads.
54 **occasion smiles upon:** good fortune grants.
56 **sits in . . . sail:** a vivid metaphor suggesting that sailing conditions are favourable.
57 **There, my . . . thee:** Polonius gives Laertes a perfunctory pat as the latter kneels before him. Note the irony of the situation. Polonius blames Laertes for delaying and then proceeds to delay him still more.
59 **character:** inscribe; **Give thy . . . tongue:** Never speak your mind.
60 (give not) **any unproportion'd . . . act:** Look before you leap.
61 **Be thou . . . vulgar:** Be friendly, but don't make yourself cheap.

Than the main voice of Denmark goes withal.
Then weigh what loss your honour may sustain,
If with too credent ear you list his songs, 30
Or lose your heart, or your chaste treasure open
To his unmaster'd importunity.
Fear it, Ophelia, fear it, my dear sister,
And keep you in the rear of your affection,
Out of the shot and danger of desire. 35
The chariest maid is prodigal enough,
If she unmask her beauty to the moon:
Virtue itself 'scapes not calumnious strokes:
The canker galls the infants of the spring
Too oft before their buttons be disclos'd, 40
And in the morn and liquid dew of youth
Contagious blastments are most imminent.
Be wary then; best safety lies in fear:
Youth to itself rebels, though none else near.
Ophelia. I shall the effect of this good lesson keep 45
As watchman to my heart; but, good my brother,
Do not as some ungracious pastors do,
Show me the steep and thorny way to heaven,
Whiles like a puff'd and reckless libertine,
Himself the primrose path of dalliance treads, 50
And recks not his own rede.
Laertes. O, fear me not;
I stay too long: but here my father comes;
Enter Polonius.
A double blessing is a double grace,
Occasion smiles upon a second leave.
Polonius. Yet here, Laertes? Aboard, aboard, for shame! 55
The wind sits in the shoulder of your sail,
And you are stay'd for. There, my blessing with thee, don't say what
And these few precepts in thy memory you think
Look thou character. Give thy thoughts no tongue,
Nor any unproportion'd thought his act; 60
Be thou familiar, but by no means vulgar; act st night
don't be rude
don't tell everything

62   **their adoption tried:** whose friendship you have tested.
63   **Grapple them . . . steel:** Bind them firmly to you, as rings of metal encircle and hold barrel staves in place; a vigorous metaphor.
64   **dull thy palm:** treat everybody, and thereby show lack of discrimination.
65   **unfledg'd:** immature; **comrade:** Q1 and Q2 read *courage,* perhaps in the sense of *hothead.*
69   **censure:** opinion.
70   **habit:** clothing, garments. (The term survives in *riding habit.*)
71   **express'd in fancy:** in the extreme of fashion.
74   **chief:** F reads *cheff.* The line implies the superiority of French over English fashions for men at that time. It has the adverbial value of *chiefly.*
77   **dulls the . . . husbandry:** prevents one from realizing the merits of thrift.
81   **season:** bring (this advice) to fruition.
59-81 The advice given by Polonius, with the exception of the last three lines, is worldly and practical, but as Professor Harry Levin points out: "It is etiquette rather than ethics" and concerns itself with outward problems. The last three lines he describes as a "magnificent non sequitur", a sound and searching piece of advice that seems out of place beside the sophisticated counsel to which it forms a climax.
83   **tend:** wait.
89   **touching:** concerning.
90   **Marry:** Well; a mild version of the oath *by Mary.*
94   **put on me:** reported to me.

Those friends thou hast, and their adoption tried,
Grapple them unto thy soul with hoops of steel,
But do not dull thy palm with entertainment
Of each new-hatch'd unfledg'd comrade; beware   65
Of entrance to a quarrel, but being in,
Bear't that the opposed may beware of thee;
Give every man thy ear, but few thy voice;
Take each man's censure, but reserve thy judgement;
Costly thy habit as thy purse can buy,   70
But not express'd in fancy; rich, not gaudy,
For the apparel oft proclaims the man,
And they in France of the best rank and station
Are of a most select and generous chief in that.
Neither a borrower nor a lender be,   75
For loan oft loses both itself and friend,
And borrowing dulls the edge of husbandry;
This above all, to thine own self be true,
And it must follow, as the night the day,
Thou canst not then be false to any man.   80
Farewell; my blessing season this in thee!
Laertes.   Most humbly do I take my leave, my lord.
Polonius.   The time invites you; go, your servants tend.
Laertes.   Farewell, Ophelia, and remember well
What I have said to you.
Ophelia.   'Tis in my memory lock'd,   85
And you yourself shall keep the key of it.
Laertes.   Farewell.   *Exit.*
Polonius.   What is't, Ophelia, he hath said to you?
Ophelia.   So please you, something touching the Lord Hamlet.
Polonius.   Marry, well bethought: 90
'Tis told me he hath very oft of late
Given private time to you, and you yourself
Have of your audience been most free and bounteous:
If it be so, as so 'tis put on me,
And that in way of caution, I must tell you,   95
You do not understand yourself so clearly

97 **behoves:** befits.

99-100 **He hath . . . me:** He has lately offered me his affection on many occasions; **tenders:** offers.

101 **green:** inexperienced. Compare *Antony and Cleopatra* (I. v. 72-73): "My salad days, /When I was green in judgement. . . ."

102 **unsifted:** untested.

106-9 Note the three meanings of "tender": *offers* (also in the form of money), *value* (regard, consider), *render;* **to crack . . . thus:** destroy the value of the word-play by overdoing it. The metaphor is taken from horsemanship; a horse's wind (or breathing) may be broken if he is run too hard. Polonius' callous attitude suggests that he is less interested in his daughter's happiness than in his own wit.

110-11 **importun'd me . . . fashion:** honourably pleaded his love for me. Ophelia timidly defends Hamlet.

112 **fashion:** Polonius rakes her with his scorn; **go to:** Don't be silly.

113 **countenance:** evidence of sincerity. Ophelia's defence of Hamlet seems pathetic.

115 **springes to . . . woodcocks:** snares to catch foolish birds; a proverb. The woodcock was reputedly a stupid bird.

116-17 **When the . . . vows:** When one is emotionally excited, one freely makes promises.

118-19 **extinct in . . . a-making:** lacking true emotion even while the promises are being made.

121 **Be something . . . presence:** Do not appear in public so much.

122-3 **Set your . . . parley:** Do not grant him interviews merely because he requests them.

125 **a larger tether:** a greater freedom.

127-31 **Do not . . . beguile:** Do not trust his promises; they may look innocent and holy (like white priestly vestments), but their real purpose is to deceive you. (Outward appearance and behaviour are treacherous); **brokers:** agents; **dye:** colour, quality; **investments:** garments; **bawds:** loose women.

As it behoves my daughter, and your honour;
What is between you? give me up the truth.
Ophelia.   He hath, my lord, of late made many tenders
   Of his affection to me.   100
Polonius.   Affection! pooh! you speak like a green girl,
   Unsifted in such perilous circumstance;
   Do you believe his tenders, as you call them?   *letters*
Ophelia.   I do not know, my lord, what I should think.
Polonius.   Marry, I will teach you: think yourself a baby,   105
   That you have ta'en these tenders for true pay,
   Which are not sterling; tender yourself more dearly,
   Or (not to crack the wind of the poor phrase,
   Running it thus) you'll tender me a fool.
Ophelia.   My lord, he hath importun'd me with love   110
   In honourable fashion.
Polonius.   Ay, fashion you may call it; go to, go to.
Ophelia.   And hath given countenance to his speech, my lord,
   With almost all the holy vows of heaven.
Polonius.   Ay, springes to catch woodcocks. I do know,   115
   When the blood burns, how prodigal the soul
   Lends the tongue vows: these blazes, daughter,   *those letters*
   Giving more light than heat, extinct in both   *are held rabbit*
   Even in their promise, as it is a-making,   *traps*
   You must not take for fire; from this time   120
   Be something scanter of your maiden presence,
   Set your entreatments at a higher rate   *don't be seen, he*
   Than a command to parley; for Lord Hamlet,   *can't marry you*
   Believe so much in him, that he is young,   *Spend time*
   And with a larger tether may he walk   125   *with others*
   Than may be given you: in few, Ophelia,
   Do not believe his vows, for they are brokers,
   Not of that dye which their investments show,
   But mere implorators of unholy suits,
   Breathing like sanctified and pious bawds,   130
   The better to beguile. This is for all;
   I would not, in plain terms, from this time forth,

You could only marry virgins

133 **slander any moment leisure:** bring scandal on any moment of leisure.
136 Ophelia's mutiny dies as it is being born.

See also p. 252.

1 **shrewdly:** keenly.
2 **eager:** biting, sharp. How do these references take us back to Scene 1? Of what importance are they?
3-4 Of what importance is this time reference?
6 **wont:** habit; S.D. **flourish:** fanfare of brass instruments; S.D. **pieces:** cannon.
8 **wake:** keep late revel; **takes his rouse:** is drinking heavily.
9 **keeps wassail:** carouses. ("Wassail" was originally an Old English salutation meaning *Health to you*); **up-spring:** riotous dance; here, object of the verb "reels".
10 **Rhenish:** Rhine wine.
11 **bray:** sound loudly.
12 **the triumph . . . pledge:** an ironic expression implying the King's glorious achievements as a drinker.
15 **to the manner born:** accustomed from birth to celebrations such as this.
16 **more honour'd . . . observance:** better ignored than observed.
18 **traduc'd, and tax'd:** slandered and censured.
19-20 **clepe:** call; **with swinish . . . addition:** give us a bad name by referring to us as pigs.

Have you so slander any moment leisure,
As to give words or talk with the Lord Hamlet.
Look to't, I charge you: come your ways.   135
Ophelia.   I shall obey, my lord.   *Exeunt.*

[handwritten: don't talk to him]

Scene 4

THE PLATFORM.

Enter Hamlet, Horatio, and Marcellus.

Hamlet.   The air bites shrewdly; it is very cold.
Horatio.   It is a nipping and an eager air.
Hamlet.   What hour now?
Horatio.   I think it lacks of twelve.
Marcellus.   No, it is struck.
Horatio.   Indeed? I heard it not: it then draws near the season 5
    Wherein the spirit held his wont to walk.
            A flourish of trumpets, and two pieces go off.
    What does this mean, my lord?
Hamlet.   The king doth wake to-night and takes his rouse,
    Keeps wassail, and the swaggering up-spring reels;
    And as he drains his draughts of Rhenish down,   10
    The kettle-drum and trumpet thus bray out
    The triumph of his pledge.
Horatio.   Is it a custom?
Hamlet.   Ay, marry, is't,
    But to my mind, though I am native here
    And to the manner born, it is a custom   15
    More honour'd in the breach than the observance.
    This heavy-headed revel east and west
    Makes us traduc'd, and tax'd of other nations;
    They clepe us drunkards, and with swinish phrase
    Soil our addition; and indeed it takes   20
    From our achievements, though perform'd at height,

[handwritten: Claudius King party drinking heavily.]

[handwritten: we might be laughing stock]

22 **the pith . . . attribute:** the essence (best part) of our reputation.
24 **vicious mole of nature:** serious natural blemish. Just as a mole disfigures the body, so such a flaw disfigures the mind.
27 **complexion:** disposition. A reference to the belief that there were four humours; namely, blood, phlegm, black bile, and yellow bile that governed the individual's temperament. Excess of any one could produce a variation from the norm, making one sanguine, phlegmatic, melancholy, or choleric.
28 **pales:** palisades; that is, defences; **forts:** defences.
29 **o'er-leavens:** gives a frivolous touch to.
30 **plausive:** praiseworthy, pleasing.
32 **livery:** badge; **nature's . . . star:** inborn or acquired by ill luck.
34 **may undergo:** is capable of.
35 **the general censure:** public opinion.
36-38 **the dram . . . scandal:** Professor G. B. Harrison labels this "the most disputed passage in all Shakespeare". He gives as its meaning, despite the corruptness of the passage: "a small proportion of evil (eale) will bring scandal on the whole substance however noble" (Penguin Shakespeare: *Hamlet*).
14-38 **But to . . . scandal:** This whole passage is omitted from F, either because it was considered undramatic or because, with the coming to England of James's queen, Anne of Denmark, it was considered unsuitable. On the other hand, it is sometimes held to be a very ironic and important speech, containing as it does a reference to the theory of the tragic flaw. In Sir Laurence Olivier's film of *Hamlet,* the speech: "So, oft . . . fault" is used as a prologue, so that its significance is highlighted. In these lines, says Granville-Barker, we have "a glimpse of the intrinsic Hamlet".
39 **ministers of grace:** good spirits.
40 **a spirit . . . damn'd:** From the beginning, Hamlet is uncertain whether the Ghost is good or evil.
43 **questionable:** provoking question.
47 **canoniz'd:** buried according to the canons (rites) of the church. Some editors say *sainted*; **hearsed:** placed in a coffin.
48 **cerements:** waxen shrouds.
49 **interr'd:** entombed.
50-51 **hath op'd . . . again:** a striking metaphor of the tomb as a great monster of stone.
52 **in complete steel:** another reference to the Ghost dressed in full armour.
53 **glimpses of the moon:** landscape seen by the fitful moonlight.
54 **we fools of nature:** we weak human beings.
55 **shake our disposition:** disturb our minds.

The pith and marrow of our attribute.
So, oft it chances in particular men,
That for some vicious mole of nature in them,
As in their birth, wherein they are not guilty,   25
(Since nature cannot choose his origin)
By the o'ergrowth of some complexion
Oft breaking down the pales and forts of reason,
Or by some habit, that too much o'er-leavens
The form of plausive manners, that these men,   30
Carrying, I say, the stamp of one defect,
Being nature's livery, or fortune's star,
His virtues else be they as pure as grace,
As infinite as man may undergo,
Shall in the general censure take corruption   35
From that particular fault: the dram of eale
Doth all the noble substance of a doubt
To his own scandal.
          Enter Ghost.
Horatio.   Look, my lord, it comes!
Hamlet.   Angels and ministers of grace defend us!
    Be thou a spirit of health, or goblin damn'd,   40
    Bring with thee airs from heaven, or blasts from hell,
    Be thy intents wicked, or charitable,
    Thou com'st in such a questionable shape,
    That I will speak to thee, I'll call thee Hamlet,
    King, father, royal Dane: O, answer me,   45
    Let me not burst in ignorance, but tell
    Why thy canoniz'd bones, hearsed in death,
    Have burst their cerements? why the sepulchre,
    Wherein we saw thee quietly interr'd
    Hath op'd his ponderous and marble jaws,   50
    To cast thee up again? What may this mean,
    That thou, dead corse, again in complete steel,
    Revisit'st thus the glimpses of the moon,
    Making night hideous, and we fools of nature
    So horridly to shake our disposition   55

56 **beyond the . . . souls:** incomprehensible.

59 **impartment:** communication.

60-61 Note the indirect stage directions.

65 **a pin's fee:** worth a pin.

71 **beetles:** juts. This is the F reading. Q1 has *beckles*; Q2, *bettles*.

73 **deprive your . . . reason:** take away your command over your reason.

75 **toys of desperation:** desperate impulses. See also *King Lear* IV. vi. 67-72.

82 **arture:** artery.

83 **hardy:** tough (in the sense of brave); **Nemean lion:** to destroy this beast was the first of the twelve labours of Hercules; **nerve:** sinew.

85 **lets:** hinders.

With thoughts beyond the reaches of our souls?
Say, why is this, wherefore, what should we do?
  Ghost beckons.
Horatio. It beckons you to go away with it,
 As if it some impartment did desire
 To you alone.
Marcellus.   Look with what courteous action **60**
 It waves you to a more removed ground:
 But do not go with it.
Horatio.   No, by no means.
Hamlet. It will not speak; then I will follow it.
Horatio. Do not, my lord.
Hamlet.   Why, what should be the fear?
 I do not set my life at a pin's fee, **65**
 And for my soul, what can it do to that,
 Being a thing immortal as itself?
 It waves me forth again, I'll follow it.
Horatio. What if it tempt you toward the flood, my lord,
 Or to the dreadful summit of the cliff **70**
 That beetles o'er his base into the sea,
 And there assume some other horrible form
 Which might deprive your sovereignty of reason,
 And draw you into madness? think of it:
 The very place puts toys of desperation, **75**
 Without more motive, into every brain
 That looks so many fathoms to the sea
 And hears it roar beneath.
Hamlet.   It waves me still;
 Go on, I'll follow thee.
Marcellus. You shall not go, my lord.
Hamlet.   Hold off your hands. **80**
Horatio. Be rul'd, you shall not go.
Hamlet.   My fate cries out,
 And makes each petty arture in this body
 As hardy as the Nemean lion's nerve.
 Still am I call'd; unhand me gentlemen,

80-86 evidence of Hamlet's physical strength and courage.
90 **Something is . . . Denmark:** How do you account for the fact that this line is sometimes left out of productions of the play? What evidence is there of moral corruption?

See also p. 253.

2 **Mark me:** Listen carefully.
4 Hamlet's warm heart goes out to the sufferings of his father.
6 **bound:** ready; in line 7, the Ghost gives it the meaning *obliged*.
3-13 references to the doctrine of purgatory.

By heaven I'll make a ghost of him that lets me: 85
I say away! go on, I'll follow thee.
                              Exeunt Ghost and Hamlet.
Horatio.   He waxes desperate with imagination.
Marcellus.   Let's follow, 'tis not fit thus to obey him.
Horatio.   Have after, to what issue will this come?
Marcellus.   Something is rotten in the state of Denmark.   90
Horatio.   Heaven will direct it.
Marcellus.   Nay, let's follow him.
                                        Exeunt.

Scene 5

ANOTHER PART OF THE PLATFORM.

Enter Ghost and Hamlet.

Hamlet.   Whither wilt thou lead me? speak; I'll go no
    further.
Ghost.   Mark me.
Hamlet.   I will.
Ghost.   My hour is almost come
    When I to sulphurous and tormenting flames
    Must render up myself.
Hamlet.   Alas, poor ghost!
Ghost.   Pity me not, but lend thy serious hearing   5
    To what I shall unfold.
Hamlet.   Speak; I am bound to hear.
Ghost.   So art thou to revenge, when thou shalt hear.
Hamlet.   What?
Ghost.   I am thy father's spirit,
    Doom'd for a certain term to walk the night,   10
    And for the day confin'd to fast in fires,
    Till the foul crimes done in my days of nature
    Are burnt and purg'd away: but that I am forbid

17 **spheres:** orbits.

18 **knotted and combined locks:** hair carefully arranged.

20 **fretful porpentine:** peevish, querulous porcupine; the porcupine with quills erect was the crest of the Sidney family.

21 **eternal blazon:** account of the other world, description of eternity.

13-22 The fact that the Ghost does not reveal what Shakespeare could not know adds to the horror of the mystery.

27 **in the best:** at best.

29-31 Hamlet's words are strangely ironic. Note that he considers revenge a natural and sacred duty. The effect of swooping speed is suggested by the words "swift" and "sweep".

32-33 **Lethe:** according to Greek mythology, the river of forgetfulness in the lower world; this simile, used to illustrate dullness, conveys a vivid picture of puffed and bloated water plants.

35 **orchard:** garden.

37 **forged process:** false report.

38 **abus'd:** deceived.

40 **my prophetic soul:** That Hamlet suspects foul play is evident (I. ii. 255-6). This line implies that he also suspected Claudius.

42 **incestuous:** Marriage with the wife of one's deceased brother was held to be within the forbidden degrees of consanguinity; **adulterate:** This line implies, as do the following lines, that Claudius and Gertrude had been intimate before the death of the elder Hamlet.

To tell the secrets of my prison-house,
I could a tale unfold whose lightest word   15
Would harrow up thy soul, freeze thy young blood,
Make thy two eyes like stars start from their spheres,
Thy knotted and combined locks to part,
And each particular hair to stand an end,
Like quills upon the fretful porpentine: 20
But this eternal blazon must not be
To ears of flesh and blood. List, list, O list!
If thou didst ever thy dear father love—
Hamlet.   O God!
Ghost.   Revenge his foul and most unnatural murder.   25
Hamlet.   Murder?
Ghost.   Murder most foul, as in the best it is,
  But this most foul, strange and unnatural.
Hamlet.   Haste me to know't, that I, with wings as swift
  As meditation, or the thoughts of love,   30
  May sweep to my revenge.
Ghost.   I find thee apt,
  And duller shouldst thou be than the fat weed
  That roots itself in ease on Lethe wharf,
  Wouldst thou not stir in this. Now, Hamlet, hear:
  'Tis given out, that sleeping in my orchard   35
  A serpent stung me; so the whole ear of Denmark
  Is by a forged process of my death
  Rankly abus'd: but know, thou noble youth,
  The serpent that did sting thy father's life
  Now wears his crown.
Hamlet.   O my prophetic soul!   40
  My uncle?
Ghost.   Ay, that incestuous, that adulterate beast,
  With witchcraft of his wit, with traitorous gifts,—
  O wicked wit, and gifts that have the power
  So to seduce!—won to his shameful lust   45
  The will of my most seeming-virtuous queen:
  O Hamlet, what a falling-off was there

50 **decline:** fall to a lower level.

51-52 **whose natural . . . mine:** The implication is that Hamlet the Elder must have been infinitely superior.

53-57 The lines show utter physical loathing and disgust; they define an insoluble paradox in human behaviour. The elder Hamlet's sense of betrayal is very strong.

59 **orchard:** See line 35.

61 **secure:** carefree, free from suspicion.

62 **hebenon:** yew or henbane.

64 **leperous distilment:** solution having effects like those of leprosy; hence, loathsome and deadly. Why did Claudius choose this method of murder? According to the old Hamlet-legend, the King was murdered at a banquet.

68 **posset:** curdle. A "posset" was a drink of hot milk to which wine or other liquor was added with a curdling effect.

69 **curd:** clot; **eager:** acid; the simile shows accurate observation on Shakespeare's part.

71-73 **And a . . . body:** And immediately, scaly scabs covered my whole body as though with leprosy; a revolting image that adds to the horror of the deed.

75 **dispatch'd:** deprived.

76 **blossoms:** very midst. One is reminded of the "primrose" metaphor.

77 **unhousel'd:** without sacrament, (*housel*—the Eucharist); **disappointed:** unprepared; **unanel'd:** unanointed, (*anele*—to give extreme unction to the dying). The arrangement of words makes the line emphatic.

80 Some editors have felt that Hamlet utters this line. Comment.

81 **nature:** "the milk of human kindness".

83 **luxury:** lust.

From me, whose love was of that dignity
That it went hand in hand even with the vow
I made to her in marriage, and to decline   50
Upon a wretch whose natural gifts were poor
To those of mine;
But virtue, as it never will be mov'd,
Though lewdness court it in a shape of heaven,
So lust, though to a radiant angel link'd,   55
Will sate itself in a celestial bed
And prey on garbage.
But soft! methinks I scent the morning air,
Brief let me be; sleeping within my orchard,
My custom always of the afternoon,   60
Upon my secure hour thy uncle stole
With juice of cursed hebenon in a vial,
And in the porches of my ears did pour
The leperous distilment, whose effect
Holds such an enmity with blood of man,   65
That swift as quicksilver it courses through
The natural gates and alleys of the body,
And with a sudden vigour it doth posset
And curd, like eager droppings into milk,
The thin and wholesome blood: so did it mine,   70
And a most instant tetter bark'd about,
Most lazar-like, with vile and loathsome crust,
All my smooth body.
Thus was I sleeping by a brother's hand
Of life, of crown, of queen, at once dispatch'd,   75
Cut off even in the blossoms of my sin,
Unhousel'd, disappointed, unanel'd,
No reckoning made, but sent to my account
With all my imperfections on my head:
O, horrible! O, horrible! most horrible!   80
If thou hast nature in thee, bear it not,
Let not the royal bed of Denmark be
A couch for luxury and damned incest.

85 **Taint not thy mind:** Let not thy mind be poisoned.

87-89 Gertrude is to be left to suffer from the pangs of conscience.

90 **uneffectual:** ineffectual; hence, faint, dim; a clear picture of the glow-worm's little spark.

93 **hold:** hold together; that is, do not break.

94 **instant:** used adverbially. (Hamlet rises from his knees.)

97 **globe:** head. (It is customary for Hamlet to press his hands against his temples.)

98-100 **table:** tablet, notebook. Memorandum books made of slate or ivory were carried by intellectual young men of the period; **fond:** foolish; **saws:** wise sayings; **pressures:** impressions; the image is that of wiping a slate clean.
pernicious: deadly—a word that can be said with great vehemence. Macbeth refers to "this pernicious hour" (IV. i. 133).

106 Claudius' hypocrisy strikes Hamlet as particularly offensive and repellent.

110 **there you are:** He has set down the description of Claudius; **to my word:** for my cue, or watchword.

112 **I have sworn't:** Hamlet kisses his sword in token of his oath.

116 **Hillo, ho, ho:** the falconer's cry. Hamlet's hysterical behaviour seems to be the result of the snapping of tension.

But, howsoever thou pursuest this act,
Taint not thy mind, nor let thy soul contrive   **85**
Against thy mother aught; leave her to heaven,
And to those thorns that in her bosom lodge
To prick and sting her. Fare thee well at once!
The glow-worm shows the matin to be near,
And 'gins to pale his uneffectual fire: **90**
Adieu, adieu, adieu! remember me.   *Exit.*
Hamlet.   O all you host of heaven! O earth! what else?
    And shall I couple hell? O, fie! Hold, hold, my
        heart,
    And you, my sinews, grow not instant old,
    But bear me stiffly up. Remember thee?   **95**
    Ay, thou poor ghost, while memory holds a **seat**
    In this distracted globe. Remember thee?
    Yea, from the table of my memory
    I'll wipe away all trivial fond records,
    All saws of books, all forms, all pressures **past**   **100**
    That youth and observation copied there,
    And thy commandment all alone shall live
    Within the book and volume of my brain,
    Unmix'd with baser matter: yes, by heaven!
    O most pernicious woman!   **105**
    O villain, villain, smiling, damned villain,
    My tables,—meet it is I set it down
    That one may smile, and smile, and be a villain,
    At least I am sure it may be so in Denmark.   *Writing.*
    So, uncle, there you are; now to my word;   **110**
    It is "Adieu, adieu! remember me."
    I have sworn't.
Horatio (*within*).   My lord, my lord!
Marcellus (*within*).   Lord Hamlet!
Horatio (*within*).   Heavens secure him!
Hamlet.   So be it!
Marcellus.   Illo, ho, ho, my lord!   **115**
Hamlet.   Hillo, ho, ho, boy! come, bird, come.

123-4 **arrant:** utter; this obvious remark suggests that Hamlet does not mean to confide in Horatio and Marcellus. Horatio rebukes him for his flippancy.

127 **without more circumstance:** without further ado.

132 **I will go pray:** It may be that Hamlet suddenly realizes his isolation and is aware of the task laid upon him.

133-5 Horatio's calm and quiet words have a sobering effect on Hamlet.

136 **by Saint Patrick:** a logical oath since St. Patrick was the keeper of purgatory. According to legend, St. Patrick found an entrance to purgatory on an island in Lough Derg and thereby convinced the Irish that there was an intermediate state between heaven and hell.

138 **an honest ghost:** "a spirit of health" rather than "a goblin damn'd" (I. iv. 40).

Enter Horatio and Marcellus.

Marcellus.   How is't, my noble lord?

Horatio.   What news, my lord?

Hamlet.   O, wonderful!

Horatio.   Good my lord, tell it.

Hamlet.   No, you will reveal it.

Horatio.   Not I, my lord, by heaven.

Marcellus.   Nor I, my lord.   120

Hamlet.   How say you, then; would heart of man once
    think it?

  But you'll be secret?

Horatio.   ⎫
            Ay, by heaven, my lord.
Marcellus. ⎭

Hamlet.   There's never a villain dwelling in all Denmark
  But he's an arrant knave.

Horatio. There needs no ghost, my lord, come from the grave 125
  To tell us this.

Hamlet.   Why, right, you are in the right,
  And so, without more circumstance at all,
  I hold it fit that we shake hands and part,
  You, as your business and desire shall point you,
  For every man hath business and desire,   130
  Such as it is, and for my own poor part,
  I will go pray.

Horatio.   These are but wild and whirling words, my lord.

Hamlet.   I'm sorry they offend you, heartily;
  Yes, faith, heartily.

Horatio.   There's no offence, my lord.   135

Hamlet.   Yes, by Saint Patrick, but there is, Horatio,
  And much offence too; touching this vision here,
  It is an honest ghost, that let me tell you:
  For your desire to know what is between us,
  O'ermaster't as you may; and now, good friends,   140
  As you are friends, scholars, and soldiers,
  Give me one poor request.

Horatio.   What is't, my lord? we will.

147   **upon my sword:** Hamlet himself had so sworn; the hilt was in the form of a cross.

150   **true-penny:** a colloquial term for an *honest fellow*.

151   **in the cellarage:** the stage direction "Ghost cries under the stage" would explain Hamlet's rather facetious remark; it was believed that spirits and devils made strange noises in the depths of the earth. Horatio and Marcellus may not hear the voice; this would add to their bewilderment.

156   **hic, et ubique:** here and everywhere.

162   **old mole:** By means of grotesque phrases, Hamlet may be trying to conceal from the others the solemnity of his interview with the Ghost. It may be that though he wished to confide in Horatio, he had to throw Marcellus off the scent. Some editors think that these incongruous phrases have been retained from the lost *Hamlet* (perhaps written by Kyd), which Shakespeare rewrote.

163   **pioner:** engineer, or military miner; **remove:** shift our ground.

165   **as a . . . welcome:** according to the ancient laws of hospitality.

167   **your philosophy:** philosophy in general. Horatio, of course, has been characterized as somewhat sceptical and "your" may refer to him. If "your" in this second sense is accepted, it suggests that Hamlet and Horatio may have engaged in arguments on the subject while at college.

169   **how strange . . . myself:** however strangely or oddly I behave.

171   Hamlet definitely implies that he intends to play the madman, possibly to gain time, perhaps to divert suspicion. Hamlet will pretend to be mad, but there will be times when it will be hard to distinguish pretence from reality. Later in the play, he speaks of himself as "punished/With a sore distraction", as though he were actually at times beyond sanity and beyond pretence.

Hamlet. Never make known what you have seen to-night.

Horatio.
Marcellus. } My lord, we will not.

Hamlet.   Nay, but swear't.

Horatio.   In faith, 145
   My lord, not I.

Marcellus.   Nor I, my lord, in faith.

Hamlet. Upon my sword.

Marcellus.   We have sworn, my lord, already.

Hamlet. Indeed, upon my sword, indeed.
      Ghost cries under the stage.

Ghost. Swear.

Hamlet. Ha, ha, boy, say'st thou so? art thou there, true-
   penny?   150
   Come on, you hear this fellow in the cellarage;
   Consent to swear.

Horatio.   Propose the oath, my lord.

Hamlet. Never to speak of this that you have seen,
   Swear by my sword.

Ghost. Swear.   155

Hamlet. *Hic, et ubique?* then we'll shift our ground.
   Come hither, gentlemen,
   And lay your hands again upon my sword:
   Swear by my sword,
   Never to speak of this that you have heard.   160

Ghost. Swear by his sword.

Hamlet. Well said, old mole! canst work i' the earth so fast?
   A worthy pioner! Once more remove, good friends.

Horatio. O day and night, but this is wondrous strange!

Hamlet. And therefore as a stranger give it welcome;   165
   There are more things in heaven and earth, Horatio,
   Than are dreamt of in your philosophy; but come,
   Here, as before, never, so help you mercy,
   (How strange or odd soe'er I bear myself,
   As I perchance hereafter shall think meet   170
   To put an antic disposition on)

[handwritten: ← he will act mad]

173 **encumber'd:** akimbo.

177 **ambiguous giving out:** suggestive behaviour and comments.

116-81 "This passage exhibits Hamlet in a state of extreme emotional instability, and with an intellect tottering on its seat" (Dover Wilson, *What Happens in 'Hamlet'*). Comment on this statement.

181 **Rest, rest, perturbed spirit:** a gentle and moving command.

187-8 **The time . . . right:** These lines express Hamlet's whole tragedy. He does not doubt that revenge is his duty, but there is a premonition of doom and disaster in the couplet. Dover Wilson calls it "a tacit confession of personal inadequacy".

189 The last line shows Hamlet's unfailing courtesy. Horatio puts around the Prince the cloak Hamlet had dropped in his pursuit of the Ghost.

See also p. 253.

That you, at such times seeing me, never shall,
With arms encumber'd thus, or this head-shake,
Or by pronouncing of some doubtful phrase,
(As "Well, well, we know," or "We could, an if we
   would," 175
Or "If we list to speak," or "There be, an if they
   might,"
Or such ambiguous giving out) to note
That you know aught of me: this do swear,
So grace and mercy at your most need help you.
Ghost. Swear. 180
Hamlet. Rest, rest, perturbed spirit! (*They swear.*) So,
   gentlemen,
With all my love I do commend me to you,
And what so poor a man as Hamlet is
May do to express his love and friending to you,
God willing, shall not lack: let us go in together, 185
And still your fingers on your lips, I pray.
The time is out of joint; O cursed spite,
That ever I was born to set it right!
Nay, come, let's go together.   *Exeunt.*

ACT II

Scene 1

TWO MONTHS LATER.
A ROOM IN POLONIUS' HOUSE.

Enter Polonius and Reynaldo.

Polonius. Give him this money, and these notes, Reynaldo.
Reynaldo. I will, my lord.
Polonius. You shall do marvellous wisely, good Reynaldo,
Before you visit him, to make inquire

7 **Danskers:** Danes. It is said that the University of Paris was a popular study centre of the Danes. In Elizabethan times, Denmark was known as *Danske*.

8 **keep:** live, dwell.

10 **encompassment and . . . question:** roundabout, casual method of questioning.

11-12 **come you . . . it:** You get closer by indirect than by direct questions; **more nearer:** a double comparative.

19-20 **put on . . . please:** accuse him of any imaginary faults you like; **rank:** gross.

23-24 **companions noted . . . liberty:** faults frequently observed among and characteristic of unfettered young men; **gaming:** gambling.

25 **fencing:** Laertes had some skill at this sport; here, the reference implies that the Parisian fencers may have been quarrelsome and that dangerous brawls may have resulted.

26 **drabbing:** frequenting brothels.

28 **season:** qualify.

30 **that he . . . incontinency:** that he goes to extremes of lechery, that his indulgence is habitual rather than occasional.

31 **quaintly:** ingeniously, artfully.

32 **taints of liberty:** touches of corruption caused by lack of restraint.

34 **a savageness . . . blood:** a wildness of undisciplined nature.

35 **of general assault:** typical of youth.

Of his behaviour.
Reynaldo.   My lord, I did intend it.   5
Polonius.   Marry, well said, very well said. Look you, sir,
    Inquire me first what Danskers are in Paris,
    And how, and who, what means, and where they keep,
    What company, at what expense, and finding
    By this encompassment and drift of question   10
    That they do know my son, come you more nearer
    Than your particular demands will touch it:
    Take you, as 'twere, some distant knowledge of him,
    As thus, "I know his father, and his friends,
    And in part him:" do you mark this, Reynaldo?   15
Reynaldo.   Ay, very well, my lord.
Polonius.   "And in part him; but," you may say, "not well:
    But if't be he I mean, he's very wild,
    Addicted so and so;" and there put on him
    What forgeries you please; marry, none so rank   20
    As may dishonour him, take heed of that,
    But, sir, such wanton, wild, and usual slips
    As are companions noted and most known
    To youth and liberty.
Reynaldo.   As gaming, my lord.
Polonius.   Ay, or drinking, fencing, swearing,   25
    Quarrelling, drabbing: you may go so far.
Reynaldo.   My lord, that would dishonour him.
Polonius.   Faith, no, as you may season it in the charge,
    You must not put another scandal on him,
    That he is open to incontinency,   30
    That's not my meaning, but breathe his faults so quaintly
    That they may seem the taints of liberty,
    The flash and outbreak of a fiery mind,
    A savageness in unreclaimed blood,
    Of general assault.
Reynaldo.   But, my good lord,—   35
Polonius.   Wherefore should you do this?
Reynaldo.   Ay, my lord,

38 **fetch of warrant:** a device that has been found to work; some editors say *justifiable scheme.*

39 **sullies:** stains, acts of disgraceful behaviour.

40 **soil'd with working:** tarnished with use.

41 **Mark you:** This short line suggests a pause for emphasis.

43 **prenominate:** aforesaid.

45 **He closes . . . consequence:** He replies as follows.

47 **according to . . . addition:** in accordance with the usage or style of address.

48 **of man and country:** befitting the individual, or typical of the land.

49-51 There is irony in the fact that Polonius is so long-winded that he loses the thread of his own discourse.

58 **o'ertook in's rouse:** overcome in his carousing; that is, he has lost consciousness.

59 **falling out:** quarrelling; **tennis:** The game was popular in the English court; Henry VIII played a good game of tennis. Shakespeare makes specific use of the terms of this game in *Henry V.*

61 **videlicet:** that is to say, namely (frequently shortened to *viz.*).

62 **your bait . . . truth:** The metaphor implies that by using false insinuations one can trick a person into revealing the truth; **carp:** a fish considered easy to catch.

63 **reach:** ability, discernment, shrewdness.

64 **with windlasses:** A windlass was a geared contrivance used to wind a crossbow. An arrangement of cords and wheels made the bending of the strong steel bow a simple if slow process; **assays of bias:** indirect approaches; the metaphor is taken from the game of bowls, where the bowl takes a curved course to reach "the jack". According to Caroline Spurgeon, Shakespeare was attracted by the subtle element in the game. He makes three times as many references to this game as he does to any other; there are in all nineteen images from bowls in his plays.

65 **By indirections . . . out:** By roundabout methods, we discover what we are trying to find out.

67 **You have me:** You understand me.

I would know that.
Polonius.   Marry, sir, here's my drift,
   And I believe it is a fetch of warrant:
   You laying these slight sullies on my son,
   As 'twere a thing a little soil'd with working,   40
   Mark you,
   Your party in converse, him you would sound,
   Having ever seen in the prenominate crimes
   The youth you breathe of guilty, be assur'd
   He closes with you in this consequence;   45
   "Good sir," (or so) or "friend," or "gentleman,"
   According to the phrase or the addition
   Of man and country.
Reynaldo.   Very good, my lord.
Polonius.   And then, sir, does he this—he does—what
   was I about to say? By the mass, I was about to say   50
   something: where did I leave?
Reynaldo.   At "closes in the consequence," at "friend or so,"
   and "gentleman."
Polonius.   At "closes in the consequence," ay, marry;
   He closes with you thus: "I know the gentleman;   55
   I saw him yesterday, or t'other day,
   Or then, or then, with such, or such, and, as you say,
   There was a' gaming, there o'ertook in's rouse,
   There falling out at tennis:" or perchance,
   "I saw him enter such a house of sale,"   60
   Videlicet, a brothel, or so forth. See you now,
   Your bait of falsehood takes this carp of truth:
   And thus do we of wisdom and of reach,
   With windlasses and with assays of bias,
   By indirections find directions out: 65
   So, by my former lecture and advice,
   Shall you my son. You have me, have you not?
Reynaldo.   My lord, I have.
Polonius.   God be wi' ye; fare ye well.
Reynaldo.   Good my lord!

70 **in yourself:** personally.

1-71 Polonius illustrates to perfection his devious methods; his spying on his son, whatever the motive (and it appears to be sheer curiosity), strikes many readers as somewhat underhand.

72 **ply his music:** indulge himself. It is probably not a literal expression.

75 **God:** changed in F to *Heaven*; by Act of Parliament in the reign of James I, the name of God could not be used on the stage.

76 **closet:** small private room.

77 **doublet all unbrac'd:** jacket (lined coat) all unfastened.

78 **foul'd:** loose and twisted (as of an anchor).

79 **down-gyved:** fallen down like fetters.

77-81 **purport:** meaning; these lines recall the description of the demented lover in *As You Like It* (III. ii. 368-71): "then your hose should be ungarter'd, your bonnet unbanded, your sleeve unbutton'd, your shoe untied, and everything about you demonstrating a careless desolation." Dover Wilson asserts that Hamlet's appearance is that of a madman rather than a lover.

89 **perusal:** study.

90 **as:** as if.

86-99 Many editors see in these lines proof of Hamlet's great love for Ophelia. His silence is enigmatic.

Polonius.   Observe his inclination in yourself.   70
Reynaldo.   I shall, my lord.
Polonius.   And let him ply his music.
Reynaldo.   Well, my lord.
Polonius.   Farewell!   *Exit Reynaldo.*
         Enter Ophelia.
                        How now, Ophelia! what's the matter?
Ophelia.   O, my lord, my lord, I have been so affrighted!
Polonius.   With what, i' the name of God?   75
Ophelia.   My lord, as I was sewing in my closet,
    Lord Hamlet, with his doublet all unbrac'd,
    No hat upon his head, his stockings foul'd,
    Ungarter'd and down-gyved to his ancle,
    Pale as his shirt, his knees knocking each other,   80
    And with a look so piteous in purport
    As if he had been loosed out of hell
    To speak of horrors, he comes before me.
Polonius.   Mad for thy love?
Ophelia.   My lord, I do not know,
    But truly I do fear it.
Polonius.   What said he?   85
Ophelia.   He took me by the wrist and held me hard;
    Then goes he to the length of all his arm,
    And with his other hand thus o'er his brow,
    He falls to such perusal of my face
    As he would draw it. Long stay'd he so;   90
    At last, a little shaking of mine arm,
    And thrice his head thus waving up and down,
    He rais'd a sigh so piteous and profound
    As it did seem to shatter all his bulk,
    And end his being: that done, he lets me go,   95
    And with his head over his shoulder turn'd,
    He seem'd to find his way without his eyes,
    For out o' doors he went without their helps,
    And to the last bended their light on me.
Polonius.   Come, go with me; I will go seek the king.   100

101 **ecstasy:** madness.
102 **whose violent . . . itself:** whose passionate quality destroys itself.
109 **access:** admittance. Polonius is very positive.
111 **coted:** observed. This is the Q2 reading; F gives *quoted*, which has the same meaning here.
112 **jealousy:** suspicion.
113 **proper to:** characteristic of.
114 **to cast . . . ourselves:** to overreach ourselves.
117-18 **which, being . . . love:** These lines are probably corrupt; Gollancz suggests the following interpretation: "If I keep Hamlet's love hidden, the hiding it may cause more grief than the disclosure may cause resentment."

See also p. 256.

1 Rosencrantz and Guildenstern have been described by Granville-Barker as "two rather lifeless strands in the play's lively fabric"; like Salanio and Salarino in *The Merchant of Venice*, they are hard to separate. Professor Harry Levin says "Their backstage nicknames are the knife and fork, partly because they are inseparable, and partly because it is their task to feed Hamlet his lines."
2 **moreover that:** beyond the fact that.
3 **provoke:** cause.
6 **sith:** since; **the exterior:** his outward appearance.
7 **should:** can.

This is the very ecstasy of love,
Whose violent property fordoes itself
And leads the will to desperate undertakings
As oft as any passion under heaven
That does afflict our natures. I am sorry.   105
What, have you given him any hard words of late?
Ophelia.   No, my good lord, but, as you did command,
I did repel his letters, and denied
His access to me.
Polonius.   That hath made him mad.
I am sorry that with better heed and judgement   110
I had not coted him: I fear'd he did but trifle
And meant to wreck thee; but beshrew my jealousy!
By heaven, it is as proper to our age
To cast beyond ourselves in our opinions
As it is common for the younger sort   115
To lack discretion. Come, go we to the king:
This must be known, which, being kept close, might move
More grief to hide than hate to utter love.
Come.   *Exeunt.*

Scene 2

A ROOM IN THE CASTLE.

Flourish. Enter King, Queen, Rosencrantz,
Guildenstern, and Attendants.

King.   Welcome, dear Rosencrantz and Guildenstern!
Moreover that we much did long to see you,
The need we have to use you did provoke
Our hasty sending. Something have you heard
Of Hamlet's transformation; so call it,   5
Sith nor the exterior nor the inward man
Resembles that it was. What it should be,
More than his father's death, that thus hath put him

11 **of so young days:** from such an early age.
12 **neighbour'd to:** associated with.
13 **vouchsafe your rest:** please to remain.
16 **occasion:** opportunity.
18 **open'd:** if it were disclosed.
1-18 Claudius is exceedingly smooth and plausible; he appears to be greatly concerned about Hamlet's condition. Dramatic irony is evident in that we know only too well what Claudius as yet does not appear to suspect.
21 **to whom . . . adheres:** to whom he is more partial or loyal.
22 **gentry:** courtesy.
24 **for the . . . hope:** in order that you may provide us with information that will help us in our desire (to cure Hamlet).
27 **of:** over.
30 **in the full bent:** fully prepared. The metaphor is from bending a bow and means *stretched tight.*
33-34 These lines emphasize the indistinguishable quality of the two, whose names suggest "garland of roses" (Rosencrantz) and "golden stars" (Guildenstern).
38 **practices:** proceedings, but the word often implies trickery; hence, the element of irony.

So much from the understanding of himself,
I cannot dream of: I entreat you both, 10
That, being of so young days brought up with him
And sith so neighbour'd to his youth and haviour,
That you vouchsafe your rest here in our court
Some little time, so by your companies
To draw him on to pleasures, and to gather 15
So much as from occasion you may glean,
Whether aught to us unknown afflicts him thus,
That open'd lies within our remedy.
Queen. Good gentlemen, he hath much talk'd of you,
And sure I am two men there are not living 20
To whom he more adheres. If it will please you
To show us so much gentry and good will
As to expend your time with us a while,
For the supply and profit of our hope,
Your visitation shall receive such thanks 25
As fits a king's remembrance.
Rosencrantz.   Both your majesties
Might, by the sovereign power you have of us,
Put your dread pleasures more into command
Than to entreaty.
Guildenstern.   But we both obey,
And here give up ourselves, in the full bent, 30
To lay our service freely at your feet
To be commanded.
King. Thanks, Rosencrantz and gentle Guildenstern.
Queen. Thanks, Guildenstern and gentle Rosencrantz:
And I beseech you instantly to visit 35
My too much changed son. Go, some of you,
And bring these gentlemen where Hamlet is.
Guildenstern. Heavens make our presence and our practices
Pleasant and helpful to him!
Queen.   Ay, amen!
    Exeunt Rosencrantz, Guildenstern, and some Attendants.
        Enter Polonius.

42 **still:** ever, always. Claudius flatters Polonius and by his skill appears to have won the old man's complete support.
47 **hunts not . . . sure:** is not as certain in pursuing the schemes of others.
51 Polonius enjoys a sense of power in keeping Claudius in suspense.
52 **fruit:** dessert, coming at the end of a meal.
55 **distemper:** mental disturbance.
56 **doubt:** suspect; **the main:** the chief cause.
58 **him:** Polonius.
60 **desires:** good wishes.
61 **our first:** Supply *audience.*
67-68 **borne in hand:** deceived, imposed upon. Macbeth implies that the hired murderers were "borne in hand" by Banquo (III. i. 81); **arrests on:** orders to desist.
69 **in fine:** in short.
71 **to give . . . arms:** to make warlike attacks.

Polonius.   The ambassadors from Norway, my good lord,   40
  Are joyfully return'd.
King.   Thou still hast been the father of good news.
Polonius.   Have I, my lord? Assure you, my good liege,
  I hold my duty as I hold my soul,
  Both to my God, and to my gracious king: 45
  And I do think, or else this brain of mine
  Hunts not the trail of policy so sure
  As it hath us'd to do, that I have found
  The very cause of Hamlet's lunacy.
King.   O, speak of that; that do I long to hear.   50
Polonius.   Give first admittance to the ambassadors;
  My news shall be the fruit to that great feast.
King.   Thyself do grace to them, and bring them in.
                    Exit Polonius.
  He tells me, my dear Gertrude, he hath found
  The head and source of all your son's distemper.   55
Queen.   I doubt it is no other but the main,
  His father's death, and our o'erhasty marriage. ← no mention of murder
King.   Well, we shall sift him.
          Re-enter Polonius, with Voltimand and Cornelius.
                    Welcome, my good friends!
  Say, Voltimand, what from our brother Norway?
Voltimand.   Most fair return of greetings and desires.   60
  Upon our first, he sent out to suppress
  His nephew's levies, which to him appear'd
  To be a preparation 'gainst the Polack,   *Denmark will attack Poland*
  But better look'd into, he truly found
  It was against your highness; whereat griev'd   65
  That so his sickness, age, and impotence
  Was falsely borne in hand, sends out arrests
  On Fortinbras, which he in brief obeys,
  Receives rebuke from Norway, and in fine
  Makes vow before his uncle never more   70
  To give the assay of arms against your majesty.
  Whereon old Norway, overcome with joy,

79-80 **on such ... down:** The document sets forth the provisions for guaranteeing Denmark's safety during Fortinbras' passage through Claudius' dominions; **It likes us well:** We warmly approve.

81 **at our ... time:** when we have more time to consider it.

86 **expostulate:** discuss, argue about.

90 **wit:** understanding.

91 **outward flourishes:** display of fine garments.

95 **more matter ... art:** more facts with fewer frills. "Art" is Polonius' forte since he clothes his ideas in the very outward flourishes he has just scorned.

98 **figure:** figure of speech, but he is mightily pleased with himself none the less.

103 **effect defective:** negative result; that is, Hamlet's madness.

Gives him three thousand crowns in annual fee
And his commission to employ those soldiers,
So levied as before, against the Polack,   75
With an entreaty, herein further shown,
     Giving a paper.
That it might please you to give quiet pass
Through your dominions for this enterprise,
On such regards of safety and allowance
As therein are set down.

King.   It likes us well,   80
And at our more consider'd time we'll read,
Answer, and think upon this business.
Meantime, we thank you for your well-took labour:
Go to your rest; at night we'll feast together:
Most welcome home!
          Exeunt Voltimand and Cornelius.
Polonius.   This business is well ended.   85
My liege, and madam, to expostulate
What majesty should be, what duty is,
Why day is day, night night, and time is time,
Were nothing but to waste night, day, and time.
Therefore, since brevity is the soul of wit   90
And tediousness the limbs and outward flourishes,
I will be brief; your noble son is mad:
Mad call I it, for, to define true madness,
What is't but to be nothing else but mad?
But let that go.
Queen.   More matter, with less art.   95
Polonius. Madam, I swear I use no art at all.
That he is mad, 'tis true: 'tis true 'tis pity,
And pity 'tis 'tis true: a foolish figure;
But farewell it, for I will use no art.
Mad let us grant him then, and now remains   100
That we find out the cause of this effect,
Or rather say, the cause of this defect,
For this effect defective comes by cause:

105 **Perpend:** Ponder. In Shakespeare, the word always has a ludicrous loftiness about it. It is followed by a pause four feet long.

85-105 Polonius is enjoying his little triumph.

108 **gather and surmise:** get the meaning, and draw your own conclusions.

109 Polonius is in his element as he imagines he has produced a solution to this thorny problem.

111 **beautified:** In Shakespeare's day, the word meant *endowed with beauty*. What meaning read into it by Polonius might justify his criticism?

113 **in her . . . bosom:** for her eye and heart alone. It may refer to the fact that she would keep the letter close to her heart.

116-18 **doubt:** have doubts about whether (the stars are fire, etc.).

119 **doubt:** question the fact that.

120 **ill at these numbers:** not skilled at writing verse. How true is Hamlet's criticism?

121 **reckon:** count, number.

123-4 **whilst this . . . him:** while this body is his. Dover Wilson suggests that the term "machine", like a number of others in this play, may have had its genesis in Timothy Bright's *A Treatise of Melancholie,* 1586, in which Bright speaks of the nature of the body as that of a kind of living instrument, tool, or engine of the soul. This is Shakespeare's only use of the word.

126 **more above:** moreover.

127 **fell out:** occurred.

130 Polonius' loyalty to Claudius is unquestioning.

131 **fain:** gladly.

132-3 Polonius' veracity may be questioned here.

Thus it remains, and the remainder thus.
Perpend;   105
I have a daughter,—have while she is mine,—
Who in her duty and obedience, mark,
Hath given me this: now gather and surmise.
     Reads.
"To the celestial and my soul's idol, the most
   beautified Ophelia,"—   110
That's an ill phrase, a vile phrase; "beautified" is a
vile phrase; but you shall hear.
     Reads.
Thus—"in her excellent white bosom, these," &c.
Queen.   Came this from Hamlet to her?
Polonius.   Good madam, stay awhile, I will be faithful.   115
     Reads.
     "Doubt thou the stars are fire,
       Doubt that the sun doth move,
       Doubt truth to be a liar,
       But never doubt I love.
"O dear Ophelia, I am ill at these numbers, I have not   120
art to reckon my groans, but that I love thee best, O
most best believe it; Adieu.
"Thine evermore, most dear lady, whilst this machine
   is to him,   HAMLET."
This in obedience hath my daughter shown me,   125
And, more above, hath his solicitings,
As they fell out by time, by means, and place,
All given to mine ear.
King.   But how hath she
Receiv'd his love?
Polonius.   What do you think of me?
King.   As of a man faithful and honourable.   130
Polonius.   I would fain prove so, but what might you think,
When I had seen this hot love on the wing,
As I perceiv'd it (I must tell you that)
Before my daughter told me, what might you,

136 **play'd the . . . table-book:** served as postman between the two. (Most editors point out that love-letters may be left in either of the places mentioned above); **table-book:** memorandum book.

137 **or given . . . winking:** winked at my heart as a hint to keep silent.

138 **idle:** indifferent.

139 **round:** directly.

140 **my young mistress:** as though she were a little girl; **bespeak:** address.

141 **out of thy star:** above thy sphere.

142 **prescripts:** orders.

143 **from his resort:** from access to her.

145 **took the . . . advice:** profited by my warnings.

148 **watch:** wakefulness, insomnia.

149 **lightness:** lightheadedness; **declension:** deterioration.

131-50 Polonius' positive confidence adds humour through its irony.

159 **the centre:** of the earth and thus of the universe, according to a Ptolemaic concept.

160 **four:** possibly *for*, though "four hours together" was a common Elizabethan phrase.

162 **loose:** release, as a greyhound from a leash; a rather unpleasant word.

163 **arras:** tapestry hangings made in Arras, France.

Or my dear majesty your queen here, think,   135
If I had play'd the desk, or table-book,
Or given my heart a winking, mute and dumb,
Or look'd upon this love with idle sight,
What might you think? No, I went round to work,
And my young mistress thus I did bespeak: 140
"Lord Hamlet is a prince out of thy star;
This must not be:" and then I prescripts gave her,
That she should lock herself from his resort,
Admit no messengers, receive no tokens;
Which done, she took the fruits of my advice;   145
And he repelled, a short tale to make,
Fell into a sadness, then into a fast,
Thence to a watch, thence into a weakness,
Thence to a lightness, and by this declension
Into the madness wherein now he raves   150
And all we mourn for.
King.   Do you think 'tis this?
Queen.   It may be, very like.
Polonius.   Hath there been such a time, I'ld fain know that,
That I have positively said " 'tis so"
When it prov'd otherwise?
King.   Not that I know.   155
Polonius (*pointing to his head and shoulder*).   Take this
    from this, if this be otherwise:
If circumstances lead me, I will find
Where truth is hid, though it were hid indeed
Within the centre.
King.   How may we try it further?
Polonius. You know, sometimes he walks four hours together 160
Here in the lobby.
Queen.   So he does, indeed.
Polonius.   At such a time I'll loose my daughter to him:
Be you and I behind an arras then;
Mark the encounter: if he love her not,
And be not from his reason fall'n thereon,   165

I'll get Hamlet to meet
Ophelia; if Hamlet is not
mad about her, cut my head.

167 **carters:** cart-horses.

168 **sadly:** seriously; **wretch:** a term of endearment mingled with pity. Othello refers to Desdemona as "excellent wretch" (III. iii. 90).

170 **board him presently:** address (tackle) him at once.

172 **God-a-mercy:** God have mercy; hence, thank God.

174 **fishmonger:** perhaps a pander, as if Hamlet thought Polonius might sacrifice Ophelia to gain his own ends. In any case, it is intended as an insult.

176 **so honest:** Here Hamlet reverts to the literal meaning: one who sells fish.

181-2 **sun breed maggots:** a common belief of the times; **a god kissing carrion:** Harrison interprets this as "good kissable flesh". Q1, Q2, and F read *good;* some editors emend it to "god". This may imply that the corruption of the world will pervert divine influence.

184 **Let her . . . sun:** perhaps an oblique reference to Claudius' lascivious eye. Dover Wilson thinks it is a scornfully ironic reference made by Hamlet to himself.

187 **How say you by that:** What do you think of that?

190 **extremity:** great pangs. (The imagination tends to boggle at this.)

193 Hamlet has a characteristic trick of repeating words or phrases in threes.

194, 196 **matter:** a) cause of dispute, b) subject matter.

197 **the satirical rogue:** perhaps the author Juvenal whose tenth satire is a description of old age.

Let me be no assistant for a state,
But keep a farm and carters.
King.   We will try it.
Queen.   But look where sadly the poor wretch comes reading.
Polonius.   Away, I do beseech you, both away:
  I'll board him presently; O, give me leave.   170
              Exeunt King, Queen, and Attendants.
          Enter Hamlet, reading.
  How does my good Lord Hamlet?
Hamlet.   Well, God-a-mercy.
Polonius.   Do you know me, my lord?
Hamlet.   Excellent well, you are a fishmonger.
Polonius.   Not I, my lord.   175
Hamlet.   Then I would you were so honest a man.
Polonius.   Honest, my lord?
Hamlet.   Ay, sir; to be honest, as this world goes, is to
  be one man pick'd out of ten thousand.
Polonius.   That's very true, my lord.   180
Hamlet.   For if the sun breed maggots in a dead dog,
  being a god kissing carrion—Have you a daughter?
Polonius.   I have, my lord.
Hamlet.   Let her not walk i' the sun: conception is a
  blessing; but not as your daughter may conceive,—   185
  friend, look to't.
Polonius (aside). How say you by that? Still harping on my
  daughter: yet he knew me not at first, he said I was
  a fishmonger: he is far gone, far gone: and truly
  in my youth I suffer'd much extremity for love;   190
  very near this. I'll speak to him again. What do
  you read, my lord?
Hamlet.   Words, words, words.
Polonius.   What is the matter, my lord?
Hamlet.   Between who?   195
Polonius.   I mean, the matter that you read, my lord.
Hamlet. Slanders, sir: for the satirical rogue says here that
  old men have grey beards, that their faces are wrinkled,

199 **purging thick amber:** discharging a sticky substance like the resin from evergreen trees.

201 **hams:** thighs and buttocks.

204-5 **old:** playing on words, Hamlet may mean *young;* on the other hand, his weariness and melancholy make him *feel* old; **if like . . . backward:** This is usually clarified by a bit of stage business: Hamlet advancing on Polonius causes him to walk backward.

197-205 This passage is a rude parody of Polonius' appearance, but Hamlet seems to be reading it and therefore it escapes being a direct insult. Hamlet uses his "madness" to express some of his true feelings.

206 **method:** meaning.

209 **pregnant:** full of meaning or significance.

210 **happiness:** an apt turn of phrase.

220 Hamlet drops the pretence of madness.

225-7 Hamlet's sincerity is shown in this glad welcome; he has no reason as yet to distrust Rosencrantz and Guildenstern.

228 **indifferent:** average, ordinary.

230 **button:** found at the very top of the cap; hence, they are not in the highest favour of Fortune.

231 Hamlet continues the metaphor.

their eyes purging thick amber and plum-tree gum,
and that they have a plentiful lack of wit, together   200
with most weak hams: all which, sir, though I most
powerfully and potently believe, yet I hold it not
honesty to have it thus set down; for yourself, sir,
shall grow old as I am, if like a crab you could go
backward.   205

Polonius (aside). Though this be madness, yet there is method ― witty
   in't.—Will you walk out of the air, my lord?

Hamlet.   Into my grave.

Polonius.

   Indeed, that's out of the air. (*aside*) How pregnant
   sometimes his replies are! a happiness that often   210
   madness hits on, which reason and sanity could
   not so prosperously be deliver'd of. I will leave
   him, and suddenly contrive the means of meeting
   between him and my daughter.—My lord, I will
   take my leave of you.   215

Hamlet.   You cannot take from me any thing that I will
   more willingly part withal: except my life, except
   my life, except my life.

Polonius.   Fare you well, my lord.

Hamlet.   These tedious old fools!   220

            Re-enter Rosencrantz and Guildenstern.

Polonius.   You go to seek the Lord Hamlet; there he is.

Rosencrantz (to Polonius).   God save you, sir! *Exit Polonius.*

Guildenstern.   My honour'd lord!

Rosencrantz.   My most dear lord!

Hamlet.   My excellent good friends! How dost thou,   225
   Guildenstern? Ah, Rosencrantz! Good lads, how
   do you both?

Rosencrantz.   As the indifferent children of the earth.

Guildenstern.   Happy, in that we are not over-happy;
   On Fortune's cap we are not the very button.   230

Hamlet.   Nor the soles of her shoe?

Rosencrantz.   Neither, my lord.

237 **strumpet:** prostitute.

239 **doomsday:** the day of judgement. Only if judgement is near will the world be virtuous. Hamlet has a strong satirical streak.

242 **prison:** Hamlet may be referring to the fact that by royal request he may not return to Wittenberg.

246 **confines:** places of confinement.

250-1 **for there . . . so:** Shakespeare may have adopted this idea from Montaigne, the French essayist, whose works in Florio's translation he evidently knew well. The philosophic aspect of Hamlet's character seems to have been drawn from Montaigne. (A copy of the *Essais* bearing Shakespeare's signature is still extant.) Lovelace, the Cavalier poet, wrote:

> Stone walls do not a prison make
> Nor iron bars a cage;
> Minds innocent and quiet take
> That for an hermitage.

John Milton expressed the same idea:

> The mind is its own place and in itself
> Can make a heaven of hell, a hell of heaven.

253 Why does Rosencrantz introduce the subject of ambition?

257 **bad dreams:** Hamlet is fencing with words, but there is an ominous quality in the remark. Does Hamlet want them to believe his madness springs from thwarted ambition? If so, why?

258-60 **for the . . . dream:** What an ambitious man considers to be substantial is only a dream's shadow; hence, it is insubstantial in the highest degree.

261-3 The emphasis is still on the unreality of ambition.

264-5 **Then are . . . shadows:** Beggars who lack ambition are therefore men having substance; kings and puffed up heroes who are ambitious are then nothing but the shadows of real men (beggars). (The king is less than the beggar; this transposition of ideas shows the nimbleness with which Hamlet's—and no doubt Shakespeare's—mind worked.)

266 **fay:** faith.

Hamlet. Then you live about her waist, or in the middle of her favours.

Guildenstern. Faith, her privates we. 235

Hamlet. In the secret parts of Fortune? O, most true; she is a strumpet. What news?

Rosencrantz. None, my lord, but that the world's grown honest.

Hamlet. Then is doomsday near: but your news is not true. Let me question more in particular: what have 240 you, my good friends, deserv'd at the hands of Fortune, that she sends you to prison hither?

Guildenstern. Prison, my lord?

Hamlet. Denmark's a prison.

Rosencrantz. Then is the world one. 245

Hamlet. A goodly one; in which there are many confines, wards and dungeons; Denmark being one o' the worst.

Rosencrantz. We think not so, my lord.

Hamlet. Why, then 'tis none to you; for there is nothing 250 either good or bad, but thinking makes it so: to me it is a prison.

Rosencrantz. Why then your ambition makes it one; 'tis too narrow for your mind.

Hamlet. O God, I could be bounded in a nut-shell, and 255 count myself a king of infinite space, were it not that I have bad dreams.

Guildenstern. Which dreams indeed are ambition; for the very substance of the ambitious is merely the shadow of a dream. 260

Hamlet. A dream itself is but a shadow.

Rosencrantz. Truly, and I hold ambition of so airy and light a quality that it is but a shadow's shadow.

Hamlet. Then are our beggars bodies, and our monarchs and outstretch'd heroes the beggars' shadows. Shall we 265 to the court? for, by my fay, I cannot reason.

Rosencrantz. ⎱
Guildenstern. ⎰ We'll wait upon you.

268 **no such matter:** by no means.
270-1 **most dreadfully attended:** (perhaps) spied upon; badly served? **in the ... friendship:** speaking frankly as one friend to another; **make you:** are you doing?
275 **too dear a halfpenny:** a halfpenny too dear.
275-7 Hamlet has become suspicious, perhaps as the result of a look or a gesture. Guildenstern's fumbling question underlines Hamlet's suspicions.
279 **any thing ... purpose:** Hamlet is scornful.
281 **your modesties:** your humble selves (irony).
282 **colour:** camouflage.
286 **consonancy:** harmony.
287 **obligation:** binding power.
288 **a better proposer:** a more eloquent speaker.
289 **even:** plain, honest.
292 **of:** upon.
295-6 **my anticipation ... discovery:** my telling you forestall your finding out.
297 **moult no feather:** not be found lacking.
298-300 **forgone all ... exercises:** given up all customary exercises; **it goes ... disposition:** I feel so depressed; **frame:** structure.
301 **a sterile promontory:** The metaphor implies barrenness, like that of a bleak, rocky headland.
302 **canopy:** covering, from the Greek word for *mosquito-net*. Compare Blanco White's sonnet with its reference to "This glorious canopy of light and blue". How does this picture of the atmosphere differ from Hamlet's? **brave:** glorious, grand.
303 **fretted:** chequered, adorned. This image of a starry sky is vividly imaginative; it emphasizes Hamlet's poetic nature as well as Shakespeare's powers of observation and originality.

Hamlet. No such matter: I will not sort you with the rest of my servants; for, to speak to you like an honest man, I am most dreadfully attended. But, in the beaten way of friendship, what make you at Elsinore? 270

Rosencrantz. To visit you, my lord, no other occasion.

Hamlet. Beggar that I am, I am even poor in thanks; but I thank you: and sure, dear friends, my thanks are too dear a halfpenny. Were you not sent for? is it 275 your own inclining? is it a free visitation? Come, come, deal justly with me: come, come; nay, speak.

Guildenstern. What should we say, my lord?

Hamlet. Any thing but to the purpose. You were sent for, and there is a kind of confession in your looks, 280 which your modesties have not craft enough to colour: I know the good king and queen have sent for you.

Rosencrantz. To what end, my lord?

Hamlet. That you must teach me. But let me conjure you, 285 by the rights of our fellowship, by the consonancy of our youth, by the obligation of our ever-preserv'd love, and by what more dear a better proposer can charge you withal, be even and direct with me, whether you were sent for, or no. 290

Rosencrantz (*aside to Guildenstern*). What say you?

Hamlet (*aside*). Nay then, I have an eye of you.—If you love me, hold not off.

Guildenstern. My lord, we were sent for.

Hamlet. I will tell you why; so shall my anticipation pre- 295 vent your discovery, and your secrecy to the king and queen moult no feather. I have of late—but wherefore I know not—lost all my mirth, forgone all custom of exercises; and indeed it goes so heavily with my disposition that this goodly frame, the 300 earth, seems to me a sterile promontory, this most excellent canopy, the air, look you, this brave o'er-hanging firmament, this majestical roof fretted with

305   **congregation of vapours:** an oppressive, foggy image.

307-8   **faculties:** mental powers; **express:** well-adapted, exact.

309   **apprehension:** power of comprehension or understanding.

310   **paragon:** model of excellence.

311   **quintessence:** fifth or highest essence of the alchemists (a word used only twice in Shakespeare). This essence would remain when the four elements of matter (fire, air, earth, water) had been removed. After this passionate flight, Hamlet returns abruptly to earth as he notes the smirking of Rosencrantz.

305-11   This magnificent passage has been referred to as "a signal illustration of the poetical resources of prose" (Verity).

305-13   These lines illustrate Hamlet's idealism and take us by contrast from the heights to the depths in a great dramatic sweep.

318   **lenten:** poor, meagre (since Lent was the season of fasting).

319   **coted:** came up with and passed. (When two greyhounds are pursuing a hare, one passes the other so as to give the hare a turn.)

321   **he that plays the king:** an oblique, satirical reference to Claudius.

323   **foil and target:** sword and shield.

324   **humorous:** full of humours, like the melancholy Jaques in *As You Like It*. Since he was crotchety, he might not "end his part in peace" but be embroiled in quarrels.

326-7   **tickle o' the sere:** easily moved to laughter, hair-triggerish. The "sere" is part of the trigger mechanism of a gun; **the lady . . . for't:** The lady shall express herself bluntly even though the rhythm suffers.

321-7   Hamlet gives us the typical roles in the typical plays of the period.

329   **were wont to:** were accustomed to.

330   **the city:** London. Shakespeare has forgotten about Denmark; several topical allusions follow. Hamlet's interest in dramatics is one of the qualities that link him with his creator. Why "tragedians"?

331   **travel:** tour; **residence:** remaining (in London).

333   **inhibition:** prohibition.

334   **innovation:** This may refer to the popularity of the child players (see below) or, as Harrison maintains, to the rebellion of Essex. The members of Shakespeare's company were somewhat implicated in the latter since they had, at the request of Essex's friends, played *Richard II* (with its abdication scene) the day before the rebellion. In this sense, "innovation" means *riot*.

335   **Do they . . . estimation:** Are they held in the same esteem?

golden fire, why, it appeareth nothing to me but a
foul and pestilent congregation of vapours. What a   305
piece of work is a man! how noble in reason! how
infinite in faculties! in form and moving how express and admirable! in action how like an angel, in
apprehension how like a god! the beauty of the
world! the paragon of animals! and yet, to me,   310
what is this quintessence of dust? man delights not
me, nor woman neither, though by your smiling you
seem to say so.

Rosencrantz.   My lord, there was no such stuff in my thoughts.

Hamlet. Why did you laugh then, when I said "man delights   315
not me"?

Rosencrantz.   To think, my lord, if you delight not in man,
what lenten entertainment the players shall receive
from you: we coted them on the way; and hither are
they coming, to offer you service.   320

Hamlet. He that plays the king shall be welcome; his majesty
shall have tribute of me; the adventurous knight
shall use his foil and target; the lover shall not sigh
gratis; the humorous man shall end his part in peace;
the clown shall make those laugh whose lungs are   325
tickle o' the sere, and the lady shall say her mind
freely, or the blank verse shall halt for't. What
players are they?

Rosencrantz.   Even those you were wont to take such
delight in, the tragedians of the city.   330

Hamlet. How chances it they travel? their residence, both
in reputation and profit, was better both ways.

Rosencrantz.   I think their inhibition comes by the
means of the late innovation.

Hamlet. Do they hold the same estimation they did when I   335
was in the city? are they so follow'd?

Rosencrantz.   No, indeed, are they not.

Hamlet.   How comes it? do they grow rusty?

340 **eyrie:** brood (of a bird of prey); **eyases:** nestlings. The metaphor has a somewhat contemptuous connotation.

341-2 **on the top of question:** at the top of their voices. The voices of the boy actors were very shrill. Another interpretation is *drowning criticism*; **tyrannically clapped:** vigorously applauded.

343 **berattle the common stages:** abuse the public stages.

344 **many wearing . . . goose-quills:** Many young gallants are afraid of being ridiculed by the satirical dramatists.

340-5 The two children's companies, which performed in private theatres, for a time put the noses of adult players out of joint. The situation was further complicated when the dramatists who wrote for the boys (Jonson and Marston) began a feud in which the adult actors of the Globe sided with Marston and the Children of Paul's. Satirical productions ridiculed members of the opposing groups until 1601, by which time the controversy had run its course. The episode is often referred to as The War of the Theatres, 1599-1601.

347-8 **escoted:** paid; **Will they . . . sing:** Will they remain in the profession only until their voices break?

349-50 **common players:** actors in the adult companies who played on the public stages.

352 **exclaim against . . . succession:** attack their own (future) profession. Shakespeare has enough foresight to realize that for the boy actors to criticize the adult actors is like cutting off their noses to spite their faces.

354 **tarre:** incite; used in dog fights.

355-7 **there was . . . question:** No money was available for a production unless the stage war was part of the plot.

359 **throwing about of brains:** controversy.

360 **carry it away:** win the day.

361 **Hercules and . . . too:** The house flag of the Globe showed Hercules with the globe on his shoulders, the motto being *Everyone is an actor*. The implication is that even the actors at the Globe suffered from the popularity of the boy players.

338-61 This passage is found in F, not in Q1 and Q2.

362 **It is . . . strange:** I am not surprised.

363 **mows:** faces (grimaces).

365 **ducats:** gold coins in value about 9 shillings each, formerly current in most European countries; **his picture in little:** Miniatures were exceedingly popular in Shakespeare's day. Possibly Rosencrantz wore one on a chain about his neck

366 **'sblood:** God's blood, a reference to the wine in the Eucharist.

362-7 Hamlet's satirical comment points up the changeable nature of human beings.

Rosencrantz.

Nay, their endeavour keeps in the wonted pace: but there is, sir, an eyrie of children, little eyases, that cry out on the top of question and are most tyrannically clapped for't: these are now the fashion, and so berattle the common stages—so they call them—that many wearing rapiers are afraid of goose-quills, and dare scarce come thither.   345

Hamlet. What, are they children? who maintains 'em? how are they escoted? Will they pursue the quality no longer than they can sing? will they not say afterwards, if they should grow themselves to common players,—as it is most like, if their means are no better,—their writers do them wrong, to make them exclaim against their own succession?   350

Rosencrantz.

Faith, there has been much to do on both sides, and the nation holds it no sin to tarre them to controversy: there was for a while no money bid for argument unless the poet and the player went to cuffs in the question.   355

Hamlet.   Is't possible?

Guildenstern. O, there has been much throwing about of brains.

Hamlet.   Do the boys carry it away?   360

Rosencrantz.

Ay, that they do, my lord; Hercules and his load too.

Hamlet.   It is not very strange, for my uncle is king of Denmark, and those that would make mows at him while my father lived, give twenty, forty, fifty, a hundred ducats a-piece, for his picture in little. 'Sblood, there is something in this more than natural if philosophy could find it out.   365

       Flourish of trumpets within.

Guildenstern.   There are the players.

Hamlet.   Gentlemen, you are welcome to Elsinore. Your hands, come then: the appurtenance of welcome is   370

340

(handwritten margin note: actors are coming)

(handwritten margin note: Hamlet knows these players)

370-2 **appurtenance of . . . ceremony:** proper accompaniment of welcome is formal ceremony; *e.g.*, the shaking of hands; **comply with . . . garb:** show formal politeness in this manner; **extent:** behaviour.

375 Hamlet pretends to give an explanation of his (so-called) madness in a deliberately madcap way.

377 **north-north-west:** Hamlet pretends that the wind affects his sanity. The whole remark suggests that he is being very subtle at the expense of Rosencrantz and Guildenstern.

378 **handsaw:** a corruption of *hernshaw* (heron), from the old proverb: "to know a hawk from a hernshaw"; that is, to make fine distinctions. The metaphor is taken from heron-hawking. Hamlet points out that he is not as mad as one might think, that he is sane enough to distinguish between friends and spies.

381-2 **swaddling clouts:** infant garments; a possible reference to senility; Hamlet's assumption of madness enables him to be rude to Polonius without being brought to task.

386 **You say right:** Hamlet pretends to be engaged in conversation with his friends in order to make fun of Polonius.

389 **Roscius:** a famous Roman comedian whose name has become a synonym for a great actor.

392 **Buz, buz:** Hamlet implies that this is stale news.

394 Probably a line from an old ballad.

395-9 **the best . . . pastoral:** Shakespeare, through Polonius (to whom such a detailed list would be meat and drink), is perhaps satirizing and exaggerating the absurd divisions of English drama. Polonius may be reading from a playbill extolling the superiorities of the company; **scene individable:** where the action takes place in one spot (unity of place); **poem unlimited:** where the action might move freely from Rome to Alexandria and back again; **Seneca cannot . . . Plautus:** Two great Latin dramatists much studied in the schools of the time. (Shakespeare is indebted to both the playwrights he has mentioned.)

400 **the law . . . liberty:** the rules of the classical school and the Elizabethan practices of Shakespeare himself. The whole passage brings out Shakespeare's zest for comedy, here at the expense of his own profession.

402 **Jephthah:** The story of Jephthah, a mighty man of valour, is told in the Book of Judges, Chapter XI. He vowed that if he were successful in leading the Israelites against the Ammonites, he would sacrifice on his return the first living creature whom he met. As he returned victorious, his only daughter came out rejoicing to meet him. Why does Hamlet refer to Polonius as Jephthah?

fashion and ceremony: let me comply with you
in this garb, lest my extent to the players, which, I tell
you, must show fairly outwards, should more appear
like entertainment than yours. You are welcome:
but my uncle-father and aunt-mother are deceived.   375
Guildenstern. In what, my dear lord?
Hamlet. I am but mad north-north-west: when the wind
    is southerly I know a hawk from a handsaw.
        Re-enter Polonius.
Polonius. Well be with you, gentlemen!
Hamlet. Hark you, Guildenstern, and you too, at each   380
    ear a hearer; that great baby you see there is not yet
    out of his swaddling clouts.
Rosencrantz. Haply he is the second time come to them, for they
    say an old man is twice a child.
Hamlet. I will prophesy; he comes to tell me of the players;   385
    mark it. You say right, sir: o' Monday morning;
    'twas so indeed.
Polonius. My lord, I have news to tell you.
Hamlet. My lord, I have news to tell you. When Roscius
    was an actor in Rome,—   390
Polonius. The actors are come hither, my lord.
Hamlet. Buz, buz!
Polonius. Upon my honour,—
Hamlet. Then came each actor on his ass,—
Polonius. The best actors in the world, either for tragedy,   395
    comedy, history, pastoral, pastoral-comical, his-
    torical-pastoral, tragical-historical, tragical-comical-
    historical-pastoral, scene individable, or poem un-
    limited: Seneca cannot be too heavy, nor Plautus
    too light; for the law of writ, and the liberty; these   400
    are the only men.
Hamlet. O Jephthah, judge of Israel, what a treasure hadst
    thou!
Polonius. What a treasure had he, my lord?
Hamlet. Why,   405

406-7 These lines and those quoted later may be found in Bishop Percy's *Reliques,* a famous collection of old ballads.

412 **follows:** Note the pun.

415 **God wot:** God knows.

418 **row:** line; here, *stanza*; **pious chanson:** so called because of the Bible story.

419 **abridgement:** entertainment and here, interruption.

420 For once, we catch a glimpse of a bright and sunny Hamlet, gay and glad in his welcome to the actors. His enthusiasm is genuine and sincere. It has also been suggested that he finds an escape from reality in this situation.

422 **valanc'd:** curtained; here, covered with a beard.

423 **to beard me:** to defy me; a play on the literal and figurative meanings.

424 **my young lady:** Boys played female parts on the English stage until 1662.

426-8 **altitude of a chopine:** height of a cork-soled shoe. Since the soles of these shoes could be from four to fifteen inches thick, the "young lady" might have "grown" considerably; **your voice . . . ring:** Before milled edges were introduced, a coin could easily be defaced. If it were chipped within the circle surrounding the device on the coin, it was no longer considered true currency. The other meaning of the pun refers to the fact that once a boy's voice had changed, he could no longer play girls' parts.

429 There is some doubt about whether this is a criticism of French falconers for their impulsiveness. Some editors assert that the French were among the best falconers in western Europe.

430 **straight:** at once.

431 **taste of your quality:** sample of your ability.

436 **caviare to the general:** a delicacy too refined for the average individual, a good thing unappreciated by the ignorant. "Caviare" is the pressed, salted roe of the sturgeon; the ordinary person does not usually appreciate it. The expression is one of many Shakespearian phrases that have become part of our language by their neat appropriateness.

437-8 **cried in . . . mine:** were superior to mine. (Some say, corresponded with mine); **digested:** arranged.

439 **modesty:** moderation.

440 **sallets:** spicy or risqué references.

> "One fair daughter, and no more,
> The which he loved passing well."

Polonius (*aside*).   Still on my daughter.

Hamlet.   Am I not i' the right, old Jephthah?

Polonius. If you call me Jephthah, my lord, I have a daughter   410
that I love passing well.

Hamlet.   Nay, that follows not.

Polonius.   What follows then, my lord?

Hamlet.   Why,

> "As by lot, God wot,"   415

and then you know,

> "It came to pass, as most like it was,"—

the first row of the pious chanson will show you
more; for look where my abridgement comes.

Enter the Players.

You are welcome, masters, welcome all. I am glad   420
to see thee well. Welcome, good friends. O, old
friend! Why, thy face is valanc'd since I saw thee
last; com'st thou to beard me in Denmark? What,
my young lady and mistress! By'r lady, your lady-
ship is nearer to heaven than when I saw you last by   425
the altitude of a chopine. Pray God your voice,
like a piece of uncurrent gold, be not crack'd within
the ring. Masters, you are all welcome. We'll
e'en to't like French falconers, fly at any thing we
see: we'll have a speech straight: come, give us a   430
taste of your quality; come, a passionate speech.

First Player.   What speech, my good lord?

Hamlet.   I heard thee speak me a speech once, but it was
never acted, or, if it was, not above once; for the
play, I remember, pleas'd not the million; 'twas   435
caviare to the general: but it was—as I received it,
and others, whose judgements in such matters cried
in the top of mine—an excellent play, well digested
in the scenes, set down with as much modesty as
cunning. I remember, one said there were no sallets   440

442 **indict the . . . affectation:** cause the author to be accused of affectation.

444-5 **handsome than fine:** The former is used in a complimentary, the latter in a critical, sense; **handsome:** naturally impressive; **fine:** artificially showy.

446 **Æneas' talk to Dido:** This is the story told in the second book of Vergil's *Æneid*, but Professor Levin believes Ovid to be the main source. Other critics maintain that it is modelled on a speech from the play *Dido* by Marlowe and Nashe, 1594.

450 **Pyrrhus:** son of Achilles, married Hermione, the daughter of Helen and Menelaus; **Hyrcanian beast:** the tiger, the proverbial embodiment in Shakespeare and other Elizabethan dramatists of hardness of heart and cruelty. Shakespeare himself was jealously referred to as a "tiger's heart wrapp'd in a player's hide". Hyrcania was a province of the ancient Persian Empire.

450-1 Hamlet's false start seems very human and natural.

450-518 This "passionate speech" has been the subject of much contradictory discussion. It is written in a strongly dramatic style, which Shakespeare himself had discarded, but it was still used by the great tragic actor, Edward Alleyn, who was the star of the rival company, the Admiral's Men. Hamlet certainly admired it. It is possible that Shakespeare himself may have acted the part, since it is traditional for the player of the Ghost to double in the role of the First Player. Note the number of end-stopped lines and the regular march of the iambic pentameter lines. 452 **sable:** heraldic for black.

454 **ominous horse:** the Trojan horse, symbolizing Troy's doom.

457 **total gules:** completely red (heraldic term) with the blood of slain foes; **trick'd:** adorned, blazoned.

459 **bak'd and . . . streets:** dried and caked by the heat of blazing streets. 460 **tyrannous:** cruel.

461 Note the rolling "r" that reverberates through the line.

462 **o'er-sized with coagulate gore:** covered with dried blood as though with glue (size).

463 **carbuncles:** red precious stones, now identified with garnets; Pyrrhus' eyes would be red and glowing fiercely.

466-7 **anon:** soon; Hamlet would hardly relish Polonius' praise, but the old man considers himself a dramatic critic of no mean stature.

468 **striking too short:** a sharp picture of the ineffectual power of the aged king; **antique:** old-fashioned; this word adds pathos.

469-70 **rebellious to . . . command:** The weakness and impotence of Priam are emphasized.

472 **his fell sword:** Pyrrhus' cruel weapon.

Hamlet wants play to be put on in which after her usbands death, a wife cries, cries but Hamlet wants to ange so that situation happens like Claudius happened. amlet will observe King to

ACT II/SCENE 2 · 93

find out whether ghost was good or bad to see truth

in the lines, to make the matter savoury, nor no matter
in the phrase that might indict the author of affectation;
but call'd it an honest method, as wholesome as
sweet, and by very much more handsome than
fine. One speech in't I chiefly lov'd: 'twas   445
Æneas' talk to Dido, and thereabout of it especially,
when he speaks of Priam's slaughter: if it live
in your memory, begin at this line; let me see, let
me see;   Claudius
"The rugged Pyrrhus, like th' Hyrcanian beast,"—   450
'Tis not so: it begins with "Pyrrhus."
"The rugged Pyrrhus, he whose sable arms,
Black as his purpose, did the night resemble,
When he lay couched in the ominous horse,
Hath now this dread and black complexion smear'd,   455
With heraldry more dismal; head to foot
Now is he total gules, horridly trick'd
With blood of fathers, mothers, daughters, sons,
Bak'd and impasted with the parching streets
That lend a tyrannous and a damned light   460
To their lord's murder: roasted in wrath and fire,
And thus o'er-sized with coagulate gore,
With eyes like carbuncles, the hellish Pyrrhus
Old grandsire Priam seeks."
So, proceed you.   465
Polonius. 'Fore God, my lord, well spoken, with good accent
and good discretion.
First Player.   "Anon he finds him
Striking too short at Greeks; his antique sword,
Rebellious to his arm, lies where it falls,
Repugnant to command: unequal match'd,   470
Pyrrhus at Priam drives, in rage strikes wide,
But with the whiff and wind of his fell sword
The unnerved father falls. Then senseless Ilium,
Seeming to feel this blow, with flaming top
Stoops to his base; and with a hideous crash   475

473-6 **unnerved:** one of Shakespeare's many contributions to the English language; **senseless Ilium . . . base:** As Priam falls, so the city crashes down; an instance of pathetic fallacy; **and with . . . ear:** Pyrrhus is momentarily stunned by the sound.

477 **declining:** falling.

479 **painted:** motionless as a painting or figure in an old tapestry.

480 **a neutral . . . matter:** one poised between the determination and the act.

482 **against some storm:** when a storm is imminent.

483 **rack:** mass of storm clouds.

484 **orb:** earth.

485 **hush:** silent; used as an adjective. Along with this adjective, the words "impasted", "mobled", "o'er-sized", and "o'er-teemed" were coined in this speech but have not achieved currency.

482-7 The elaborate (Vergilian?) simile creates a clear picture.

488 **Cyclops' hammers:** The Cyclopes assisted Vulcan in his task of creating the armour of the gods.

489 **for proof eterne:** to withstand assaults forever.

490 **remorse:** pity; **bleeding:** blood-stained; a sombre personification.

492 **strumpet:** prostitute.

493 **synod:** assembly, specially of the gods.

494 **fellies:** pieces of wood used to form the rim of a wheel.

495 **the round nave:** the hub.

492-6 The picture of Fortune with a wheel to suggest mutability is a traditional one.

497 Polonius' interruption seems dramatically sound.

499 **jig:** farcical interlude; **tale of bawdry:** a risqué story.

501 **mobled:** muffled, a dialect word; perhaps with her head covered by a scarf (*mob-cap*). The word is strange to Hamlet, but Polonius sets himself up as an authority in approving of it.

506 **bisson rheum:** blinding tears; **clout:** rag, cloth; still used in the expression *dish-clout*.

508 **o'er-teemed:** worn out with child-bearing.

Takes prisoner Pyrrhus' ear, for, lo! his sword,
Which was declining on the milky head
Of reverend Priam, seem'd i' the air to stick;
So, as a painted tyrant, Pyrrhus stood,
And like a neutral to his will and matter,   480
Did nothing.
But as we often see, against some storm,
A silence in the heavens, the rack stand still,
The bold winds speechless, and the orb below
As hush as death, anon the dreadful thunder   485
Doth rend the region, so after Pyrrhus' pause
Aroused vengeance sets him new a-work;
And never did the Cyclops' hammers fall
On Mars's armour, forg'd for proof eterne,
With less remorse than Pyrrhus' bleeding sword   490
Now falls on Priam.
Out, out, thou strumpet, Fortune! All you gods,
In general synod take away her power,
Break all the spokes and fellies from her wheel,
And bowl the round nave down the hill of heaven   495
As low as to the fiends!"
Polonius.   This is too long.
Hamlet.   It shall to the barber's, with your beard.
Prithee, say on: he's for a jig, or a tale of bawdry,
or he sleeps: say on, come to Hecuba.   500
First Player.   "But who, ah! who, had seen the mobled
queen—"
Hamlet.   "The mobled queen"?
Polonius.   That's good; "mobled queen" is good.
First Player.
"Run barefoot up and down, threatening the flames   505
With bisson rheum, a clout upon that head
Where late the diadem stood, and for a robe,
About her lank and all o'er-teemed loins,
A blanket in the alarm of fear caught up:
Who this had seen, with tongue in venom steep'd   510

510-11 **Who this . . . pronounc'd:** Anyone who had seen this would, speaking with the utmost bitterness, have denounced the power of Fortune.

513 **malicious sport:** as if he were enjoying it.

517-18 **would have . . . gods:** would have made the blazing stars weep and roused compassion in the gods.

519 **whether he . . . colour:** how he has turned pale. Note the indirect stage directions.

523 **bestow'd:** provided with lodging.

524 **abstract and . . . time:** summary and short history of the period. The drama reflects the age.

528 **bodkin:** dagger. Some editors prefer *bodykins,* a reference to the bread of the Holy Sacrament.

528-32 **whipping:** the usual punishment for beggars; another of Hamlet's references to the general depravity of man.

540-1 **study:** commit to memory; **some dozen or sixteen lines:** It is almost impossible to discover the passages that Hamlet is supposed to have inserted in the play within the play. Suffice it to say that he supposedly worked the lines in so well that they were indistinguishable from the fabric. The important thing is that the idea occurred to him on this occasion and appealed to his ingenious and creative brain.

544-5 **look you . . . not:** See that you do not make fun of him (as Hamlet had done). Either the Players might get into trouble or Hamlet feels that his example is not one to follow.

'Gainst Fortune's state would treason have pronounc'd;
But if the gods themselves did see her then,
When she saw Pyrrhus make malicious sport
In mincing with his sword her husband's limbs,
The instant burst of clamour that she made,   515
Unless things mortal move them not at all,
Would have made milch the burning eyes of heaven
And passion in the gods."

Polonius.   Look, whether he has not turn'd his colour, and has
tears in's eyes. Prithee, no more.   520

Hamlet.   'Tis well; I'll have thee speak out the rest of this
soon. Good my lord, will you see the players well
bestow'd? Do you hear, let them be well us'd, for
they are the abstract and brief chronicles of the time:
after your death you were better have a bad epitaph   525
than their ill report while you live.

Polonius.   My lord, I will use them according to their desert.

Hamlet.   God's bodkin, man, much better: use every man
after his desert, and who shall 'scape whipping?
Use them after your own honour and dignity; the   530
less they deserve, the more merit is in your bounty.
Take them in.

Polonius.   Come, sirs.

Hamlet. Follow him, friends: we'll hear a play to-morrow.
(*exit Polonius with all the Players but the First.*) Dost   535
thou hear me, old friend; can you play the Murder
of Gonzago?

First Player.   Ay, my lord.

Hamlet.   We'll ha't to-morrow night. You could, for
need, study a speech of some dozen or sixteen   540
lines, which I would set down and insert in't, could
you not?

First Player.   Ay, my lord.

Hamlet.   Very well. Follow that lord, and look you mock
him not. [*exit First Player.*] My good friends, I'll   545
leave you till night: you are welcome to Elsinore.

548 **alone:** said with relief, as though he could be himself without pretence.

549-607 Hamlet's second great soliloquy is inspired by the First Player's eloquence. Its substance, as well as the impassioned delivery of it, reminds him of how little he has accomplished since his vow to the Ghost. Besides creating a strong dramatic moment in the play, it further reveals Hamlet's character and advances the plot in that it forecasts the attempt to establish Claudius' guilt. Is Hamlet's plan merely a device to postpone action?

549 **rogue:** an idle vagrant. (The old meaning is appropriate here.)

550 **monstrous:** outrageously wrong.

551 **dream of passion:** imaginary emotion.

552 **conceit:** conception of the part.

553 **her working:** the soul's emotion; **wann'd:** grew pale.

554 **distraction in's aspect:** agitation in his expression.

555-6 **his whole . . . conceit:** all his physical powers adapting themselves to his interpretation.

560 **cue for passion:** the motive for strong feeling.

562 **general:** public.

563 **appal the free:** fill the innocent with fear.

564-5 **confound:** throw into perplexity, confuse, stupefy; **amaze indeed . . . ears:** bewilder or stupefy the senses of seeing and hearing.

567 **muddy-mettled:** lacking a fiery spirit; **peak:** mope without acting.

568 **like John-a-dreams . . . cause:** John the dreamer, barren of plans for revenge.

570 **property:** possessions.   571 **defeat:** ruin, destruction.

572-5 **pate:** head; **beard:** It is probable that Richard Burbage, who first played the role, had a beard, but modern Hamlets are invariably clean-shaven; **Who calls . . . lungs:** All these acts would be challenges demanding some response.

577 **'Swounds:** God's wounds. Instead of denying that he would show the white feather, Hamlet admits that he must be a coward. His mood of despair makes him exaggerate his own weaknesses.

578 **pigeon-liver'd:** The liver was the seat of courage, but it was believed that doves lacked gall (secreted by the liver), and that they owed their gentleness to this fact.

579 **to make oppression bitter:** to make him suffer.

580 **the region kites:** the birds of prey in the area. Shakespeare's knowledge of birds seems to have been wide and accurate.

581 **offal:** carrion; **bawdy:** obscene.

Rosencrantz.   Good my lord!
Hamlet.   Ay, so, God be wi' ye! [*exeunt Rosencrantz and
    Guildenstern.*] Now I am alone.
  O, what a rogue and peasant slave am I!
  Is it not monstrous that this player here,   550
  But in a fiction, in a dream of passion,
  Could force his soul so to his own conceit
  That from her working all his visage wann'd,
  Tears in his eyes, distraction in's aspect,
  A broken voice, and his whole function suiting   555
  With forms to his conceit? and all for nothing,
  For Hecuba!
  What's Hecuba to him, or he to Hecuba,
  That he should weep for her? What would he do,
  Had he the motive and the cue for passion   560
  That I have? He would drown the stage with tears
  And cleave the general ear with horrid speech,
  Make mad the guilty, and appal the free,
  Confound the ignorant, and amaze indeed
  The very faculties of eyes and ears.   565
  Yet I,
  A dull and muddy-mettled rascal, peak,
  Like John-a-dreams, unpregnant of my cause,
  And can say nothing: no, not for a king,
  Upon whose property and most dear life   570
  A damn'd defeat was made. Am I a coward,
  Who calls me villain, breaks my pate across,
  Plucks off my beard, and blows it in my face,
  Tweaks me by the nose, gives me the lie i' the throat,
  As deep as to the lungs? who does me this?   575
  Ha!
  'Swounds, I should take it: for it cannot be
  But I am pigeon-liver'd, and lack gall
  To make oppression bitter, or ere this
  I should have fatted all the region kites   580
  With this slave's offal: bloody, bawdy villain,

582 **kindless:** unnatural.

583 In Sir John Gielgud's production, Hamlet in hysterical frenzy thrust his dagger into the door through which the King had departed and sank to the floor in shamed exhaustion. ("O vengeance" marks the emotional climax of the soliloquy.)

587-8 **must like . . . drab:** He pours scorn on himself, as though he were only a screaming woman of the streets.

589 **scullion:** no prince, but a washer of dishes and pots in the kitchen.

590 **about, my brains:** set to work, "Wits, to your work!" (Dowden).

593 **presently:** immediately.

594 **malefactions:** evil deeds.

599 **tent him to the quick:** probe him to the soul; **blench:** flinch.

600-602 Hamlet may be rationalizing, but all the beliefs of the time pointed to the idea that ghosts were evil.

603 **melancholy:** This term implies not so much a mood as a disease. Bradley maintains that it was this malady that kept Hamlet from carrying out his revenge. Nowadays, an individual suffering from manic depression would require psychiatric treatment.

605 **abuses:** deceives.

606-7 **relative:** conclusive, relevant; **catch the conscience of the king:** test his guilt; **the play's . . . king:** These lines provide a dramatic conclusion to the soliloquy, the scene, and the act. As the curtain falls, Hamlet snatches up a pen from the council table and begins to write furiously. This provides a brilliant curtain.

See also p. 257.

tragic flaw - failure to act?

Remorseless, treacherous, lecherous, kindless villain!
O, vengeance!
Why, what an ass am I! This is most brave,   *Revenge with*   585
That I, the son of a dear father murder'd,   *words!*
Prompted to my revenge by heaven and hell,
Must like a whore unpack my heart with words,
And fall a-cursing like a very drab,
A scullion!
Fie upon't! foh! About, my brains! Hum, I
  have heard   *the play which*   590
That guilty creatures, sitting at a play,   *Claudius will see*
Have by the very cunning of the scene   *will be all about the murder*
Been struck so to the soul, that presently   *he will be shocked by*
They have proclaim'd their malefactions;   *what he'll see that he*
For murder, though it have no tongue, will speak   *will* 595 *know*
With most miraculous organ. I'll have these players *whether he is guilty*
Play something like the murder of my father   *by his expression,*
Before mine uncle, I'll observe his looks,   *and then I'll know what*
I'll tent him to the quick; if he do blench,   *to do*
I know my course. The spirit that I have seen   600
May be a devil, and the devil hath power
To assume a pleasing shape; yea, and perhaps
Out of my weakness, and my melancholy,
As he is very potent with such spirits,
Abuses me to damn me; I'll have grounds   605
More relative than this; the play's the thing
Wherein I'll catch the conscience of the king.

                                                    Exit.

1 **drift of conference:** roundabout questioning, leading him on in cunning talk.
2 **puts on this confusion:** assumes this deliberate madness. (Claudius here implies that he is aware that Hamlet's madness is not genuine.)
3 **grating:** disturbing.
1-4 Note the interrupted scene.
7 **forward to be sounded:** inclined to be questioned.
8 **crafty madness:** an apt description. Why?
12 **but with . . . disposition:** with strained politeness.
13-15 **niggard of . . . reply:** slow to converse, but ready to answer our questions. (Rosencrantz and Guildenstern give a false report of the interview. How can this be explained?) **assay him to:** attempt to get him to join in (so that he will no longer brood over thwarted ambition).
17 **o'er-raught:** overtook.
22 **beseech'd:** besought.

ACT III

Scene 1

THE NEXT DAY.
A ROOM IN THE CASTLE.

*Enter King, Queen, Polonius, Ophelia, Rosencrantz,
and Guildenstern.*

King.   And can you, by no drift of conference,
  Get from him why he puts on this confusion,
  Grating so harshly all his days of quiet
  With turbulent and dangerous lunacy?
Rosencrantz.   He does confess he feels himself distracted,   5
  But from what cause he will by no means speak.
Guildenstern.   Nor do we find him forward to be sounded,
  But, with a crafty madness, keeps aloof,
  When we would bring him on to some confession
  Of his true state.
Queen.   Did he receive you well?   10
Rosencrantz.   Most like a gentleman.
Guildenstern.   But with much forcing of his disposition.
Rosencrantz.   Niggard of question, but of our demands
  Most free in his reply.
Queen.   Did you assay him
  To any pastime?   15
Rosencrantz.   Madam, it so fell out that certain players
  We o'er-raught on the way; of these we told him,
  And there did seem in him a kind of joy
  To hear of it: they are here about the court,
  And, as I think, they have already order   20
  This night to play before him.
Polonius.   'Tis most true,
  And he beseech'd me to entreat your majesties
  To hear and see the matter.

24-25 Note the dramatic irony. Claudius little suspects the purpose of the play.

26 **give him a further edge:** sharpen his appetite (for these pleasures).

29 **closely:** secretly (without Hamlet's knowledge of the actual sender).

31 **affront:** encounter, meet face to face.

32 **lawful espials:** spies justifiably curious.

33 **bestow:** place.

40 **wildness:** distraction.

41 **wonted:** accustomed.

44 **this book:** evidently a book of prayers or devotions.

45-46 **that show . . . loneliness:** that your being alone may be explained by the fact that you seem to be praying.

47-49 **that with . . . himself:** that with the outward appearance of religion we conceal the most wicked thoughts; an attack on hypocrisy, which sounds odd coming from Polonius.

50 **smart:** sharp; **How smart . . . conscience:** This is the first time the King has made any reference to his guilt. The metaphor of the scourge of conscience is very vivid.

51-53 **The harlot's . . . word:** The exaggerated make-up of the prostitute is just as ugly as the haggard cheek beneath it; similarly, my hypocritical attitude is just as repulsive as the deed I have committed.

54 **O heavy burthen:** This insight into Claudius' feelings makes him a more sympathetic character.

56-88 Hamlet's most famous soliloquy brings out his philosophic quality of mind, as well as showing his brilliant imagination and introspective nature. The prevailing mood is one of frustration; the high excitement and intensity of purpose shown in the preceding soliloquy have vanished. Professor Harrison comments on its agnosticism; Professor Levin emphasizes the fact that "in introspection, his mentor is Montaigne", whose phraseology (in Florio's translation) and philosophy "reverberate" throughout the play in general and the soliloquies in particular. The passage contains lines that have become part of the splendid heritage of our language.

56 **To be . . . question:** "A like expression of utter weariness is not to be found in the rest of human literature" (Dover Wilson, *What Happens in 'Hamlet'*); **not to be:** to end life by suicide; **the question:** in the sense of a philosophical subject; in Q1, the King says "See where he comes poring upon a book."

58 **the slings . . . fortune:** Fortune is represented as cruelly violent in attack; **slings:** field-guns, culverin.

King. With all my heart; and it doth much content me
  To hear him so inclin'd.   25
  Good gentlemen, give him a further edge,
  And drive his purpose into these delights.
Rosencrantz. We shall, my lord.
                    Exeunt Rosencrantz and Guildenstern.
King.   Sweet Gertrude, leave us too,
  For we have closely sent for Hamlet hither,
  That he, as 'twere by accident, may here   30
  Affront Ophelia: her father and myself,
  Lawful espials,
  Will so bestow ourselves that, seeing unseen,
  We may of their encounter frankly judge,
  And gather by him, as he is behav'd,   35
  If't be the affliction of his love or no
  That thus he suffers for.
Queen.   I shall obey you.
  And for your part, Ophelia, I do wish
  That your good beauties be the happy cause
  Of Hamlet's wildness; so shall I hope your virtues 40
  Will bring him to his wonted way again,
  To both your honours.
Ophelia.   Madam, I wish it may.   *Exit Queen.*
Polonius. Ophelia, walk you here. Gracious, so please you,
  We will bestow ourselves. (*to Ophelia*) Read on this
    book,
  That show of such an exercise may colour   45
  Your loneliness. We are oft to blame in this,—
  'Tis too much prov'd—that with devotion's visage
  And pious action we do sugar o'er
  The devil himself.
King (aside).   O, 'tis too true!
  How smart a lash that speech doth give my conscience! 50
  The harlot's cheek, beautied with plastering art,
  Is not more ugly to the thing that helps it
  Than is my deed to my most painted word:

See p. 104 for notes on ll. 54-58.

59 The mixed metaphor is a famous one; it does, however, imply the quixotic gallantry of trying to face unbelievable odds. The "sea of troubles" suggests wave after wave of misfortune.

57-60 to endure or to escape? 61 **no more:** merely this.

63 **that flesh is heir to:** "Man is born to trouble as the sparks fly upward"; **consummation:** completion.

64 Note the effect secured by the word "devoutly".

65 **rub:** obstacle, difficulty. The metaphor is the second in the play drawn from the game of bowls. In bowling, the "rub" is anything that interferes with the true course of the bowl.

67 **shuffled off this mortal coil:** got rid of this human fuss. Some editors see in it a reference to the body as a coil of rope, sloughed off like a snakeskin in death.

68 **respect:** consideration.

69 **calamity of so long life:** sufferers from calamity so long-lived.

70 **whips and . . . time:** harsh criticism and contempt of the world. Life is pictured as a beadle (parish officer) whose duty it was to whip offenders through the streets.

71 **contumely:** scorn, insolent language.

72 F reads *dispriz'd,* under-valued; "despis'd" is the Q2 reading.

73-74 **office:** those in office; **spurns that . . . takes:** the insults offered by inferior men to those who are quietly worthy.

70-74 Some have seen in these lines possible references by Shakespeare to himself.

75 **his quietus make:** secure his own release; a legal term for the final settlement of an account.

76 **bare:** mere; **bodkin:** dagger; **fardels:** burdens.

77 **to grunt . . . life:** Note the imitative quality; the line suggests a picture of man as a beast of burden. "Grunt"=*groan.*

78 **something after death:** Did Hamlet believe in immortality?

79-80 **bourn:** limit, boundary. (The passage seems to be in contradiction to the appearance of the Ghost); **the undiscover'd . . . returns:** a memorable picture of death in all its finality. Shakespeare implies that Hamlet does not believe in the authenticity of the Ghost at this point.

83 **conscience:** habit of reasoning, speculative thought.

84 **native hue of resolution:** natural colour of courage. Note the metaphor drawn from physical health.

86 **of great pitch and moment:** of momentous importance. The "pitch" was the highest point in a falcon's flight before it swooped. F reads *pith,* value or significance.

87 **with this regard:** because this is reflected upon; **their currents turn awry:** as a river loses itself in a marsh or swamp.

O heavy burthen!
Polonius.　I hear him coming: let's withdraw, my lord.　　55
　　　　　　　Exeunt King and Polonius.
　　Enter Hamlet.
Hamlet.　To be, or not to be, that is the question;
　Whether 'tis nobler in the mind to suffer
　The slings and arrows of outrageous fortune,　　*Contemplating*
　Or to take arms against a sea of troubles,　　*suicide*
　And by opposing, end them. To die; to sleep,　　60
　No more, and by a sleep to say we end
　The heart-ache, and the thousand natural shocks
　That flesh is heir to; 'tis a consummation
　Devoutly to be wish'd. To die, to sleep;
　To sleep; perchance to dream; ay, there's the rub;　　65
　For in that sleep of death what dreams may come,
　When we have shuffled off this mortal coil,
　Must give us pause; there's the respect　　*What's after death.*
　That makes calamity of so long life:
　For who would bear the whips and scorns of time,　　70
　The oppressor's wrong, the proud man's contumely,
　The pangs of despis'd love, the law's delay,
　The insolence of office, and the spurns
　That patient merit of the unworthy takes,
　When he himself might his quietus make　　75
　With a bare bodkin? who would fardels bear,
　To grunt and sweat under a weary life,
　But that the dread of something after death,
　The undiscover'd country, from whose bourn
　No traveller returns, puzzles the will,　　80
　And makes us rather bear those ills we have　　*If he kills*
　Than fly to others that we know not of?　　*himself, then it*
　Thus conscience does make cowards of us all,　　*no way back*
　And thus the native hue of resolution
　Is sicklied o'er with the pale cast of thought,　　85
　And enterprises of great pitch and moment
　With this regard their currents turn awry

88 **Soft you now:** Wait a moment, hush!

89-90 **Nymph, in . . . remember'd:** Lady, in your prayers, ask forgiveness for my sins. There is a theatrical tradition that Ophelia should be kneeling when Hamlet enters. Explain how this may have developed. Some critics find in Hamlet's attitude merely a strained politeness, as though he were addressing a stranger. "My sins" may be said sardonically.

91 The humble rebuke implied in the line adds pathos, though ironically it is partly Ophelia's own fault that she has not seen Hamlet.

95-96 Ophelia's gesture angers Hamlet because he cannot but be touched by the forlornness of it.

99 **perfume:** the affection of the giver; metaphorically, the gift might be the blossom.

101 Note the contrast. (One imagines that Hamlet's gifts would be truly valuable, but not ostentatious.)

103 **honest:** chaste, virtuous; Hamlet's laughter is mirthless. If, as Sir John Gielgud believes (following Dover Wilson), Hamlet heard Polonius say: "I'll loose my daughter to him", it is easy to explain, though not to justify, the prince's attitude.

107-8 **That if . . . beauty:** Dover Wilson paraphrases this as follows: "If you were the chaste maiden you pretend to be, you would not allow your beauty to be used as bait in this fashion" (*What Happens in 'Hamlet'*).

109 **commerce:** association. F reads *converse,* discourse.

115 **once:** before the remarriage of Gertrude.

111-15 Hamlet indicates that the more beautiful a woman is, the more difficult it is for her to be virtuous in view of the fact that she will have greater temptations. Beauty has greater power than virtue and will more likely destroy it than the reverse. This, he says, was once an apparent contradiction, but there is proof of it now (in his mother's, and perhaps Ophelia's, behaviour).

117-19 **virtue cannot . . . it:** The branch (of virtue) cannot be so grafted on to the original tree (of human evil) as to overcome (eliminate) all the wickedness of the old; **we shall relish of it:** We shall retain some traces of the old stock. Hamlet speaks harshly, perhaps through a sense of guilt. Has he betrayed Ophelia?

120 Ophelia, pitiful and fragile, can only confess her love for Hamlet.

And lose the name of action. Soft you now,
The fair Ophelia! Nymph, in thy orisons
Be all my sins remember'd.
Ophelia.   Good my lord, 90
How does your honour for this many a day?
Hamlet.   I humbly thank you, well, well, well.
Ophelia.   My lord, I have remembrances of yours,
That I have longed long to re-deliver;
I pray you now receive them.
Hamlet.   No, not I; 95
I never gave you aught.
Ophelia.   My honour'd lord, you know right well you did,
And with them words of so sweet breath compos'd
As made the things more rich: their perfume lost,
Take these again; for to the noble mind 100
Rich gifts wax poor when givers prove unkind.
There, my lord.
Hamlet.   Ha, ha! are you honest?
Ophelia.   My lord?
Hamlet.   Are you fair? 105
Ophelia.   What means your lordship?
Hamlet.   That if you be honest and fair, your honesty should
admit no discourse to your beauty.
Ophelia.   Could beauty, my lord, have better commerce than
with honesty? 110
Hamlet.   Ay, truly; for the power of beauty will sooner
transform honesty from what it is to a bawd than the
force of honesty can translate beauty into his likeness:
this was sometime a paradox, but now the time gives
it proof. I did love you once. 115
Ophelia.   Indeed, my lord, you made me believe so.
Hamlet.
You should not have believ'd me, for virtue cannot
so inoculate our old stock but we shall relish of it;
I lov'd you not.
Ophelia.   I was the more deceiv'd. 120

121 If Hamlet cannot marry her, he prefers her to withdraw from the world. Another meaning of "nunnery" is *house of ill-fame*. If this interpretation is accepted, Hamlet is implying that Ophelia is no better than a prostitute.

122 **indifferent:** moderately.

128 **crawling:** suggests that man is but a worm.

129 **arrant:** utter.

122-30 Hamlet's confession may be intended to show that Ophelia is foolish to love such a person; he may also be trying to get her to confess that she is dishonest in helping to trick him.

131 Hamlet's abrupt question may result: a) from having heard Polonius' remark (II. ii. 162), or b) from just having caught a glimpse of Polonius. It is almost impossible to believe that he did not know of Polonius' whereabouts.

132 A slight pause before Ophelia's remark would emphasize her poor little lie. Most readers sympathize with her in this dilemma of divided loyalties. Should she betray her father or the man she loves?

133-4 Hamlet's reply, as he thrusts Ophelia away from him, is obviously intended for Polonius.

138 **calumny:** slander.

136-42 Hamlet is enraged by Ophelia's apparent betrayal; his speech is a savage attack not only on her but on all women.

143 Ophelia assumes that Hamlet is mad.

144 **your paintings:** Hamlet in his misogyny lashes out at women's make-up.

146-8 **jig, you amble:** dance and move in a suggestive, sexual manner; **lisp:** talk artificially; **nickname:** use coarse language to describe; **make your . . . ignorance:** justify your lack of modesty by saying that you did not know.

149-50 a reference to Gertrude and Claudius. How can this obvious warning to Claudius be explained?

151 S.D. **Exit:** Certain actors of the role of Hamlet engage in some bit of stage business that, though unseen by Ophelia, illustrates Hamlet's love for her.

154 **expectancy and rose:** hope and symbol of perfection. The rose was the emblem of the Tudors; Shakespeare took great delight in flowers as the many references in his plays attest; **fair:** made so by his presence.

Hamlet. Get thee to a nunnery; why wouldst thou be a breeder of sinners? I am myself indifferent honest, but yet I could accuse me of such things that it were better my mother had not borne me: I am very proud, revengeful, ambitious, with more offences 125 at my beck than I have thoughts to put them in, imagination to give them shape, or time to act them in. What should such fellows as I do crawling between earth and heaven? We are arrant knaves, believe none of us; go thy ways to a nunnery. 130 Where's your father?

Ophelia. At home, my lord.

Hamlet. Let the doors be shut upon him, that he may play the fool no where but in's own house. Farewell.

Ophelia. O, help him, you sweet heavens! 135

Hamlet. If thou dost marry, I'll give thee this plague for thy dowry: be thou as chaste as ice, as pure as snow, thou shalt not escape calumny. Get thee to a nunnery, farewell. Or, if thou wilt needs marry, marry a fool, for wise men know well enough what 140 monsters you make of them. To a nunnery, go, and quickly too, farewell.

Ophelia. Heavenly powers restore him!

Hamlet. I have heard of your paintings well enough; God hath given you one face, and you make yourselves 145 another: you jig, you amble, and you lisp, you nickname God's creatures, and make your wantonness your ignorance. Go to, I'll no more on't, it hath made me mad. I say we will have no more marriage; those that are married already, all but one shall live, 150 the rest shall keep as they are. To a nunnery, go.

Exit.

Ophelia. O, what a noble mind is here o'erthrown!
The courtier's, soldier's, scholar's, eye, tongue,
    sword,
The expectancy and rose of the fair state,

155   **glass of . . . form:** mirror of good taste and model for others to follow.

152-6   Ophelia's lament gives a vivid picture of the kind of person Hamlet had once been: gifted, versatile, the white hope of Denmark. Hamlet combined the attributes (talents) of the man of the world, the man of action, and the man of intellect.

158   **suck'd the . . . vows:** listened eagerly to his sweet declarations (another mixed metaphor).

160   The simile of the discordant bells is appropriate and effective. F reads *time* for "tune".

161   **feature:** figure; **blown:** full-blown, in full bloom.

162   **blasted with ecstasy:** destroyed by madness.

164   **love:** Claudius' scorn is marked; **affections:** state of mind, emotions.

165-6   **nor what . . . not:** the emphatic use of the double negative.

166-9   **doubt:** suspect; **disclose:** the breaking of the shell when the fledgling is hatched; **for to prevent:** to forestall; the metaphor suggests imminent danger. "Melancholy" is thought of as a bird in the nest.

172   Ethelred the Unready first paid tribute to the Danes in 994 on condition that they refrain from raiding the coast of England.

173   **haply:** perhaps.

174   **variable objects:** change of surroundings. England is seen as a health resort.

175   **something:** somewhat, used adverbially. Claudius acts with energy and despatch in this emergency.

177   **fashion of himself:** his usual self.

178-80   Polonius is unwilling to admit that his theory was unsound and shows this in his unfeeling remarks to Ophelia.

185   **grief:** grievance; **round:** blunt.

186-7   **And I'll . . . conference:** concealed where I can hear what is said; a typical Polonius scheme; **find him not:** does not discover what is the matter with him.

The glass of fashion, and the mould of form,   155
The observ'd of all observers, quite, quite down,
And I of ladies most deject and wretched,
That suck'd the honey of his music vows;
Now see that noble and most sovereign reason,
Like sweet bells jangled out of tune, and harsh,   160
That unmatch'd form, and feature of blown youth,
Blasted with ecstasy: O, woe is me,
To have seen what I have seen, see what I see!
            Re-enter King and Polonius.
King.   Love! his affections do not that way tend,
    Nor what he spake, though it lack'd form a little,   165
    Was not like madness. There's something in his soul
    O'er which his melancholy sits on brood,
    And I do doubt the hatch and the disclose
    Will be some danger: which for to prevent,
    I have in quick determination   170
    Thus set it down;—he shall with speed to England,
    For the demand of our neglected tribute:
    Haply the seas, and countries different,
    With variable objects, shall expel
    This something-settled matter in his heart,   175
    Whereon his brains still beating puts him thus
    From fashion of himself. What think you on't?
Polonius.   It shall do well: but yet do I believe
    The origin and commencement of his grief
    Sprung from neglected love. How now, Ophelia?   180
    You need not tell us what Lord Hamlet said,
    We heard it all. My lord, do as you please;
    But if you hold it fit, after the play,
    Let his queen mother all alone entreat him
    To show his grief; let her be round with him;   185
    And I'll be plac'd, so please you, in the ear
    Of all their conference. If she find him not,
    To England send him; or confine him where
    Your wisdom best shall think.

190 The final line has an ominous ring. See also p. 260.

1-4 **the speech:** presumably the one Hamlet had composed. A rehearsal is apparently in progress. The First Player, according to Dover Wilson, is to take the part of Lucianus; **as I . . . you:** He had himself spoken it as he wished it delivered; **trippingly on the tongue:** smoothly, without stumbling over the words; **mouth it:** say the words without regard to the meaning; **I had . . . lines:** I had as soon have the speech bellowed by one who cared only about the sound; **saw the air:** gesture violently.

8 **temperance:** self-control. The paradox of acting is that the cool intellect controls the expression of great emotion; the actor is "acting" rather than "living" the part, though he must convey the impression that he is doing the latter.

9-10 **robustious:** violent, blustering; **periwig-pated:** wearing a wig; only actors wore wigs at this time. Both adjectives are imitative; **tear a . . . rags:** This suggests an over-emotional, melodramatic display. "Tear to rags" implies furious, almost insane, activity.

11 **groundlings:** the rabble standing in the pit (on the *ground* floor).

12-13 **capable of . . . dumb-shows:** able to appreciate only unintelligible pantomime. Hamlet's condemnation of the dumb-show implies that he is not responsible for the one later presented; "inexplicable" may mean *without words to explain them.*

14 **Termagant:** imaginary Mohammedan god depicted in the morality plays as noisy and ranting. An actor "o'erdoing Termagant" or "out-heroding Herod" would be going to the most furious extremes. Nowadays, "termagant" refers to a brawling woman.

15 **Herod:** This biblical figure who appeared in the miracle plays was also depicted as a violent, raging tyrant.

1-15 Here, in a singularly significant way, Hamlet seems to be a projection of Shakespeare, who had doubtless advised members of his company to show smoothness and moderation.

17-20 **Be not . . . nature:** The golden mean is Shakespeare's ideal here; an actor should show by his gestures that he understands the meaning of his lines, but he must at all costs be natural; **modesty:** moderation.

21-23 **from:** alien from, contrary to; **the purpose . . . nature:** Shakespeare (Hamlet) here states, once and for all, the basic principle of great acting; **hold as . . . nature:** show human nature the ideal. 24 **scorn:** that which should be scorned, folly.

25-26 **the very . . . pressure:** society its real self; **come tardy off:** underdone.

King.   It shall be so:
   Madness in great ones must not unwatch'd go. *+ true* 190
                                    Exeunt.

Purpose to his madness

Scene 2

A HALL IN THE CASTLE.

Enter Hamlet and three of the Players.

Hamlet. Speak the speech, I pray you, as I pronounc'd it
   to you, trippingly on the tongue; but if you mouth
   it as many of your players do, I had as lief the town-
   crier spoke my lines; nor do not saw the air too
   much with your hand thus, but use all gently, for in   5
   the very torrent, tempest, and, as I may say, whirl-
   wind of your passion, you must acquire and beget
   a temperance, that may give it smoothness. O, it
   offends me to the soul to hear a robustious periwig-
   pated fellow tear a passion to tatters, to very rags,   10
   to split the ears of the groundlings, who for the most
   part are capable of nothing but inexplicable dumb-
   shows, and noise: I would have such a fellow
   whipp'd for o'erdoing Termagant; it out-herods
   Herod: pray you, avoid it.   15
First Player. I warrant your honour.
Hamlet. Be not too tame neither, but let your own discretion be your tutor, suit the action to the word, the
   word to the action, with this special observance,
   that you o'erstep not the modesty of nature: for   20
   anything so o'erdone is from the purpose of playing,
   whose end, both at the first, and now, was and is, to
   hold as 'twere the mirror up to nature, to show
   virtue her own feature, scorn her own image, and
   the very age and body of the time his form and   25
   pressure. Now this overdone, or come tardy off,

giving direction on acting

28 **censure:** judgement.

29 **in your allowance:** as you must agree.

31-32 **not to . . . profanely:** that is, what follows is said in all sincerity and seriousness.

35 **nature's journeymen:** not nature herself but her unskilled workers who have not yet become master craftsmen.

37 **abhominably:** abominably. This is a pun on the derivation *ab homine;* they did not appear to be men at all.

38 **indifferently:** more or less.

40-43 **let those . . . them:** Shakespeare attacks the practice of ad-libbing among the comedians of the time; there may be a dig here at Will Kempe, the greatest comic actor of the period, who was with a rival troupe; **for there . . . laugh:** a reference to the bad habit of coming out of character; **barren:** brainless, dull.

45-47 Shakespeare's (Hamlet's) objection is a logical one; he also emphasizes indirectly the importance of team-play in a company.

1-48 The advice to the players is of special interest not only to actors of *Hamlet* and actors in general, but also to students of Shakespeare; the creator and the created are one.

48-49 **piece of work:** masterpiece (said gaily).

50 **presently:** at once.

54 **S.D. Enter Horatio:** Horatio has not been on stage since Act I, Scene 5.

56-57 **thou art . . . withal:** You are as honest or well-balanced a man as I have ever encountered. Hamlet's appreciation of his friend's quality springs from the fact that he (Hamlet) lacks stability.

though it make the unskilful laugh, cannot but make the judicious grieve, the censure of which one must in your allowance o'erweigh a whole theatre of others. O, there be players that I have seen play, 30 and heard others praise, and that highly, not to speak it profanely, that neither having the accent of Christians, nor the gait of Christian, pagan, nor man, have so strutted and bellow'd, that I have thought some of nature's journeymen had made 35 men, and not made them well, they imitated humanity so abhominably.

First Player. I hope we have reform'd that indifferently with us.

Hamlet. O, reform it altogether; and let those that play 40 your clowns speak no more than is set down for them: for there be of them that will themselves laugh, to set on some quantity of barren spectators to laugh too, though in the mean time some necessary question of the play be then to be consider'd: that's 45 villainous, and shows a most pitiful ambition in the fool that uses it. Go, make you ready.

          Exeunt Players.
   Enter Polonius, Rosencrantz, and Guildenstern.
How now, my lord? will the king hear this piece of work?

Polonius. And the queen too, and that presently.   50

Hamlet. Bid the players make haste.   *Exit Polonius.* Will you two help to hasten them?

Rosencrantz. ⎫
Guildenstern. ⎭ Ay, my lord.

   Exeunt Rosencrantz and Guildenstern.
Hamlet. What ho! Horatio!
   Enter Horatio.
Horatio. Here, sweet lord, at your service.   **55**
Hamlet. Horatio, thou art e'en as just a man
 As e'er my conversation cop'd withal.

Hamlet lacks stability

60 **revenue:** The accent is on the second syllable.
62 **candied tongue . . . pomp:** Sugary words flatter the rich man
and his ridiculous display.
63-64 **and crook . . . fawning:** kneel readily (act obsequiously)
where something is to be gained from such behaviour. The
image in these lines is that of a spaniel trying to curry favour
with its master. The understood subject of "crook" is *flatterer.*
58-64 Hamlet is satirical in his criticism of human hypocrisy. He
may have Rosencrantz and Guildenstern in mind.
66 **election:** choice.
67-70 Horatio's stoic qualities and strength of character are admired by Hamlet.
71 **blood:** passion, impulse; **commedled:** So Q2; F reads *com-
mingled.* The meaning is the same.
72-73 **a pipe . . . please:** The metaphor suggests the image of a
weak character.
74 **passion's slave:** a person at the mercy of his impulses.
76 Hamlet feels that he has been too garrulous, perhaps too
unreserved, and has embarrassed Horatio.
78-79 **the circumstance . . . death:** Hamlet has evidently confided in
Horatio, contrary to his original intentions.
81 **the very . . . soul:** with your keenest powers of observation.
82 **occulted:** secret, hidden.
83 **unkennel:** reveal; **one speech:** Hamlet's lines.
84 **a damned ghost:** Hamlet had earlier expressed the fear that the
Ghost was evil.
86 **stithy:** smithy. "Vulcan" was the blacksmith of the gods; his
forge was in Mount Etna (a volcano).
87 **for I . . . face:** By using this metaphor, Hamlet suggests how
intently he plans to watch Claudius.
89 **in censure . . . seeming:** in judgement of his appearance.
90-91 **If he . . . theft:** Horatio implies that he will not take his
eyes from Claudius; no action or gesture on the part of the
King will escape him.

Horatio.   O, my dear lord,—
Hamlet.   Nay, do not think I flatter,
  For what advancement may I hope from thee,
  That no revenue hast but thy good spirits,   60
  To feed and clothe thee? Why should the poor be
  flatter'd?
  No, let the candied tongue lick absurd pomp,
  And crook the pregnant hinges of the knee
  Where thrift may follow fawning. Dost thou hear?
  Since my dear soul was mistress of her choice,   65
  And could of men distinguish her election,
  Hath seal'd thee for herself, for thou hast been
  As one, in suffering all, that suffers nothing,
  A man that fortune's buffets and rewards
  Hast ta'en with equal thanks: and blest are those   70
  Whose blood and judgement are so well commedled
  That they are not a pipe for fortune's finger
  To sound what stop she please. Give me that man
  That is not passion's slave, and I will wear him
  In my heart's core, ay, in my heart of heart,   75
  As I do thee. Something too much of this.
  There is a play to-night before the king;
  One scene of it comes near the circumstance
  Which I have told thee of my father's death:
  I prithee, when thou seest that act a-foot,   80
  Even with the very comment of thy soul
  Observe my uncle; if his occulted guilt
  Do not itself unkennel in one speech,
  It is a damned ghost that we have seen,
  And my imaginations are as foul   85
  As Vulcan's stithy. Give him heedful note;
  For I mine eyes will rivet to his face,
  And after we will both our judgements join
  In censure of his seeming.
Horatio.   Well, my lord:
  If he steal aught the whilst this play is playing,   90

92 **be idle:** play the madman.

94 **fares:** in the double sense of *does* and *eats*.

95 **of the chameleon's dish:** The chameleon, a small lizard, was reputed to live on air.

96 **promise-cramm'd:** perhaps a reference to the succession (I. ii. 108-9); **capons:** castrated cocks; the fowl so treated is more easily fattened and hence makes better eating. There may be a hint that the King is feeding Hamlet ("air": heir?) empty promises.

98-99 **I have . . . mine:** I can make nothing of your answer; the words have nothing to do with me.

100-101 **nor mine now:** Now that I have spoken them, they do not belong to me; **My lord . . . say:** Plays were performed at Oxford and Cambridge. (It is tempting to imagine Polonius as an undergraduate.)

102-3 Polonius, proud of his histrionic talent, walks into the trap Hamlet sets. (Hamlet has no doubt frequently heard of Polonius' triumphs.)

105-6 Shakespeare may have been referring here to his own play *Julius Cæsar;* Cæsar (historically) was murdered close to Pompey's theatre.

107-8 **calf:** implies callow immaturity; Hamlet's pun is as bad as those Polonius himself is addicted to.

111-20 The exchange between Hamlet and Ophelia is no doubt intended to be heard by Polonius. It would support his theory concerning the cause of Hamlet's "madness". Hamlet's coarseness may spring from bitterness, but it is not in good taste by modern standards.

And 'scape detecting, I will pay the theft.

Hamlet. They are coming to the play: I must be idle: *must be*
Get you a place. *mad*

       Danish march. A flourish.

*Enter King, Queen, Polonius, Ophelia, Rosencrantz,
Guildenstern, and other Lords attendant, with the Guard
carrying torches.*

King. How fares our cousin Hamlet?

Hamlet. Excellent, i' faith, of the chameleon's dish: I eat   95
   the air, promise-cramm'd: you cannot feed capons
   so.

King. I have nothing with this answer, Hamlet; these
   words are not mine.

Hamlet. No, nor mine now. [*to Polonius*] My lord, you   100
   play'd once i' the university, you say?

Polonius. That did I, my lord, and was accounted a good
   actor.

Hamlet. What did you enact?

Polonius. I did enact Julius Cæsar, I was killed i' the   *Foreshadowing* 105
   Capitol, Brutus kill'd me.

Hamlet. It was a brute part of him to kill so capital a calf
   there. Be the players ready?

Rosencrantz. Ay, my lord, they stay upon your patience.

Queen. Come hither, my dear Hamlet, sit by me.   110

Hamlet. No, good mother, here's metal more attractive.

Polonius (to the King). O, ho! do you mark that?   *— Mad for Ophelia*

Hamlet. Lady, shall I lie in your lap?

      Lying down at Ophelia's feet.

Ophelia. No, my lord.

Hamlet. I mean, my head upon your lap?   115

Ophelia. Ay, my lord.

Hamlet. Do you think I meant country matters?

Ophelia. I think nothing, my lord.

Hamlet. That's a fair thought to lie between maids' legs.

Ophelia. What is, my lord?   120

Hamlet. Nothing.

125 **your only jig-maker:** creator of coarse, farcical interludes, a reference to his previous conversation.

128 Ophelia's correction indicates the lapse of time, about which Shakespeare has been vague up to this point. Hamlet too has let time slip by.

129-30 **so long:** Hamlet is satirical; **Nay then . . . sables:** Let the devil go into mourning; I'll wear rich furs. Hamlet is presumably still wearing black. There is a play on the meaning of "sable", the heraldic black, and "sables", valuable brown furs. Since they were worn by well-to-do elderly gentlemen, Hamlet implies that much time must have elapsed.

134-6 **suffer not thinking on:** be forgotten; **with the . . . forgot:** a line from an old ballad, based on the suppression of May Day revels by the Puritans. The hobby-horse was a feature of the Morris (Moorish) dances, brought back by John of Gaunt from Spain. The ballad laments the disappearance of the hobby-horse, a man who pranced about inside a stuffed replica of the horse's head and torso.

131-6 Hamlet is cynical about human love and loyalty; we are all selfish and forgetful. Even the great are forgotten in six months' time, unless churches are built in honour of their memory; here, masses for their souls may keep remembrance of them alive.

136 S.D. **dumb-show:** here, a rehearsal in pantomime of the action to be performed in the play. Why the King does not stop the performance immediately after the dumb-show can perhaps be explained by the fact that he is conversing with Polonius about Hamlet. (Granville-Barker believes that Claudius did watch the dumb-show and maintained his composure until the scene of the poisoning.) Since the dumb-show was used, as Hamlet points out, to entertain the groundlings, it might be ignored by the more intellectual part of the audience.

138 **miching mallecho:** sneaking misdeed.

139 **imports the argument:** indicates the subject matter; S.D. **Prologue:** the actor who speaks the prologue or introduction; he was dressed in black with a laurel wreath on his head since originally the poet-author performed this role.

140-1 **cannot keep counsel:** cannot keep a secret.

Ophelia. You are merry, my lord.

Hamlet. Who, I?

Ophelia. Ay, my lord.

Hamlet. O God, your only jig-maker. What should a man   125
do but be merry? for look you how cheerfully my
mother looks, and my father died within's two hours.

Ophelia. Nay, 'tis twice two months, my lord.

Hamlet. So long? Nay then, let the devil wear black, for
I'll have a suit of sables. O heavens! die two   130
months ago, and not forgotten yet? Then there's
hope a great man's memory may outlive his life half
a year: but, by'r lady, he must build churches then,
or else shall he suffer not thinking on, with the hobby-
horse, whose epitaph is, "For, O, for, O, the hobby-   135
horse is forgot."

      The trumpets sound. The dumb-show enters.

*Enter a King and a Queen, the Queen embracing him, and
he her. He takes her up, and declines his head upon her
neck: he lies him down upon a bank of flowers: she,
seeing him asleep, leaves him. Anon comes in another
man, takes off his crown, kisses it, pours poison in the
sleeper's ears, and leaves him. The Queen returns, finds
the King dead, makes passionate action. The Poisoner
with some three or four come in again, seem to condole
with her. The dead body is carried away. The Poisoner
woos the Queen with gifts: she seems harsh awhile, but
in the end accepts love.*   *Exeunt.*

Ophelia. What means this, my lord?

Hamlet. Marry, this is miching mallecho; it means mischief.

Ophelia. Belike this show imports the argument of the play.

      Enter Prologue.

Hamlet. We shall know by this fellow: the players cannot   140
keep counsel; they'll tell all.

Ophelia. Will he tell us what this show meant?

Hamlet. Ay, or any show that you will show him: be not

146 **naught:** shameless (licentious).

148 **stooping to your clemency:** asking your indulgence. The Prologue frequently apologized for the supposed shortcomings of the play.

150 **posy of a ring:** motto inscribed in a ring; *e.g., The Merchant of Venice* (V. i. 150): "Love me, and leave me not."

152 Another gibe at the frailty of the sex.

153 ff. The style of the play within the play is formal and stilted. The rhyming couplets remind us of Shakespeare's earlier period and are said to be typical of earlier Elizabethan tragedy, which was modelled on that of Seneca. It may be that Shakespeare adopted this style in order to provide a distinct contrast with the freer-flowing blank verse of *Hamlet.*

153 **Phoebus' cart:** the sun chariot.

154 **Neptune's salt wash:** the domain of the god of the sea; **Tellus' orbed ground:** the earth, spherical in shape.

157 **Hymen:** god of marriage.

158 **commutual:** reciprocally.

153-60 Note the classical allusions; an involved way of stating that the Player Queen and the Player King have been married for thirty years. If this is supposed to refer to Hamlet's mother and father, it might help us to deduce his age.

163 **distrust:** am anxious about.

165 **hold quantity:** are proportionate.

166 **in neither . . . extremity:** Fear and love are entirely absent, or else both are found to an extreme degree.

168 **And as . . . so:** Because my love is great, so is my fear.

172 **operant:** active; **leave to do:** cease to perform.

175 **confound:** as it were, damn.

you asham'd to show, he'll not shame to tell you
what it means.   145

Ophelia.   You are naught, you are naught: I'll mark the play.

Prologue.   For us and for our tragedy,
                        Here stooping to your clemency,
                        We beg your hearing patiently.

Hamlet.   Is this a prologue, or the posy of a ring?   150

Ophelia.   'Tis brief, my lord.

Hamlet.   As woman's love.
                    Enter two Players, King and Queen.

Player King.   Full thirty times hath Phœbus' cart gone round
    Neptune's salt wash and Tellus' orbed ground,
    And thirty dozen moons with borrow'd sheen   155
    About the world have times twelve thirties been,
    Since love our hearts, and Hymen did our hands,
    Unite commutual in most sacred bands.

Player Queen.   So many journeys may the sun and moon
    Make us again count o'er ere love be done!   160
    But, woe is me, you are so sick of late,
    So far from cheer and from your former state,
    That I distrust you. Yet, though I distrust,
    Discomfort you, my lord, it nothing must:
    For women's fear and love hold quantity,   165
    In neither ought, or in extremity;
    Now, what my love is, proof hath made you know,
    And as my love is siz'd, my fear is so:
    Where love is great, the littlest doubts are fear,
    Where little fears grow great, great love grows there.   170

Player King.   Faith, I must leave thee, love, and shortly too;
    My operant powers their functions leave to do:
    And thou shalt live in this fair world behind,
    Honour'd, belov'd; and haply one as kind
    For husband shalt thou—

Player Queen.   O, confound the rest   175
    Such love must needs be treason in my breast: — *leaving*
    In second husband let me be accurst,

179   **wormwood:** bitter words (for Claudius? for Gertrude?).
180   **instances:** motives, inducements.
181   **respects of thrift:** considerations of gain.
186-9   **Purpose is . . . be:** The implication here is that our intentions (unripe fruit) may be good, but we tend to forget them (ripe fruit falling to the ground). The retentive aspect of the memory is like the force that holds the fruit to the tree.
190-3   **Most necessary . . . lose:** Our resolves are debts to ourselves. Why embarrass ourselves with inconvenient payments (Dowden)? We make good resolutions in the heat of the moment, but as our enthusiasm wanes, our resolves fade. The lines remind us of Hamlet's delay in securing his revenge.
194-5   The intensity of the emotions prevents the purpose from being carried into effect.
196-7   Where the capacity for emotion is great, the individual swings from happiness to despair on the slightest provocation. Shakespeare's quick mind delighted in turns of expression that entailed contrast and compression.
198-9   The world is not permanently static; therefore, our affections may change with worldly advancement.
200-201   Does a man fall in love with a wealthy heiress for her own sake, or does he love her because he loves her wealth?
202   Shakespeare had seen and read of numerous instances; he may be thinking of the fall of the Earl of Essex.
204   **tend:** depend.
207   **seasons him his enemy:** ripens him into his enemy.
200-207   This is a theme to which Shakespeare frequently refers; it is a satire on human hypocrisy.
209-11   No matter what we plan, the outcome is always different from our anticipations.
213   **die thy thoughts:** Let thy thoughts (of a second marriage) die.
184-213   It has been suggested that the lines written by Hamlet are incorporated in this speech.

None wed the second but who kill'd the first.   *riddle*

Hamlet (aside).   That's wormwood.

Player Queen.   The instances that second marriage move   180
  Are base respects of thrift, but none of love: *I'm loyal, I wouldn't*
  A second time I kill my husband dead,   *marry again*
  When second husband kisses me in bed.

Player King.   I do believe you think what now you speak,
  But what we do determine, oft we break.   185
  Purpose is but the slave to memory,
  Of violent birth, but poor validity:
  Which now, the fruit unripe, sticks on the tree,
  But fall unshaken when they mellow be.
  Most necessary 'tis that we forget   190
  To pay ourselves what to ourselves is debt:
  What to ourselves in passion we propose,
  The passion ending, doth the purpose lose.
  The violence of either grief or joy,
  Their own enactures with themselves destroy: 195
  Where joy most revels, grief doth most lament;
  Grief joys, joy grieves, on slender accident.
  This world is not for aye, nor 'tis not strange
  That even our loves should with our fortunes change:
  For 'tis a question left us yet to prove,   200
  Whether love lead fortune, or else fortune love.
  The great man down, you mark his favourite flies;
  The poor advanc'd makes friends of enemies:
  And hitherto doth love on fortune tend:
  For who not needs shall never lack a friend,   205
  And who in want a hollow friend doth try
  Directly seasons him his enemy.
  But, orderly to end where I begun,
  Our wills and fates do so contrary run,
  That our devices still are overthrown,   210
  Our thoughts are ours, their ends none of our own:
  So think thou wilt no second husband wed,
  But die thy thoughts when thy first lord is dead.   *Soon as I'm gone*

215 **Sport and . . . night:** May I be deprived of pleasure by day and rest by night. (The subjunctive mood is used throughout the Player Queen's speech.)

216 **desperation:** despair.

217 **anchor's cheer:** hermit's scanty food.

218-19 **Each opposite . . . destroy:** May all my hopes be blasted just as a joyful face may turn white with sudden fear.

222 **it:** this resolution.

225 **rock:** soothe (as in a cradle).

228 **protest:** make protestations of her love.

229 Hamlet may emphasize "her" in order to point out the contrast between his mother and the Player Queen.

230 **argument:** subject, story. This question implies that Claudius had not been watching the pantomime; **no offence:** nothing offensive.

232-3 Hamlet speaks with airy innocence.

235 The title seems singularly appropriate; **Marry:** a mild oath, originally *by Mary;* **tropically:** figuratively, metaphorically. A *trope* is a metaphor or figure of speech. (There may be a pun on "trap".)

236 **image:** representation. Shakespeare may be referring to an actual play.

238 **knavish:** villainous.

239 **free:** free from guilt.

240-1 **let the . . . unwrung:** Let him who is guilty flinch; our consciences are clear; **gall'd jade:** a nag whose shoulders are rubbed raw by the saddle; **withers:** ridge between the shoulders.

242 Hamlet was Claudius' nephew. Lucianus is sometimes dressed like Hamlet.

243 **chorus:** one who explains; in Greek drama, a group performing this function.

244-5 The interpreter at an Elizabethan "Punch and Judy" show explained the action to the onlookers. So Hamlet could explain Ophelia's love if he could see her thoughts manifested as puppets being manipulated by the operator (Polonius?).

Player Queen.   Nor earth to me give food, nor heaven light!
  Sport and repose lock from me day and night!   215
  To desperation turn my trust and hope,
  An anchor's cheer in prison be my scope!
  Each opposite, that blanks the face of joy,
  Meet what I would have well and it destroy!
  Both here and hence pursue me lasting strife,   220
  If, once a widow, ever I be wife!
Hamlet.   If she should break it now!
Player King.   'Tis deeply sworn. Sweet, leave me here a while;
  My spirits grow dull, and fain I would beguile
  The tedious day with sleep.   *Sleeps.*
Player Queen.   Sleep rock thy brain,   225
  And never come mischance between us twain!   *Exit.*
Hamlet.   Madam, how like you this play?
Queen.   The lady doth protest too much, methinks.
Hamlet.   O, but she'll keep her word.
King.   Have you heard the argument? Is there no offence   230
  in't?
Hamlet.   No, no, they do but jest, poison in jest; no offence
  i' the world.
King.   What do you call the play?
Hamlet.   The Mouse-trap. Marry, how? Tropically. This   235
  play is the image of a murder done in Vienna: Gon-
  zago is the duke's name, his wife, Baptista: you
  shall see anon, 'tis a knavish piece of work, but
  what of that? your majesty, and we that have free
  souls, it touches us not: let the gall'd jade wince,   240
  our withers are unwrung.
      Enter Lucianus.
  This is one Lucianus, nephew to the king.
Ophelia.   You are as good as a chorus, my lord.
Hamlet.   I could interpret between you and your love, if I
  could see the puppets dallying.   245
Ophelia.   You are keen, my lord, you are keen.
Hamlet.   It would cost you a groaning to take off mine edge.

249 **Begin, murderer:** It has been suggested that these may be the lines composed by Hamlet; hence, his excitement.

250 **pox:** syphilis; **leave thy damnable faces:** Stop grimacing.

251 **the croaking . . . revenge:** This line from an old play simply means *hurry up and begin.*

253 **confederate season:** propitious or favourable moment.

255 **Hecate:** goddess of black magic and the dark side of the moon; **ban:** curse.

256 **dire property:** dread power.

257 **wholesome:** healthy.

252-7 These may be the lines written by Hamlet.

260 **anon:** right away, immediately.

262 ff.   Note the indirect stage directions.

263 **false fire:** the explosion of blank cartridges; many critics believe that the remark is ironic. Has Claudius been frightened by a mere play? Another theory is that the lines written by Hamlet may have shown how the murderer got the love of Gonzago's wife. In this case, Hamlet would be annoyed that the King had not waited for the climax of the play.

268 **stricken:** shot; **weep:** There is a poetic tradition that the wounded deer will shed tears at the point of death.

268-71 The words of the old ballad seem singularly appropriate.

272 **forest of feathers:** Plumes were popular on the Elizabethan stage.

273-5 **turn Turk:** make a complete change for the worse, as from Christian to Moslem. (The Elizabethans were intolerant of other faiths); **Provincial roses:** rosettes from Provence in Southern France, famous for its roses; **raz'd:** with the leather slashed to form a pattern; **fellowship in . . . players:** a partnership in a company of actors; **cry:** a pack of hounds, so named because of the yelping made when they are in pursuit.

272-5 Hamlet's excitement is hysterical; he seems more stimulated intellectually by the success of his scheme than by the establishment of the King's guilt.

276 **share:** Elizabethan actors were paid from the proceeds according to the number of shares they owned.

278 **Damon:** one of a pair of loyal friends in an old classical tale.

279-80 **dismantled was . . . himself:** Hamlet refers to his father as Jove in III. iv. 56. The elder Hamlet was also bereft of his throne.

Ophelia. Still better and worse.

Hamlet. So you mis-take your husbands. Begin, murderer,
pox, leave thy damnable faces, and begin; come,   250
the croaking raven doth bellow for revenge.

Lucianus. Thoughts black, hands apt, drugs fit, and time
agreeing;
Confederate season, else no creature seeing;
Thou mixture rank, of midnight weeds collected,
With Hecate's ban thrice blasted, thrice infected,   255
Thy natural magic, and dire property,
On wholesome life usurps immediately.

Pours the poison into the sleeper's ear.

Hamlet. He poisons him i' the garden for his estate, his
name's Gonzago, the story is extant, and written
in very choice Italian, you shall see anon how the   260
murderer gets the love of Gonzago's wife.

Ophelia. The king rises.

Hamlet. What, frighted with false fire?   *King admits guilt*

Queen. How fares my lord?

Polonius. Give o'er the play.   265

King. Give me some light. Away!   *Turning point-crisis*

Polonius. Lights, lights, lights.

Exeunt all but Hamlet and Horatio.

Hamlet. Why, let the stricken deer go weep,   *Now king will hunt Hamlet*
The hart ungalled play;
For some must watch, while some must sleep: 270
Thus runs the world away.
Would not this, sir, and a forest of feathers—if the
rest of my fortunes turn Turk with me—with Pro-
vincial roses on my raz'd shoes, get me a fellowship
in a cry of players?   275

Horatio. Half a share.

Hamlet. A whole one, I.
For thou dost know, O Damon dear,
This realm dismantled was
Of Jove himself; and now reigns here   280

281   **pacock:** F, Q1, and Q2 read *paiocke;* rendered by most editors as *pajock.* The peacock was considered to be the epitome of many negative qualities such as vanity, lechery, and pride. Sir Henry Irving, the great Victorian actor, plucked apart a fan of peacock feathers in order to add validity to the comment. Some actors of the role tear up the manuscript of the play within the play. (Hamlet may have been acting as prompter.) He delivers his lines from Claudius' throne, into which he has flung himself.

283-4   Hamlet is no longer in doubt with regard to his uncle's guilt.

288   **recorder:** a kind of flute or flageolet with a mouthpiece. It was the chief Elizabethan wind instrument and had a sweet, solemn tone.

290   **perdy:** a corruption of *par Dieu.*

292   **vouchsafe:** condescend to grant.

293   Hamlet dons his antic disposition.

296   **marvellous distemper'd:** extremely upset.

297   Hamlet's question has an acid edge.

298   **choler:** a) anger, b) biliousness, the choleric temperament being caused by an excess of bile.

301   **purgation:** cleansing, both physically and spiritually; purification.

303   **frame:** order.

305   **pronounce:** speak out.

308   Hamlet bows with exaggerated courtesy.

312   **pardon:** permission to go.

       A very, very—pacock.

Horatio.   You might have rhym'd.

Hamlet.   O good Horatio, I'll take the ghost's word for a
thousand pound. Didst perceive?

Horatio.   Very well, my lord.   285

Hamlet.   Upon the talk of the poisoning?

Horatio.   I did very well note him.

Hamlet.   Ah, ha! Come, some music! come, the recorders!
        For if the king like not the comedy,
        Why then, belike, he likes it not, perdy.   290
Come, some music!

      Re-enter Rosencrantz and Guildenstern.

Guildenstern.   Good my lord, vouchsafe me a word with you.

Hamlet.   Sir, a whole history.

Guildenstern.   The king, sir,—

Hamlet.   Ay, sir, what of him?   295

Guildenstern.   Is in his retirement marvellous distemper'd.

Hamlet.   With drink, sir?

Guildenstern.   No, my lord, with choler.

Hamlet.   Your wisdom should show itself more richer to
signify this to the doctor; for, for me to put him   300
to his purgation would perhaps plunge him into
more choler.

Guildenstern. Good my lord, put your discourse into some frame,
and start not so wildly from my affair.

Hamlet.   I am tame, sir; pronounce.   305

Guildenstern.

The queen, your mother, in most great affliction of
spirit, hath sent me to you.

Hamlet.   You are welcome.

Guildenstern.

Nay, good my lord, this courtesy is not of the right
breed. If it shall please you to make me a whole-   310
some answer, I will do your mother's commandment: if not, your pardon and my return shall be
the end of business.

321 **amazement and admiration:** bewilderment and astonishment.

323 **no sequel . . . of:** nothing to follow.

325 **closet:** small room, specially for private interviews.

327 **were she . . . mother:** There is an ironic implication that the closer the relationship, the less the necessity for obedience.

328 **trade:** business.

330 **by these . . . stealers:** Hamlet swears by uplifted hands. The Anglican catechism says: "Keep my hands from picking and stealing."

331 **distemper:** derangement.

332 **bar the . . . liberty:** lock yourself in mentally and thus prevent a cure; speaking of his grievances would give him relief. Another interpretation is: "Your reticence may lead to your being shut up like a madman" (Dover Wilson, New Shakespeare *Hamlet.*)

334 **Sir, I lack advancement:** Hamlet pretends that thwarted ambition is the cause of his apparent madness; he knows that his sycophantic friends will tell Claudius everything.

337 **while the grass grows:** "While the grass grows, the steed starves." The old proverb implies that Hamlet must cool his heels while Claudius reigns, and wait indefinitely for the throne.

338 **musty:** stale.

339-41 **to withdraw with you:** to speak a word with you in private; **go about:** try, attempt; **recover the wind of:** get to windward of; **toil:** pit or net. The metaphor is drawn from hunting. If the hunter is upwind, the deer picks up the scent and dashes in the opposite direction, where the snares have been placed.

342-3 **O, my . . . unmannerly:** Because I must boldly perform my duty, I have to be rude to a friend. (If my sense of duty makes me too rude, it is my love for you that causes it.)

Hamlet. Sir, I cannot.

Guildenstern. What, my lord?   315

Hamlet. Make you a wholesome answer; my wit's dis-
eas'd: but, sir, such answer as I can make, you shall
command, or rather, as you say, my mother: therefore
no more, but to the matter; my mother, you say,—

Rosencrantz.

Then thus she says; your behaviour hath struck her   320
into amazement and admiration.

Hamlet. O wonderful son, that can so astonish a mother!
But is there no sequel at the heels of this mother's
admiration? Impart.

Rosencrantz.

She desires to speak with you in her closet ere you   325
go to bed.

Hamlet. We shall obey, were she ten times our mother.
Have you any further trade with us?

Rosencrantz. My lord, you once did love me.

Hamlet. So I do still, by these pickers and stealers.   330

Rosencrantz.

Good my lord, what is your cause of distemper?
You do surely bar the door upon your own liberty,
if you deny your griefs to your friend.

Hamlet. Sir, I lack advancement.   *— still pretends*

Rosencrantz.

How can that be, when you have the voice of the   335
king himself for your succession in Denmark?

Hamlet. Ay, sir, but "while the grass grows,"—the proverb
is something musty.

         Re-enter Players with recorders.

O, the recorders! let me see one. To withdraw
with you:—why do you go about to recover the   340
wind of me, as if you would drive me into a toil?

Guildenstern. O, my lord, if my duty be too bold, my love is too
unmannerly.

350 **touch:** fingering.
351 **It is as easy as lying:** therefore, Guildenstern should be able to do it; **govern these ventages:** control these openings.
354 **stops:** openings.
365 **fret:** Note the play on the double meaning: a) annoy, b) equip with horizontal bars that act as a guide to the fingers of a lute player (technical meaning). You can go through the motions, but you cannot produce a melody; you can annoy me, but you cannot penetrate my secret. Sir John Gielgud confesses that he cannot resist the temptation to break the recorder across his knee by way of climax.
369 **presently:** at once.
370 **yonder cloud:** Hamlet is in a royal palace, but because the Elizabethan theatre was open to the sky, the reference does not seem incongruous; Hamlet uses a piece of the recorder as a telescope and deliberately plays the fool with Polonius, who probably believes that it is dangerous to cross a madman.

Hamlet.   I do not well understand that. Will you play
  upon this pipe?   345
Guildenstern.   My lord, I cannot.
Hamlet.   I pray you.
Guildenstern.   Believe me, I cannot.
Hamlet.   I do beseech you.
Guildenstern.   I know no touch of it, my lord.   350
Hamlet.   It is as easy as lying: govern these ventages with
  your fingers and thumbs, give it breath with your
  mouth, and it will discourse most eloquent music;
  look you, these are the stops.
Guildenstern.
  But these cannot I command to any utterance of   355
  harmony; I have not the skill.
Hamlet.   Why, look you now how unworthy a thing you
  make of me! You would play upon me, you would
  seem to know my stops, you would pluck out the
  heart of my mystery, you would sound me from my   360
  lowest note to the top of my compass; and there
  is much music, excellent voice, in this little organ, yet
  cannot you make it speak. 'Sblood, do you think
  I am easier to be play'd on than a pipe? Call me
  what instrument you will, though you can fret me,   365
  yet you cannot play upon me.
           Re-enter Polonius.
  God bless you, sir!
Polonius.   My lord, the queen would speak with you, and
  presently.
Hamlet. Do you see yonder cloud that's almost in shape of   370
  a camel?
Polonius.   By the mass and 'tis, like a camel indeed.
Hamlet.   Methinks it is like a weasel.
Polonius.   It is back'd like a weasel.
Hamlet.   Or like a whale.   375
Polonius.   Very like a whale.
Hamlet. Then I will come to my mother by and by. (*aside*)

378   **to the . . . bent:** to the extreme limit, (till I can bear it no longer).

379   **I will, say so:** Some editors give this line to Polonius and omit the comma.

381   **witching:** time for magic or witches, bewitching; hence, midnight.

382   **yawn:** open their jaws (to release the dead).

383   **contagion:** disease-bearing fumes; **could I . . . blood:** Hamlet says "could" not *will*.

387   **Nero:** a Roman emperor notorious for his cruelty; he is said to have engineered the murder of his mother.

389   **speak daggers:** utter sharp, piercing words. The picture kindles the imagination.

390   **My tongue . . . hypocrites:** in the sense that the bitterness of the soul will not be honestly expressed.

391   **shent:** blamed, rebuked.

392   **to give them seals:** to confirm them by action.

See also p. 262.

2   **range:** rove unchecked.

3   **commission:** written instructions.

5   **the terms . . . estate:** my position as King.

7   **provide:** prepare.

1-7   The King acts with customary decision. Since he openly discusses the threat to his life implied by Lucianus, it is obvious that *the court* has taken his interpretation of the murder of Gonzago. *The theatre audience* sees in it, of course, a re-enactment of the murder of the elder Hamlet by Claudius. It seems logical to assume that Claudius grasps both meanings.

9   **bodies:** subjects. The image seems to be that of plants taking nourishment from a sustaining source.

11   **peculiar:** individual.

They fool me to the top of my bent. I will come
by and by. Leave me, friends. I will, say so.
                        Exeunt all but Hamlet.

"By and by" is easily said.   380
'Tis now the very witching time of night,
When churchyards yawn, and hell itself breathes out   *Now he can*
Contagion to this world: now could I drink hot blood, *kill Claudius*
And do such bitter business as the day
Would quake to look on. Soft! now to my mother.   385
O heart, lose not thy nature, let not ever
The soul of Nero enter this firm bosom;
Let me be cruel, not unnatural:
I will speak daggers to her, but use none;
My tongue and soul in this be hypocrites;   390
How in my words soever she be shent,
To give them seals never my soul consent!   *Exit.*

Scene 3

A ROOM IN THE CASTLE.

Enter King, Rosencrantz, and Guildenstern.

King.   I like him not, nor stands it safe with us   *Will sent him*
  To let his madness range. Therefore prepare you;   *away*
  I your commission will forthwith dispatch,
  And he to England shall along with you:
  The terms of our estate may not endure   5
  Hazard so near us as doth hourly grow
  Out of his lunacies.
Guildenstern.   We will ourselves provide:
  Most holy and religious fear it is
  To keep those many many bodies safe
  That live and feed upon your majesty.   10
Rosencrantz. The single and peculiar life is bound
  With all the strength and armour of the mind

13 **noyance:** harm.
14 **weal:** welfare. One of Shakespeare's beliefs was that the power and the person of the sovereign provided stability and held society together.
15 **cease of majesty:** death of a king.
16 **gulf:** whirlpool.
17 **massy:** massive.
20 **mortis'd:** joined, a term in carpentry. A "mortise" is a hole in a framework designed to receive the end of some other part.
21 **annexment:** addition; **petty consequence:** trivial result.
22 **attends the . . . ruin:** is included in the violent downfall.
23 **general:** of all the people.
24 **arm:** prepare.
25 The image is that of a prisoner shackled at the ankles.
28 **arras:** (accent on first syllable) rich tapestry, formerly hung round walls of rooms; Arras, a town in Artois in the north of France, was famous for the fabric; **convey:** conceal. There was space for a person between the wall and the tapestry.
29 **process:** the proceedings; **tax him home:** reprove him soundly.
30 It was Polonius who suggested the scheme that he now diplomatically attributes to Claudius.
33 **of vantage:** from an advantageous position. Dover Wilson gives the meaning *in addition*.
36 **rank:** foul.
37 **primal eldest curse:** first and most ancient curse, pronounced on Cain for the murder of Abel.
39 **though inclination . . . will:** though desire be as strong as determination. He wishes to pray.
42 **in pause:** in doubt.

To keep itself from noyance, but much more
That spirit upon whose weal depends and rests
The lives of many. The cease of majesty   15
Dies not alone, but like a gulf doth draw
What's near it with it. It is a massy wheel,
Fix'd on the summit of the highest mount,
To whose huge spokes ten thousand lesser things
Are mortis'd and adjoin'd, which when it falls,   20
Each small annexment, petty consequence,
Attends the boisterous ruin. Never alone
Did the king sigh, but with a general groan.

whichever affects kings affects all people

King. Arm you, I pray you, to this speedy voyage,
For we will fetters put about this fear,   25
Which now goes too free-footed.

Hamlet will be guarded

Rosencrantz. ⎫   We will haste us.
Guildenstern. ⎭

        Exeunt Rosencrantz and Guildenstern.
        Enter Polonius.
Polonius. My lord, he's going to his mother's closet:
Behind the arras I'll convey myself,
To hear the process: I'll warrant she'll tax him home:
And, as you said, and wisely was it said,   30
'Tis meet that some more audience than a mother,
Since nature makes them partial, should o'erhear
The speech of vantage. Fare you well, my liege;
I'll call upon you ere you go to bed,
And tell you what I know.

will listen to Hamlet

King.   Thanks, dear my lord.   35
                            Exit Polonius.
O, my offence is rank, it smells to heaven.
It hath the primal eldest curse upon't,
A brother's murder. Pray can I not;
Though inclination be as sharp as will,
My stronger guilt defeats my strong intent,   40
And like a man to double business bound,
I stand in pause where I shall first begin,

The whole situation smells.

43-47 Claudius here reminds us of *Macbeth* II. ii. 60-63 and V. i. 48-49, where the blood-stained hand is a dominant image; **Whereto serves . . . offence:** Where is there an opportunity for mercy except in the presence of sin?

48 **twofold force:** Forgive us our trespasses and lead us not into temptation.

55 Note the three motives.

56 **offence:** the thing acquired by sin; here, the crown.

57 **currents:** courses.

58 **Offence's gilded . . . justice:** Filled with gold, the hand of the offender can bribe those in authority, so that there appears to be one law for the well-to-do, another for the poor. Justice is thereby thrust aside.

59-60 **the wicked . . . law:** That which was ill-gotten (stolen, dishonestly achieved) is used to hush up the theft and prevent justice from being done.

61 **shuffling:** evasion; **lies:** exists, a legal term.

63 **even to . . . forehead:** to the last jot and tittle.

64 **what rests:** What remains?

65-66 Understand *do* after "can" in these lines.

68 **limed:** caught in bird lime, a sticky substance spread on twigs to entangle birds that were eaten as food.

69 **engag'd:** closely stuck. Shakespeare had no doubt often watched these pitiful struggles in his native Warwickshire. A modern equivalent would be flies on fly-paper, though the purpose is different; **make assay:** make an onset or attack (to win him to repentance).

36-72 That Claudius is not a hardened sinner is brought out in these lines where we feel a certain sympathy for him in his dilemma, murderer though he is. Perhaps Shakespeare does this so that we shall not want Hamlet to murder him. The fact that Claudius does have a conscience links him with Macbeth in the earlier stages of that tragedy. In Sir John Gielgud's production, Hamlet picked up Claudius' sword, which the King had taken off as he knelt to pray.

73 **pat:** without any trouble, opportunely.

75 **That would be scann'd:** That needs to be carefully examined.

And both neglect. What if this cursed hand
Were thicker than itself with brother's blood,
Is there not rain enough in the sweet heavens   45
To wash it white as snow? Whereto serves mercy
But to confront the visage of offence?
And what's in prayer but this twofold force,
To be forestalled ere we come to fall,
Or pardon being down? Then I'll look up;   50
My fault is past. But O, what form of prayer
Can serve my turn? "Forgive me my foul murder"?
That cannot be, since I am still possess'd
Of those effects for which I did the murder,
My crown, mine own ambition and my queen.   55
May one be pardon'd and retain the offence?
In the corrupted currents of this world
Offence's gilded hand may shove by justice,
And oft 'tis seen the wicked prize itself
Buys out the law: but 'tis not so above;   60
There is no shuffling, there the action lies
In his true nature, and we ourselves compell'd
Even to the teeth and forehead of our faults
To give in evidence. What then? what rests?
Try what repentance can: what can it not?   65
Yet what can it when one can not repent?
O wretched state! O bosom black as death!
O limed soul, that struggling to be free
Art more engag'd! Help, angels! make assay!
Bow, stubborn knees, and, heart with strings of steel,   70
Be soft as sinews of the new-born babe!
All may be well.   *Retires and kneels.*
    Enter Hamlet.
Hamlet.   Now might I do it pat, now a' is a-praying;
And now I'll do it, and so he goes to heaven,
And so am I reveng'd. That would be scann'd;   75
A villain kills my father, and for that,
I, his sole son, do this same villain send

78 **to heaven:** The pause is full of meaning.

79 **hire and salary:** in other words, mere payment, simple justice. According to Professor Harrison, revenge demanded much more. Q1 reads: "this is a benefit/And not revenge."

80 **grossly:** Hamlet's father was technically in a state of sin; **full of bread:** not fasting and not penitent.

81 **broad blown:** in full bloom; **flush:** full of vigour.

82 **audit:** account. The steward of an estate must give the owner periodically an account of receipts and expenditures. This is a recurring Shakespearian image.

83 **in our . . . thought:** according to our human point of view. Dover Wilson: "as all evidence and speculation shows".

84 **'Tis heavy with him:** He has severe punishment to endure.

88 **a more horrid hent:** a more horrible opportunity.

90 Claudius had married within the forbidden degrees.

91 **at game:** gambling.   92 **relish:** trace.   95 **stays:** waits.

96 **physic:** medicine. The fact that Claudius was at prayer saved his life temporarily, postponing the inevitable end as a drug that brings some relief but does not cure the disease.

73-98 Hamlet's speech is puzzling. Perhaps he simply does not want to kill the King and uses the fact that Claudius is praying as an excuse for further delay. Some critics assert that he did not want a hole-in-corner revenge but a public one, in which Claudius' treachery would be exposed to all. Others have felt that his desire to make Claudius suffer in the after-life is unworthy of Hamlet. Still others see in it his fatal habit "of thinking too precisely on the event"; when he begins to rationalize, his will to act is paralysed. However, by Elizabethan standards at least, his behaviour is intelligible. Many modern readers feel the same way. It has also been argued that this is the turning point of the play, since Hamlet's failure allows the initiative to pass to the King. Claudius, of course, had already made his plan, though we are not as yet aware that it entails Hamlet's death. Claudius' final couplet is ironic, since Hamlet spared him in the belief that he was praying. There is a dramatic moment when Claudius sees that his sword is gone. See also p. 263.

1 **straight:** immediately.   2 **broad:** unrestrained.

4 **heat:** anger; **sconce:** hide. Some editions read *silence*. Q1 has: "I'll shroud myself behind the arras." As with Reynaldo, Polonius cannot resist telling the Queen what to say.

5 Hamlet's triple cry may be an interpolation by Burbage. It serves to create excitement and to show his angry mood.

6 **fear me not:** Don't worry about me (I. iii. 51)

To heaven.
O, this is hire and salary, not revenge.
He took my father grossly, full of bread,
With all his crimes broad blown, as flush as May;
And how his audit stands who knows save heaven?
But in our circumstance and course of thought,
'Tis heavy with him: and am I then reveng'd,   85
To take him in the purging of his soul,
When he is fit and season'd for his passage?
No.
Up, sword, and know thou a more horrid hent,
When he is drunk, asleep, or in his rage,
Or in the incestuous pleasure of his bed,   90
At game, a-swearing, or about some act
That has no relish of salvation in't,
Then trip him, that his heels may kick at heaven,
And that his soul may be as damn'd and black
As hell whereto it goes. My mother stays: 95
This physic but prolongs thy sickly days.   *Exit.*
King (*rising*).   My words fly up, my thoughts remain below:
      Words without thoughts never to heaven go.   *Exit.*

Scene 4

THE QUEEN'S CLOSET.

Enter Queen and Polonius.

Polonius.   He will come straight; look you lay home to him,
      Tell him his pranks have been too broad to bear with,
      And that your grace hath screen'd and stood between
      Much heat and him. I'll sconce me even here.
      Pray you, be round with him.
Hamlet (*within*).   Mother, mother, mother!   5
Queen.   I'll warrant you; fear me not.
      Withdraw, I hear him coming.

11 **idle:** foolish.

9-12 This exchange increases the atmosphere of tension.

14 **rood:** cross.

19 **glass:** mirror.

24 **for a ducat:** I'll bet a ducat. Life is cheap; the alliteration on the letter "d" adds to the intensity; S.D. **a pass:** a thrust; a fencing term. Hamlet's impulsive gesture shows that it was not cowardice that kept him from murdering Claudius. His question shows that he acted in the hope that it was his uncle behind the arras.

30 The Queen's startled question implies that she was innocent of the murder of Hamlet's father, though Hamlet had insinuated that she was an accomplice; S.D. **discovers:** discloses, reveals.

31 **wretched:** hateful. Comment on this as an epitaph for Polonius.

33 **busy:** officious, as of a busybody. Sir John Gielgud states that the killing of Polonius is, to him, the turning point of the play.

34 Note the indirect stage direction.

Polonius - self centered

Polonius hides behind the arras.
Enter Hamlet.

Hamlet. Now, mother, what's the matter?

Queen. Hamlet, thou hast thy father much offended.

Hamlet. Mother, you have my father much offended. 10

Queen. Come, come, you answer with an idle tongue.

Hamlet. Go, go, you question with a wicked tongue.

Queen. Why, how now, Hamlet?

Hamlet. What's the matter now?

Queen. Have you forgot me?

Hamlet. No, by the rood, not so:
You are the queen, your husband's brother's wife, 15
And—would it were not so!—you are my mother.

Queen. Nay, then, I'll set those to you that can speak.

Hamlet. Come, come, and sit you down; you shall not budge;
You go not till I set you up a glass
Where you may see the inmost part of you. 20

Queen. What wilt thou do? thou wilt not murder me? *— He is old, so will attack me*
Help, ho!

Polonius (behind). What, ho! help, help, help!

Hamlet (drawing). How now! a rat? Dead for a ducat,
dead! *Makes a pass through the arras.*

Polonius (behind). O, I am slain! *Falls and dies.*

Queen. O me, what hast thou done? 25

Hamlet. Nay, I know not, is it the king? *— Suspects it was king*

Queen. O, what a rash and bloody deed is this!

Hamlet. A bloody deed; almost as bad, good mother,
As kill a king, and marry with his brother.

Queen. As kill a king? *— She didn't know king was killed.*

Hamlet. Ay, lady, 'twas my word. 30
Lifts up the arras and discovers Polonius.
Thou wretched, rash, intruding fool, farewell;
I took thee for thy better; take thy fortune;
Thou find'st to be too busy is some danger.
Leave wringing of your hands: peace! sit you down,
And let me wring your heart, for so I shall, 35

37 **braz'd:** covered with brass.

38 **proof:** impenetrable (as of armour); **sense:** feeling.

40 **act:** Hamlet probably has incest and adultery in mind. Mrs. Patrick Campbell is quoted by Sir John Gielgud as saying " 'The point about Gertrude in the closet scene is not that she didn't know Claudius was a murderer, but that she doted on him so much that she wouldn't have minded if he had been.' This seems to me feminine and shrewd."

41 **that:** as; **blurs:** disfigures, tarnishes.

42 **the rose:** symbol of natural loveliness and perfection.

44 **sets a blister:** brands as a harlot.

46-47 **from the . . . soul:** desecrates the solemn marriage contract **sweet religion:** solemn marriage ceremony.

48 **rhapsody:** meaningless sound.

49 **this solidity . . . mass:** heaven's face, perhaps the moon.

50 **as against the doom:** as though in preparation for doomsday.

51 **the act:** the marriage of Gertrude to Claudius. Hamlet believes that his mother has outraged decency in her behaviour.

52 **index:** prologue, corresponding to our table of contents. In his anger and contempt, Hamlet has probably been shouting.

53 **Look here . . . this:** Granville-Barker recommends the use of miniatures on chains as necklaces in this episode: Hamlet wears that of his father, the Queen that of Claudius. Sir John Gielgud, following the tradition of Sir Henry Irving, paints his pictures in words and makes us see them in the mind's eye. Dover Wilson feels that the lines indicate full-length portraits.

54 **counterfeit presentment:** portraits.

56 **Hyperion:** the sun-god; **front of Jove:** forehead.

57 **Mars:** god of war; the Ghost appeared in full armour.

58 **station:** attitude in standing, noble bearing.

59 **new-lighted on . . . hill:** The line has a lightness that suggests the fleet-footed messenger of the gods.

61-62 **where every . . . man:** All the gods affirmed the fact that the elder Hamlet was a man of the noblest qualities. Hamlet thought of his father as godlike in all his attributes.

64 **mildew'd ear:** a blighted ear of corn. Mildew is a destructive growth of minute fungi.

65 **blasting:** infecting, destroying; **wholesome:** healthy.

66 **leave:** cease.

67 **batten:** feed gluttonously; **moor:** as opposed to "this fair mountain", a tract of open, waste ground, wild and desolate. Q2 has *Moor,* which suggests a dark skin, unpopular among Elizabethans.

69 **hey-day:** youthful high spirits and passionate impulses.

If it be made of penetrable stuff,
If damned custom have not braz'd it so,
That it be proof and bulwark against sense.
Queen.　What have I done, that thou dar'st wag thy tongue
　　In noise so rude against me?
Hamlet.　　　　　　　　　　Such an act　　　　　　40
　　That blurs the grace and blush of modesty,
　　Calls virtue hypocrite, takes off the rose
　　From the fair forehead of an innocent love,
　　And sets a blister there, makes marriage vows
　　As false as dicers' oaths, O, such a deed　　　　45
　　As from the body of contraction plucks
　　The very soul, and sweet religion makes
　　A rhapsody of words: heaven's face does glow;
　　Yea this solidity and compound mass,
　　With heated visage, as against the doom,　　　　50
　　Is thought-sick at the act.
Queen.　　　　　　　　Ay me, what act,
　　That roars so loud and thunders in the index?
Hamlet.　Look here, upon this picture, and on this,
　　The counterfeit presentment of two brothers.
　　See what a grace was seated on this brow;　　　55
　　Hyperion's curls, the front of Jove himself,
　　An eye like Mars, to threaten and command,
　　A station like the herald Mercury
　　New-lighted on a heaven-kissing hill;
　　A combination and a form indeed,　　　　60
　　Where every god did seem to set his seal
　　To give the world assurance of a man:
　　This was your husband. Look you now what follows:
　　Here is your husband, like a mildew'd ear,
　　Blasting his wholesome brother. Have you eyes?　65
　　Could you on this fair mountain leave to feed,
　　And batten on this moor? Ha! have you eyes?
　　You cannot call it love, for at your age
　　The hey-day in the blood is tame, it's humble,

Your old king was great

but Cladius is rotten

71 **sense:** perception.

72 **motion:** emotion, impulse.

73 **apoplex'd:** suffering from apoplexy; hence, paralysed.

74-75 **Nor sense . . . choice:** Perception was never so enslaved by insanity that it did not retain some power of discrimination.

77 **cozen'd:** cheated; **hoodman-blind:** blind-man's-buff.

79 **sans:** without (a fully anglicized word in Shakespeare's day).

81 **could not so mope:** could not be so dull and stupid.

82-86 **rebellious hell . . . fire:** If middle age can be the victim of its passions, youth need not show any self-control; **mutine:** mutiny, rebel; **proclaim no . . . charge:** (Let youth) show no shame when driven by the energy of passionate lust.

87 **frost:** age, when judgement should be in control.

88 **reason pandars will:** Reason, instead of disciplining desire, caters to it.

90 **grained:** dyed, ingrained.

91 **leave their tinct:** give up their dye.

92 **enseamed:** defiled.

97 **twentieth part the tithe:** a twentieth of a tenth; that is, a two-hundredth.

98 **precedent:** former; **a Vice of kings:** a caricature or clown of a king. In the old morality plays, the Vice was the buffoon; equipped with a dagger of lath, he pared his nails and be-laboured the devil, who eventually carried him off to hell.

99 **cutpurse:** thief. The purse was often attached to a belt from which it could be snipped. The term implies that Claudius is a usurper.

And waits upon the judgement, and what judgement 70
Would step from this to this? Sense sure you have,
Else could you not have motion, but sure that sense
Is apoplex'd, for madness would not err,
Nor sense to ecstasy was ne'er so thrall'd
But it reserv'd some quantity of choice, 75
To serve in such a difference. What devil was't
That thus hath cozen'd you at hoodman-blind?
Eyes without feeling, feeling without sight,
Ears without hands or eyes, smelling sans all,
Or but a sickly part of one true sense 80
Could not so mope. O shame! where is thy blush?
Rebellious hell,
If thou canst mutine in a matron's bones,
To flaming youth let virtue be as wax
And melt in her own fire; proclaim no shame 85
When the compulsive ardour gives the charge,
Since frost itself as actively doth burn,
And reason pandars will.
Queen.   O Hamlet, speak no more:
Thou turn'st my very eyes into my soul,
And there I see such black and grained spots 90
As will not leave their tinct.
Hamlet.   Nay, but to live
In the rank sweat of an enseamed bed,
Stew'd in corruption, honeying and making love
Over the nasty sty,—
Queen.   O, speak to me no more;
These words like daggers enter in my ears; 95
No more, sweet Hamlet!
Hamlet.   A murderer and a villain,
A slave that is not twentieth part the tithe
Of your precedent lord, a Vice of kings,
A cutpurse of the empire and the rule,
That from a shelf the precious diadem stole 100
And put it in his pocket!

102 **a king . . . patches:** wearing the motley (parti-coloured) dress of the professional fool. The expression has become proverbial; **S.D. Enter Ghost:** According to Q1, it appears in its night (or dressing) gown. It is interesting to speculate why it appears at this particular juncture. When was it last seen? At this point, the great actor David Garrick was said to have knocked over a chair; this traditional bit of stage business was so effective that it is sometimes still used.

40-102 Hamlet is merciless in his denunciation of the King. Some of the speeches in this section suggest that Hamlet's love for his mother is so great as to be abnormal; from them arises the theory that he is a victim of the Oedipus complex. However, against this it must be stated that he did not feel jealousy or resentment concerning his own father's affection for Gertrude.

105 **he's mad:** The Ghost is visible to Hamlet; whether the audience should also see it is a moot point.

107 **laps'd in . . . passion:** having wasted time and allowed feeling to cool. "Time" can also mean *circumstance,* and "laps'd" can mean *taken prisoner.*

108 **important:** urgent.

111 "Purpose" is compared to a dull knife.

112 **amazement:** terror.

113 **step between . . . soul:** soothe her fears.

114 **conceit:** imagination. The Ghost's concern for Gertrude is in keeping with the picture that we have been given of the elder Hamlet.

118 **incorporal:** immaterial, having no substance.

120 **in the alarm:** when the alarm is raised (the sleeping soldiers leap up).

121 **bedded:** lying flat; **like life in excrements:** Nails and hair are represented as being alive.

122 **start, stand:** attracted into the plural by the noun immediately preceding them. Hamlet's appearance, his eyes wild, his hair on end and dishevelled, can easily be imagined.

123 **distemper:** disturbance of mind, madness.

125 **glares:** stares (not with anger).

126-7 **His form . . . capable:** His appearance and the wrongs he has suffered combined would move the very stones if the tale were told.

128-9 **convert my stern effects:** prevent me from carrying out my grim resolves.

130 **want true colour:** will lose its justification, or lack the red hue of blood, implying courage. Hamlet may lose his nerve.

132 Why can Gertrude neither see nor hear the Ghost?

Queen. No more!
Hamlet. A king of shreds and patches—
    Enter Ghost.
  Save me and hover o'er me with your wings,
    You heavenly guards! What would your gracious
      figure?
Queen. Alas, he's mad! 105
Hamlet. Do you not come your tardy son to chide,
    That, laps'd in time and passion, lets go by
    The important acting of your dread command?
  O, say!
Ghost. Do not forget: this visitation 110
    Is but to whet thy almost blunted purpose.
    But look, amazement on thy mother sits;
    O, step between her and her fighting soul:
    Conceit in weakest bodies strongest works,
    Speak to her, Hamlet.
Hamlet. How is it with you, lady? 115
Queen. Alas, how is't with you,
    That you do bend your eye on vacancy,
    And with the incorporal air do hold discourse?
    Forth at your eyes your spirits wildly peep;
    And, as the sleeping soldiers in the alarm, 120
    Your bedded hair, like life in excrements,
    Start up and stand an end. O gentle son,
    Upon the heat and flame of thy distemper
    Sprinkle cool patience. Whereon do you look?
Hamlet. On him, on him. Look you how pale he glares! 125
    His form and cause conjoin'd, preaching to stones,
    Would make them capable. Do not look upon me,
    Lest with this piteous action you convert
    My stern effects: then what I have to do
    Will want true colour; tears perchance for blood. 130
Queen. To whom do you speak this?
Hamlet. Do you see nothing there?
Queen. Nothing at all; yet all that is I see.

134   **how it steals away:** Note the verbs that have been used to describe the movement of the Ghost. What is implied by the verb "steals"?

135   **habit:** dress, garb.

137   **coinage:** invention.

138-9   **This bodiless . . . in:** Madness is very crafty in creating such figments.

141   **healthful music:** rhythm of well being, an interesting metaphor.

143   **I the . . . re-word:** I will express the meaning in different words. Some editors say *repeat in the same words.* Which would be the better test of sanity?

144   **would gambol from:** be unable to take seriously.

145   **Lay not . . . soul:** Do not deceive your soul with that consoling thought; **unction:** salve, ointment.

146   **that not . . . speaks:** that it is my madness, not your sin, speaking.

147-9   **It will . . . unseen:** Surface healing will conceal the dangerous infection beneath. The dominating image in *Hamlet,* according to Spurgeon, is that of an ulcer or tumour. Account for this.

151-2   **And do . . . ranker:** Manure scattered on weeds will make the growth more luxuriant; so the Queen is exhorted not to add sin to sin.

153   **pursy:** corpulent. The image suggests bloated loose living.

154-5   **Virtue itself . . . good:** Vice is so powerful that virtue must bow and coax in order to get its permission to reform wickedness—a cynical comment on the standards of the court.

161   **who all . . . eat:** which destroys all feeling. Repetition takes the edge off any experience.

162-5   **of habits devil:** the evil genius of our (bad) habits; **is angel . . . on:** has its finer side in that the more we perform a good action the more habitual it becomes, just as a garment becomes more comfortable with use.

Hamlet.   Nor did you nothing hear?
Queen.   No, nothing but ourselves.
Hamlet.   Why, look you there! look, how it steals away!
    My father, in his habit as he liv'd!   135
    Look, where he goes, even now out at the portal!
                                            Exit Ghost.
Queen.   This is the very coinage of your brain:
    This bodiless creation ectasy
    Is very cunning in.
Hamlet.   Ecstasy!
    My pulse, as yours, doth temperately keep time,   140
    And makes as healthful music: it is not madness
    That I have utter'd; bring me to the test,
    And I the matter will re-word, which madness
    Would gambol from. Mother, for love of grace,
    Lay not that flattering unction to your soul,   145
    That not your trespass but my madness speaks:
    It will but skin and film the ulcerous place,
    Whiles rank corruption, mining all within,
    Infects unseen. Confess yourself to heaven,
    Repent what's past, avoid what is to come,   150
    And do not spread the compost on the weeds
    To make them ranker. Forgive me this my virtue:
    For in the fatness of these pursy times
    Virtue itself of vice must pardon beg,
    Yea, curb and woo for leave to do him good.   155
Queen.   O Hamlet, thou hast cleft my heart in twain.   You broke my heart in two
Hamlet.   O, throw away the worser part of it,
    And live the purer with the other half.
    Good night: but go not to my uncle's bed;
    Assume a virtue, if you have it not.   160
    That monster, custom, who all sense doth eat,
    Of habits devil, is angel yet in this,
    That to the use of actions fair and good
    He likewise gives a frock or livery,
    That aptly is put on. Refrain to-night,   165

168 **use almost . . . nature:** Habit can almost alter an inborn characteristic.

169 A word such as "quell" or *master* is usually inserted here, although a verb is missing in Q2.

171 **desirous to be blest:** repentant.

174 **to punish . . . this:** to make me guilty of this man's murder (and thus place me in the King's power); **this with me:** (to punish) this man by having me murder him.

175 **their:** its (heaven's); **scourge and minister:** the lash and the wielder of the lash.

176 **bestow:** dispose of.

178 **I must . . . kind:** Hamlet sees himself as a surgeon who heals by using the knife.

180 **What shall I do:** in Q1, the Queen says: "I will conceal, consent, and do my best/What stratagem soe'er thou shalt devise."

181 **by no means:** by any means. (Note the negative command.)

182 **blowt:** soft-bodied, bloated.

183 **wanton:** lascivious(ly); **mouse:** a term of endearment.

184 **reechy:** filthy, dirty; from *reek*, smoke or vapour.

186 **ravel all . . . out:** unravel.

190 **paddock:** toad; **gib:** gib or Gilbert cat, tomcat.

191 **dear concernings:** matters of such importance to him.

194 **famous ape:** The story has not been traced, but it evidently deals with an ape that tried to fly by jumping out of a birdcage (woven basket).

195 **to try conclusions:** to repeat the experiment. It will be best for Gertrude to say nothing.

And that shall lend a kind of easiness
To the next abstinence; the next more easy;
For use almost can change the stamp of nature,
And either [quell] the devil, or throw him out
With wondrous potency. Once more, good
    night: 170
And when you are desirous to be blest,
I'll blessing beg of you. For this same lord,
    Pointing to Polonius.
I do repent: but heaven hath pleas'd it so
To punish me with this, and this with me,
That I must be their scourge and minister.   175
I will bestow him, and will answer well
The death I gave him. So, again, good night;
I must be cruel, only to be kind:
Thus bad begins, and worse remains behind.
One word more, good lady.
Queen.   What shall I do?   180
Hamlet.   Not this, by no means, that I bid you do:
Let the blowt king tempt you again to bed,
Pinch wanton on your cheek, call you his mouse,
And let him, for a pair of reechy kisses,
Or paddling in your neck with his damn'd fingers,   185
Make you to ravel all this matter out,
That I essentially am not in madness,
But mad in craft; 'twere good you let him know;
For who, that's but a queen, fair, sober, wise,
Would from a paddock, from a bat, a gib,   190
Such dear concernings hide! who would do so?
No, in despite of sense and secrecy,
Unpeg the basket on the house's top,
Let the birds fly, and like the famous ape,
To try conclusions, in the basket creep   195
And break your own neck down.
Queen.   Be thou assur'd, if words be made of breath
And breath of life, I have no life to breathe

200-201 Some critics wonder how Hamlet and Gertrude know this, but he was probably informed, since originally he was to go to England for his health. No doubt Claudius informed Gertrude also.

204 **mandate:** command; **sweep my way:** clear my path.

205 **marshal me to knavery:** lead me on to villainy; **Let it work:** Let it follow its course.

206-8 **to have . . . petar:** to cause the engineer to be blown up by his own bomb; that is, to cause a person to perish by his own devices. Evil thus becomes a boomerang. The expression has become a household word; **'t shall . . . but:** it will be a strange thing if I do not; **delve one . . . mines:** Countermining was used in siege warfare.

210 **crafts:** schemes.

211 **set me packing:** hasten my departure.

212 **lug the guts:** The expression seems exceedingly coarse and crude nowadays; Hamlet may be using it deliberately to reinforce his contempt for Polonius. Perhaps the crudeness conceals his real feelings of aversion?

215 **prating:** chattering.

213-15 These lines have a sardonic irony. It is especially ironic that the epitaph should contain a pun.

216 **to draw toward an end:** a play on words; "draw" in the sense of *drag;* the whole expression means *to bring to a conclusion.*

217 S.D. **severally:** separately.

See also p. 264.

This scene is properly a continuation of the preceding one. (The division into acts and scenes was not made until 1676; though arbitrary, it is still followed by most editors. The stage direction of F at this point is *Enter King.*)

1 **profound:** in a double sense, both heartfelt and significant.

2 **translate:** interpret.

Handwritten annotations:

Hamlet tells Gertrude that she should tell Claudius that Hamlet's actions are mad, not him.

What thou hast said to me.

Hamlet.   I must to England; you know that?

Queen.   Alack,   200
   I had forgot: 'tis so concluded on.

What comes around, goes around

Hamlet.   There's letters seal'd: and my two schoolfellows, *something will happen.*
   Whom I will trust as I will adders fang'd,
   They bear the mandate; they must sweep my way,
   And marshal me to knavery. Let it work;   205
   For 'tis the sport to have the enginer

People die at their own devices

   Hoist with his own petar, and 't shall go hard
   But I will delve one yard below their mines,
   And blow them at the moon: O, 'tis most sweet
   When in one line two crafts directly meet.   210
   This man shall set me packing:
   I'll lug the guts into the neighbour room.
   Mother, good night indeed: this counsellor
   Is now most still, most secret, and most grave,
   Who was in life a foolish prating knave.   215
   Come, sir, to draw toward an end with you.
   Good night, mother.

               Exeunt severally; Hamlet dragging in Polonius.

ACT IV

Scene 1

A ROOM IN THE CASTLE.

Enter King, Queen, Rosencrantz, and Guildenstern.

King.   There's matter in these sighs, these profound heaves;
   You must translate, 'tis fit we understand them.
   Where is your son?

Queen.   Bestow this place on us a little while.

               Exeunt Rosencrantz and Guildenstern.

11 **brainish apprehension:** headstrong conception.

12 The Queen's estimate of Polonius seems rather vapid.

7-12 Gertrude in attributing the murder to Hamlet's madness is doing her best to shield her son.

13 Claudius' reaction is a selfish, though perceptive, one.

16 **answer'd:** explained.

17 **providence:** foresight.

18 **kept short:** kept under control, restrained; **out of haunt:** out of society. Claudius is now prepared to accept Hamlet's "madness" as a reason for getting rid of him. The reference to "our love" is highly hypocritical.

21 **foul disease:** The disease image is the dominant one in *Hamlet*. How can this be explained?

22 **divulging:** becoming known publicly.

23 **pith:** strength.

25 **ore:** precious metal, vein of gold.

26 **among a mineral:** in a mine.

27 **he weeps . . . done:** The Queen may be fabricating to show Hamlet's "remorse"; it seems unlikely that Hamlet would shed tears.

32 **countenance:** sanction, make the best of.

33 **join you . . . aid:** get some assistance.

36 **speak fair:** Speak gently (so as not to antagonize).

Ah, mine own lord, what have I seen to-night!   5
King.   What, Gertrude? How does Hamlet?
Queen.   Mad as the sea and wind when both contend
   Which is the mightier, in his lawless fit,
   Behind the arras hearing something stir,
   Whips out his rapier, cries "A rat, a rat!"   10
   And in this brainish apprehension kills
   The unseen good old man.
King.   O heavy deed!
   It had been so with us, had we been there;
   His liberty is full of threats to all,
   To you yourself, to us, to every one;   15
   Alas, how shall this bloody deed be answer'd?
   It will be laid to us, whose providence
   Should have kept short, restrain'd, and out of haunt,
   This mad young man: but so much was our love,
   We would not understand what was most fit,   20
   But, like the owner of a foul disease,
   To keep it from divulging, let it feed
   Even on the pith of life. Where is he gone?
Queen.   To draw apart the body he hath kill'd:
   O'er whom his very madness, like some ore   25
   Among a mineral of metals base,
   Shows itself pure; he weeps for what is done.
King.   O Gertrude, come away!
   The sun no sooner shall the mountains touch,
   But we will ship him hence: and this vile deed   30
   We must, with all our majesty and skill,
   Both countenance and excuse. Ho, Guildenstern!
         Re-enter Rosencrantz and Guildenstern.
   Friends both, go join you with some further aid;
   Hamlet in madness hath Polonius slain,
   And from his mother's closet hath he dragg'd him: 35
   Go seek him out, speak fair, and bring the body
   Into the chapel. I pray you, haste in this.
            Exeunt Rosencrantz and Guildenstern.

38 **we'll call . . . friends:** Claudius wishes to have the support of his council in his move to send Hamlet away.

40 **So haply slander:** These words were suggested by a later editor, since both F and Q2 leave the half-line blank.

42 **blank:** the white mark at the centre of a target.

40-44 The slightest murmur of false, malicious report carries its poisoned message to the ends of the earth as inevitably and as directly as the cannon ball reaches its mark; but perhaps the charge will not strike us and will instead be spent on the invulnerable air. (If we are fortunate, we won't be blamed.)

See also p. 268.

6 **compounded:** mixed.

11 **that I . . . own:** that I can follow your advice and not keep my own secret.

12-13 **demanded of:** questioned by; **sponge:** Hamlet's scornful contempt for the sycophantic courtiers is evident in the sound and meaning of the word; **replication:** answer, reply (a legal term).

15 **countenance:** patronage, favour.

16 **authorities:** powers; **officers:** servants.

17-18 **like an ape:** Q1 reads *as an ape doth nuttes;* Q2, *like an apple.* The idea is clear in either case. Dover Wilson suggests that the groundlings of the time gnawed on small apples or pippins.

Come, Gertrude, we'll call up our wisest friends,
And let them know both what we mean to do
And what's untimely done. [So haply slander]   40
Whose whisper o'er the world's diameter
As level as the cannon to his blank
Transports his poison'd shot, may miss our name
And hit the woundless air. O, come away!
My soul is full of discord and dismay.   *Exeunt.*   45

Scene 2

ANOTHER ROOM IN THE CASTLE.

Enter Hamlet.

Hamlet.   Safely stow'd.
Rosencrantz
Guildenstern } [*within*].   Hamlet! Lord Hamlet.
Hamlet.   But soft, what noise? who calls on Hamlet?
   O, here they come.
         Enter Rosencrantz and Guildenstern.
Rosencrantz. What have you done, my lord, with the dead body? 5
Hamlet.   Compounded it with dust, whereto 'tis kin.
Rosencrantz.   Tell us where 'tis, that we may take it thence,
   And bear it to the chapel.
Hamlet.   Do not believe it.
Rosencrantz.   Believe what?   10
Hamlet. That I can keep your counsel and not mine own.
   Besides, to be demanded of a sponge, what replica-
   tion should be made by the son of a king?
Rosencrantz.   Take you me for a sponge, my lord?
Hamlet. Ay, sir; that soaks up the king's countenance, his   15
   rewards, his authorities. But such officers do the
   king best service in the end: he keeps them, like
   an ape, in the corner of his jaw, first mouth'd, to
   be last swallow'd: when he needs what you have

23-24 **a knavish . . . ear:** Hamlet may have transposed his adjectives; in this case, the foolish speech is his; the knavish ear, Rosencrantz's. If it is taken as it stands, it means that a wicked speech is lost upon a fool, an expression said to be a proverb.

27-28 **The body . . . body:** Polonius is with the King, my father, but the King, my uncle, is still alive (as yet!).

29-30 **A thing . . . nothing:** Psalm 144: "Man is like a thing of nought." Macbeth says that life is "a tale/Told by an idiot . . . Signifying nothing" (V. v. 26-28).

30-31 Hamlet darts off stage as he utters this cry from the game of hide-and-seek. The fox is Polonius, for whom they are all looking.

See also p. 268.

4 **of:** by; **distracted:** unstable. Some editors see in this line a reference to the ill-starred Earl of Essex, whose character, brilliant, temperamental, impulsive, may have been Shakespeare's inspiration for the character of Hamlet.

6 **scourge is weigh'd:** punishment is considered.

7 **bear:** keep.

9 **deliberate pause:** the result of careful consideration.

10 **appliance:** remedy; the proverb is familiar.

glean'd, it is but squeezing you, and, sponge, you   20
shall be dry again.

Rosencrantz.   I understand you not, my lord.

Hamlet.   I am glad of it: a knavish speech sleeps in a foolish
ear.

Rosencrantz.
My lord, you must tell us where the body is, and   25
go with us to the king.

Hamlet.   The body is with the king, but the king is not
with the body. The king is a thing—

Guildenstern.   A thing, my lord?

Hamlet.   Of nothing: bring me to him. Hide fox, and   30
all after.   *Exeunt.*

Scene 3

ANOTHER ROOM IN THE CASTLE.

Enter King, attended.

King.   I have sent to seek him, and to find the body.
How dangerous is it that this man goes loose!   *INDECISION?*
Yet must not we put the strong law on him;
He's loved of the distracted multitude,
Who like not in their judgement, but their eyes;   5
And where 'tis so, the offender's scourge is weigh'd,
But never the offence. To bear all smooth and
    even,
This sudden sending him away must seem   *We have to make*
Deliberate pause: diseases desperate grown   *Hamlet's depart look*
By desperate appliance are reliev'd,   *Smooth*   10
Or not at all.
        Enter Rosencrantz and others.
                How now! what hath befall'n?

Rosencrantz.   Where the dead body is bestow'd, my lord,
We cannot get from him.

21-22 **politic worms:** crafty maggots; the phrase is unpleasantly suggestive, reminding one of Polonius' devious schemes in life; **your:** the; **emperor:** one who dines luxuriously.

20-22 The speech contains oblique allusions to the Diet of Worms, 1521, where the young Emperor Charles V was confronted by the "troublesome monk" Martin Luther, professor of theology at the University of Wittenberg. See I. ii. 113.

24-25 **variable service:** different courses.

27-28 **eat:** an old form of the past participle, pronounced *et*; the logic is irrefutable. The old Yorkshire song "On Ilkla Moor Baht 'At" represents the same idea in a light-hearted way.

31 **progress:** state journey of a sovereign.

20-31 Satire and cynicism are combined in this rather grisly passage.

33 **send thither:** a hint that Claudius will not be able to go himself.

41 **tender:** cherish, are concerned for.

43 **with fiery quickness:** with hot haste.

44 **at help:** favourable.

45 **tend:** wait in readiness; **bent:** prepared, as of a bow.

46 The question mark after "For England?" as suggested by F seems illogical since Hamlet knew. Q2 prints a period. Why is Hamlet so complacent?

death levels everyone

King.   But where is he?

Rosencrantz.   Without, my lord, guarded to know your pleasure.

King.   Bring him before us.   15

Rosencrantz.   Ho, bring in my lord.

            Enter Hamlet guarded.

King.   Now, Hamlet, where's Polonius?

Hamlet.   At supper.

King.   At supper, where?

Hamlet. Not where he eats, but where he is eaten: a certain   20
    convocation of politic worms are e'en at him. Your
    worm is your only emperor for diet: we fat all crea-
    tures else to fat us, and we fat ourselves for maggots:
    your fat king and your lean beggar is but variable
    service, two dishes, but to one table: that's the end.   25

King.   Alas, alas!

Hamlet. A man may fish with the worm that hath eat of a
    king, and eat of the fish that hath fed of that worm.

King.   What dost thou mean by this?

Hamlet.   Nothing but to show you how a king may go a   30
    progress through the guts of a beggar.

King.   Where is Polonius?

Hamlet.   In heaven; send thither to see: if your messenger
    find him not there, seek him i' the other place
    yourself; but if indeed you find him not within   35
    this month, you shall nose him as you go up the
    stairs into the lobby.

King.   Go seek him there.   *To some Attendants.*

Hamlet.   He will stay till you come. *Exeunt Attendants.* — He will wait

King.   Hamlet, this deed, for thine especial safety,   40
    Which we do tender, as we dearly grieve
    For that which thou hast done, must send thee hence
    With fiery quickness: therefore prepare thyself;
    The bark is ready, and the wind at help,
    The associates tend, and every thing is bent   45
    For England.

Hamlet.   For England.

48 **cherub:** The cherubim were gifted with knowledge; as the sentinels of heaven, they were also endowed with keen eyesight. Hamlet implies that he has an inkling of Claudius' designs. How do you account for this remark?

51-53 Hamlet's ever-so-polite logic infuriates the King as it is intended to do.

54 **at foot:** at his heels.

57 **leans on:** depends on.

58 **hold'st at aught:** dost value at all.

60 **cicatrice:** scar of a wound. (There is no trace of this incident in the play.)

61 **free:** willing (no longer enforced by the sword).

62 **coldly set:** undervalue, regard with indifference, esteem lightly.

63 **process:** mandate.

64 **congruing:** agreeing.

65 **present:** immediate.

66 **the hectic:** consumptive fever.

68 **were ne'er begun:** So in F. Q2 reads *will ne'er begin*.

See also p. 268.

"A back drop suggests a barren stretch of plain with gnarled trees breaking the grey expanse. Fortinbras talks with one of his captains and there is a sound of martial music in the distance" (Gilder). Another production made effective use of a Viking ship silhouetted against a sunset sky.

3 **conveyance:** conduct, escort, convoy.

King.   Ay, Hamlet.

Hamlet.   Good.

King. So is it, if thou knew'st our purposes.

Hamlet. I see a cherub that sees them. But, come, for
  England! Farewell, dear mother.

King. Thy loving father, Hamlet. ⸺   50

Hamlet. My mother; father and mother is man and wife,
  man and wife is one flesh, so my mother. Come,
  for England!   *Exit.*

King. Follow him at foot, tempt him with speed aboard,
  Delay it not; I'll have him hence to-night: 55
  Away! for every thing is seal'd and done
  That else leans on the affair: pray you, make haste;
                    Exeunt Rosencrantz and Guildenstern.
  And, England, if my love thou hold'st at aught—
  As my great power thereof may give thee sense,
  Since yet thy cicatrice looks raw and red   60
  After the Danish sword; and thy free awe
  Pays homage to us, thou mayst not coldly set
  Our sovereign process, which imports at full,
  By letters congruing to that effect,
  The present death of Hamlet. Do it, England;   65
  For like the hectic in my blood he rages,
  And thou must cure me: till I know 'tis done,
  Howe'er my haps, my joys were ne'er begun.   *Exit.*

*The letters say
that Hamlet
should be killed*

Scene 4

THE NEXT DAY.
A PLAIN IN DENMARK.

Enter Fortinbras with his army over the stage.

Fortinbras. Go, captain, from me greet the Danish king;
  Tell him that by his license Fortinbras
  Craves the conveyance of a promis'd march

*Going through Denmark
to Poland as arranged before*

1-4 These lines recall II. ii. 76-80.

6 **in his eye:** in his presence, used specially of royalty.

8 **softly:** slowly.

1-8 The brief appearance of Fortinbras at this time prepares us for his re-entrance at the end of the play. His previous activities were dwelt on in Act I and Act II; hence, we are not entirely taken by surprise at his appearance. A dramatic stage effect has been gained by having Fortinbras remain in a shadow on a higher platform while Hamlet speaks below.

9 **powers:** troops.

11 **How purpos'd:** What is their destination?

15 **the main of Poland:** Poland in general.

20 **five ducats, five:** The repetition implies contempt. A gold ducat was equivalent to about 9s. 4d.; a silver ducat to 3s. 6d. (Onions). The latter was an Italian coin; the former was in use in most European countries; **farm:** rent, lease.

22 **a ranker rate:** a higher value; **in fee:** (to be held) in absolute possession, freehold.

17-22 This short speech etches the Captain briefly but decisively for us. The patch of ground, it is believed, refers to the sand-dunes of Ostend, which were defended as a symbol, not for their military value, by an Anglo-Dutch force under Sir Francis Vere against a Spanish force ten times larger. This stage of the defence lasted from July 2, 1601, to the spring of 1602.

26 **debate the question:** suffice to settle the matter.

27 **imposthume:** abscess, purulent (discharging pus) swelling.

32 **occasions:** occurrences; **inform against me:** accuse me.

34 **market:** employment.

this land is for honour
The others are ready

Over his kingdom. You know the rendezvous.
If that his majesty would aught with us,   5
We shall express our duty in his eye;
And let him know so.
Captain.   I will do't, my lord.
Fortinbras.   Go softly on.   *Exeunt Fortinbras and Soldiers.*

They are going to Poland

Enter Hamlet, Rosencrantz, Guildenstern, and others.

Hamlet.   Good sir, whose powers are these?
Captain.   They are of Norway, sir.   10
Hamlet.   How purpos'd, sir, I pray you?
Captain.   Against some part of Poland.
Hamlet.   Who commands them, sir?
Captain.   The nephew to old Norway, Fortinbras.
Hamlet.   Goes it against the main of Poland, sir,   15
Or for some frontier?
Captain.   Truly to speak, and with no addition,
We go to gain a little patch of ground
That hath in it no profit but the name.
To pay five ducats, five, I would not farm it;   20
Nor will it yield to Norway or the Pole
A ranker rate, should it be sold in fee.

fate of Poland Sending many men — war?

Hamlet.   Why then the Polack never will defend it.
Captain.   Yes, it is already garrison'd.
Hamlet.   Two thousand souls and twenty thousand ducats   25
Will not debate the question of this straw:
This is the imposthume of much wealth and peace,
That inward breaks, and shows no cause without
Why the man dies. I humbly thank you, sir.
Captain.   God be wi' you, sir.   *Exit.*
Rosencrantz.   Will't please you go, my lord?   30
Hamlet.   I'll be with you straight, go a little before.
                    Exeunt all but Hamlet.
How all occasions do inform against me,
And spur my dull revenge! What is a man,
If his chief good and market of his time
Be but to sleep and feed? a beast, no more.   35

36-37 **large discourse . . . after:** intelligence that can consider both past and future; power of wide-ranging reflection.

39 **fust:** grow mouldy, taste of the cask.

40 **bestial oblivion:** forgetfulness like that of an animal; **craven scruple:** cowardly feeling of doubt.

41 **event:** outcome, consequence; **of thinking . . . event:** This line is sometimes taken to represent the essence of Hamlet's character and to explain the cause of his delay.

42 **quarter'd:** divided into four; hence, analysed.

45 **sith:** since.

46 **gross:** palpable, obvious.   47 **charge:** cost.

48 **delicate:** not robust; **tender:** young.

49 **puff'd:** inspired.

50 **makes mouths . . . event:** mocks the uncertainties of war.

53-56 **an egg-shell:** What could be more fragile or more worthless? **Rightly to . . . stake:** (Note that the "not" modifies "is".) True greatness does not consist in fighting over mere trifles, but in fighting at once and for a trifle if honour is in question. "Fighting for trifles is mere pugnacity, not greatness; but it *is* greatness to fight instantly and for a trifle when honour is at stake" (Dover Wilson, New Shakespeare *Hamlet*).

58 **blood:** feelings.

60 **twenty thousand men:** It is characteristic of Hamlet that in his excitement he should confuse the two thousand men with the twenty thousand ducats.

61 **trick of fame:** trifle of reputation.

62 **go to . . . beds:** How clearly the simile suggests the eagerness with which they seek death!

63 **whereon the . . . cause:** not large enough to hold the men who are fighting for it. (The irony is marked.)

64 **not tomb enough:** It is known that Vere was encamped in an old church-yard outside Ostend; **continent:** receptacle.

32-66 Sir John Gielgud's delivery of these lines was memorable as the following passage testifies: "Very quietly the noble music of the lines reflects the new stage in Hamlet's progress. Though he is concerned with his delays, self-accusatory, warring still with his own shortcomings and weaknesses, his tone is firm, the timbre of his voice strong and resonant, his few gestures clear cut, decisive. He is as merciless as ever in his judgement of himself, yet he can think of his shortcomings without the hysterical despair of his Hecuba musings. . . . Though he exhorts himself as ever to action . . . his growing resolution has, this time, an inner assurance" (Gilder).

See also p. 269.

Sure, he that made us with such large discourse,
Looking before and after, gave us not
That capability and god-like reason
To fust in us unus'd. Now, whether it be
Bestial oblivion, or some craven scruple   40
Of thinking too precisely on the event,— *tragic flaw*
A thought which, quarter'd, hath but one part wisdom
And ever three parts coward,—I do not know
Why yet I live to say "this thing's to do,"
Sith I have cause, and will, and strength, and means   45
To do't. Examples gross as earth exhort me;
Witness this army of such mass and charge,
Led by a delicate and tender prince,
Whose spirit with divine ambition puff'd
Makes mouths at the invisible event,   50
Exposing what is mortal and unsure
To all that fortune, death, and danger dare,
Even for an egg-shell. Rightly to be great
Is not to stir without great argument,
But greatly to find quarrel in a straw   55
When honour's at the stake. How stand I then,
That have a father kill'd, a mother stain'd,
Excitements of my reason and my blood,
And let all sleep, while to my shame I see
The imminent death of twenty thousand men,   60
That for a fantasy and trick of fame
Go to their graves like beds, fight for a plot
Whereon the numbers cannot try the cause,
Which is not tomb enough and continent
To hide the slain? O, from this time forth,   65
My thoughts be bloody, or be nothing worth!

Exit.

S.D. **Gentleman:** F discards the "Gentleman" and gives his speeches to Horatio.

2 **importunate:** persistent; **distract:** mad, distracted.

6 **spurns enviously at straws:** literally, kicks angrily at straws in her path; perhaps a way of saying that she is irritable about trifles. The former conveys a picture of childish frustration.

7 **is nothing:** has no meaning.

8-9 **Yet the . . . collection:** Still, the disconnected incoherence of her speech causes the listener to make deductions.

10 **botch the . . . thoughts:** make a clumsy attempt at fitting the words to match their ideas. They read into her words what they would like to find there.

11-13 **which, as . . . unhappily:** Her distracted behaviour gives the impression that some great unhappiness has befallen her.

15 **ill-breeding:** suspicious.

18 **toy:** trifle; **amiss:** calamity.

19-20 **artless jealousy:** unskilful suspicion; **so full . . . spilt:** A guilty conscience gives itself away through its own fears, which create suspicion. (The image is that of a trembling hand, which, over-anxious, is very likely to spill the contents of a bowl.) "Spill" also has the meaning of *destroy*.

20 S.D. F reads "Enter Ophelia distracted"; Q1, "Enter Ophelia playing on a Lute, and her hair downe singing."

25 **cockle hat:** The pilgrim wore a cockle-shell in his hat to indicate that he had visited the shrine of St. James of Compostella in the north-west of Spain. A lover might also describe himself as a pilgrim worshipping at his lady's shrine and be so attired.

26 **shoon:** shoes, an archaic plural.

27 **imports:** is the meaning of.

Ophelia's father is dead -Polonius, and her
boyfriend is mad.

Scene 5

A FEW DAYS LATER.
ELSINORE. A ROOM IN THE CASTLE.

Enter Queen, Horatio, and a Gentleman.

Queen.   I will not speak with her.
Gentleman.   She is importunate, indeed distract:
  Her mood will needs be pitied.
Queen.   What would she have?
Gentleman.   She speaks much of her father, says she hears
  There's tricks i' the world, and hems and beats her heart,   5
  Spurns enviously at straws, speaks things in doubt,
  That carry but half sense: her speech is nothing,
  Yet the unshaped use of it doth move
⌊ The hearers to collection; they aim at it,
  And botch the words up fit to their own thoughts;   10
  Which, as her winks, and nods, and gestures yield them,
  Indeed would make one think there might be thought,
  Though nothing sure, yet much unhappily.
Horatio.   'Twere good she were spoken with, for she may strew
  Dangerous conjectures in ill-breeding minds.   15
  Let her come in.   *Exit Gentleman.*
Queen (aside).   To my sick soul, as sin's true nature is,
  Each toy seems prologue to some great amiss:
  So full of artless jealousy is guilt,
  It spills itself in fearing to be spilt.   20
          Enter Ophelia.
Ophelia.   Where is the beauteous majesty of Denmark?⌋
Queen.   How now, Ophelia?
Ophelia (sings).   How should I your true love know
                  From another one?
                  By his cockle hat and staff   25
                  And his sandal shoon.
Queen.   Alas, sweet lady, what imports this song?

28 Ophelia stamps her foot. In Sir John Gielgud's production, she appeared in a yellow chiffon gown touched up with orange. An orange stocking had been drawn like a glove over her left hand and arm. Bold and dishevelled, she was the reverse of the gentle, winsome Ophelia of earlier scenes.

31 **turf:** a clod of earth.

36 **larded:** garnished.

37 **not:** Although later editors omit the "not" in the interests of euphony, it is found in Q1, Q2, and F. Its presence in the line causes a jolt that is in keeping with Ophelia's disordered reasoning.

38 **true-love showers:** the tears of the faithful beloved.

40-41 **God 'ild you:** God yield or reward you; **owl was . . . daughter:** The reference is to an old Gloucestershire legend; according to it, Jesus once entered a baker's shop and asked for bread. When the baker's wife offered him a large piece, her daughter objected, crying "Heugh, heugh, heugh" and was turned into an owl for her meanness. Walter de la Mare's poem "The Owl" deals with this legend. Ophelia speaks pertly to the King.

42 **God be at your table:** a blessing uttered by a guest at a meal. It may be connected with the previous reference to bread.

43 **conceit:** imaginative fancies.

46 **Saint Valentine's day:** According to an old English custom, the first man seen by a girl on the morning of February 14 was considered to be her true-love or Valentine. Birds were believed to mate on this day.

51 **dupp'd:** opened. The latch was lifted *up*. (*Don, doff,* and *dout* are analogous formations.)

56 **By Gis:** By Jesus.

59 **By cock:** By God.

Ophelia is mad
irony - Hamlet's taking madness made Ophelia mad.

Ophelia.   Say you? nay, pray you, mark.
　(*sings*) He is dead and gone, lady,
　　　　He is dead and gone,　　　　　　　　　30
　　　　　At his head a grass-green turf,
　　　　　　At his heels a stone.
　O ho!
Queen.   Nay, but Ophelia,—
Ophelia.　　　　　　　　Pray you, mark.
　(*sings*) White his shroud as the mountain snow,—
　　　　Enter King.
Queen.   Alas, look here, my lord.　　　　　　　35
Ophelia (*sings*).　　　Larded all with sweet flowers;
　　　　　Which bewept to the grave did not go
　　　　　　With true-love showers.
King.   How do you, pretty lady?
Ophelia.
　Well, God 'ild you! They say the owl was a baker's　40
　daughter; Lord, we know what we are, but know
　not what we may be. God be at your table!
King.   Conceit upon her father.
Ophelia.   Pray, let's have no words of this, but when they
　ask you what it means, say you this:　　　　　45
　(*sings*) To-morrow is Saint Valentine's day,
　　　　　All in the morning betime,
　　　　And I a maid at your window,
　　　　　To be your Valentine.
　　　　Then up he rose, and donn'd his clothes,　50
　　　　　And dupp'd the chamber-door,
　　　　Let in the maid, that out a maid
　　　　　Never departed more.
King.   Pretty Ophelia!
Ophelia.   Indeed, without an oath, I'll make an end on't:　55
　(*sings*) By Gis and by Saint Charity,
　　　　　Alack, and fie for shame!
　　　　Young men will do't, if they come to't,
　　　　　By cock, they are to blame.

60 **tumbled:** dishonoured, deprived of virginity.

64 **an:** if.

46-64 The suggestiveness of this song creates an element of tragic irony, since it is so unlike the Ophelia we knew earlier. Perhaps Hamlet's coarse, brutal speech has preyed on her mind. (One theory is that Hamlet had betrayed Ophelia.)

65 The King's question implies that time has passed. When would Ophelia's breakdown have become complete?

66-71 These lines suggest the combination of little girl and princess.

73-74 How does Claudius account for Ophelia's madness? To what extent is his reasoning valid?

76-77 **they come . . . battalions:** In modern parlance, "It never rains but it pours." The military metaphor is a graphic one.

78-79 Note Claudius' explanation of Hamlet's banishment; there is an element of hypocrisy here; **muddied:** confused. The picture of muddy water is easy to visualize.

80 **thick:** not clear; **unwholesome:** foul, in the sense of suspicious.

81 **greenly:** unskilfully, foolishly, as if lacking in judgement.

82 **in hugger-mugger:** secretly and hastily.

83 **divided from herself:** an apt description of madness, perhaps suggesting schizophrenia. Of what importance is our "judgement" according to Claudius?

87 **feeds on this wonder:** is filled with amazement; **keeps himself in clouds:** remains aloof, occupied with gloomy thoughts.

88-89 **and wants . . . death:** and lacks not tale-bearers to fill his mind with poisonous explanations concerning the death of Polonius.

90-92 **wherein necessity . . . ear:** in which, lack of definite knowledge will force the speaker to make charges against the King himself. The image is that of accusations whispered from one person to another.

    Quoth she, before you tumbled me,   **60**
        You promised me to wed.
He answers:
        So would I ha' done, by yonder sun,
        An thou hadst not come to my bed.
King.   How long hath she been thus?   **65**
Ophelia. I hope all will be well, we must be patient, but I
cannot choose but weep to think they would lay
him i' the cold ground. My brother shall know
of it, and so I thank you for your good counsel.
Come, my coach! Good night, ladies, good   **70**
night; sweet ladies, good night, good night.   *Exit.*
King.   Follow her close, give her good watch, I pray you.
                                        Exit Horatio.
O, this is the poison of deep grief; it springs
All from her father's death, and now behold!
O Gertrude, Gertrude,   **75**
When sorrows come, they come not single spies,
But in battalions. First, her father slain;
Next, your son gone, and he most violent author
Of his own just remove; the people muddied,
Thick and unwholesome in their thoughts, and
    whispers   **80**
For good Polonius' death: and we have done but
    greenly,
In hugger-mugger to inter him: poor Ophelia
Divided from herself, and her fair judgement,
Without the which we are pictures, or mere beasts;
Last, and as much containing as all these,   **85**
Her brother is in secret come from France,
Feeds on this wonder, keeps himself in clouds,
And wants not buzzers to infect his ear
With pestilent speeches of his father's death;
Wherein necessity, of matter beggar'd,   **90**
Will nothing stick our person to arraign
In ear and ear. O my dear Gertrude, this,

93 **murdering-piece:** small cannon loaded with little bullets, nails, old iron, etc.

94 **gives me superfluous death:** is more than enough to kill me.

95 **Switzers:** the royal bodyguard. Swiss mercenaries were well known throughout Europe, as shown by an old saying: "Law, logicke, and the Switzers, may be hired to fight for anybody." The Pope retains a Swiss guard in modern times.

97 **overpeering of his list:** rising above its boundaries. The lists were the palisades surrounding a tilting ground.

98 **eats not the flats:** swallows not the low-lying lands; **impiteous:** usually interpreted as *impetuous,* perhaps *pitiless.*

99 **in a riotous head:** with a band of rioters.

100 **the rabble:** Shakespeare does not have much sympathy for this segment of the population. The ease with which Laertes rouses the mob suggests that Hamlet might also have done so had he so desired.

101 **as:** as if.

102-3 **word:** promise; **antiquity forgot . . . word:** The established order is sanctioned and supported by age and habit. The mob disregards this fact in being ready to overthrow the King.

107 **How cheerfully . . . cry:** The followers of Laertes are compared to hounds giving tongue as they pursue the wrong scent; people are blaming Claudius for Polonius' death.

108 **counter:** following the scent in the wrong direction.

110 Laertes' question drips with scorn.

111-12 Is Shakespeare trying to show how easily a mob may be manipulated?

116 **cuckold:** a husband whose wife has been unfaithful to him.

117 **here:** Laertes in his excitement illogically strikes his own forehead. Another interpretation is that "here" means *at this moment;* **unsmirched:** unstained. This is the only reference in the play to Polonius' wife.

115-18 In answer to the Queen's request, "Calmly", Laertes implies that if he is calm, he is not his father's true son. This is a time for righteous anger.

    Like to a murdering-piece, in many places
    Gives me superfluous death.   *A noise within.*
Queen.   Alack, what noise is this?
King.   Attend! Where are my Switzers? Let them guard
    the door.   95
          Enter a Messenger.
    What is the matter?
Messenger.   Save yourself, my lord:
    The ocean, overpeering of his list,
    Eats not the flats with more impiteous haste
    Than young Laertes in a riotous head
    O'erbears your officers: the rabble call him lord;   100
    And, as the world were now but to begin,
    Antiquity forgot, custom not known,
    The ratifiers and props of every word,
    They cry "Choose we; Laertes shall be king!"
    Caps, hands and tongues applaud it to the clouds,   105
    "Laertes shall be king, Laertes king!"
Queen.   How cheerfully on the false trail they cry!
          Noise within.
    O, this is counter, you false Danish dogs!
King.   The doors are broke.
          Enter Laertes, armed; Danes following.
Laertes.   Where is this king? Sirs, stand you all without.   110
Danes.   No, let's come in.
Laertes.   I pray you, give me leave.
Danes.   We will, we will. *They retire without the door.*
Laertes.   I thank you: keep the door. O thou vile king,
    Give me my father!
Queen.   Calmly, good Laertes.
Laertes. That drop of blood that's calm proclaims me bastard, 115
    Cries cuckold to my father, brands the harlot
    Even here, between the chaste unsmirched brow
    Of my true mother.
King.   What is the cause, Laertes,
    That thy rebellion looks so giant-like?

120 Note the indirect stage direction; **fear our person:** fear for me. The King's courage is admirable.

121 **there's such . . . king:** The theory of the divine right of kings is an anachronism in this play, but the belief was strongly held in Shakespeare's time. According to G. B. Harrison, Elizabeth I showed supreme confidence at the time of the Essex uprising. When she heard that Essex was winning some support, she exclaimed that He that placed her in that seat would preserve her in it. On another occasion when the royal barge was accidentally struck by a shot, she "came to the open place of the barge, and bad them never feare, for if the shot were made at her, they durst not shoot againe . . . (she) was as all princes are or should be, so full of divine fulnesse that guiltie mortalitie durst not behold her but with dazzled eyes" (Chettle).

122 **that treason . . . would:** Treason dare not openly show its true aims.

123 **acts little . . . will:** cannot carry out its intentions.

130 **grace:** divine forgiveness.

132 **both the . . . negligence:** I hold heaven and earth in contempt.

134 **throughly:** thoroughly.

128-34 Laertes' blunt determination provides an obvious contrast to Hamlet's inaction.

135 **my will:** nothing but my own will.

136 **husband:** manage with prudence.

140 **swoopstake:** indiscriminately, like a gambler who draws in the whole stake at once.

144 **life-rendering pelican:** According to the old fable, the bird fed its young with its own blood; it has thus become a sacrificial symbol.

145 **repast:** feed.

148 **sensibly:** feelingly.

149 **level:** plain; **'pear:** appear. Q2 has *peare;* F, *pierce.*

Let him go, Gertrude; do not fear our person: 120
There's such divinity doth hedge a king,
That treason can but peep to what it would,
Acts little of his will. Tell me, Laertes,
Why thou art thus incens'd: let him go, Gertrude:
Speak, man.   125
Laertes.   Where is my father?
King.   Dead.
Queen.   But not by him.
King.   Let him demand his fill.
Laertes.   How came he dead? I'll not be juggled with:
To hell, allegiance! vows, to the blackest devil!
Conscience and grace, to the profoundest pit!   130
I dare damnation: to this point I stand,
That both the worlds I give to negligence,
Let come what comes; only I'll be reveng'd
Most throughly for my father.
King.   Who shall stay you?
Laertes.   My will, not all the world: 135
And for my means, I'll husband them so well,
They shall go far with little.
King.   Good Laertes,
If you desire to know the certainty
Of your dear father, is't writ in your revenge
That, swoopstake, you will draw both friend and foe,   140
Winner and loser?
Laertes.   None but his enemies.
King.   Will you know them then?
Laertes.   To his good friends thus wide I'll ope my arms;
And, like the kind life-rendering pelican,
Repast them with my blood.
King.   Why, now you speak   145
Like a good child and a true gentleman.
That I am guiltless of your father's death,
And am most sensibly in grief for it,
It shall as level to your judgement 'pear

151 S.D. **Re-enter Ophelia:** An early edition gives the following stage direction: "Enter Ophelia, fantastically drest with Straws and Flowers." Other editors prefer the suggestion that the flowers are imaginary.

153 **sense and virtue:** perceptive power.

155 **the beam:** the balance of the scale. Justice will be more than done.   **158 mortal:** subject to death.

159 **Nature is fine:** Natural affection is delicate in its workings.

160 **instance:** token. (Ophelia's sanity has followed Polonius to his grave as proof of her affection.)

152-61 Laertes' expression of grief, though ostentatious, is sincere.

163 **Hey non . . . nonny:** a nonsense refrain common in old ballads.

165 **my dove:** perhaps Laertes, whom of course she does not recognize, or more likely, an imaginary bird.

168-70 These lines may be snatches of an old spinning song; the rhythm of the wheel fits that of the melody. Some editors believe that "you call him a-down-a" refers to Polonius' downfall in death.

170-1 **It is . . . daughter:** By stage tradition, Ophelia looks at Claudius and starts away from him in horror. The reference has not been identified.

172 **This nothing's . . . matter:** This incoherent talk moves me more deeply than a sensible speech would.

173-83 The flowers mentioned have specific meanings and are presented to the appropriate person.

173 **rosemary:** a symbol of remembrance used at weddings and funerals; thinking perhaps of Hamlet, Ophelia presents this to Laertes. In Stratford-on-Avon on Shakespeare's birthday, sprigs of rosemary are worn in his memory.

174 **pansies:** from *pensée* and therefore a symbol of thoughts, especially thoughts of love. These too she gives to Laertes.

176 **document:** lesson.

178 **fennel:** stands for flattery. (Gladiators ate fennel to renew their strength); **columbines:** for faithlessness in wedlock. Both are given to Claudius, who stole the love of his brother's wife. Dramatic irony adds a poignant touch to this speech.

179 **rue:** symbol of repentance (for the Queen) and sorrow (for herself).

181 **with a difference:** with a different implication (a heraldic term); **daisy:** symbol of dissembling or deceit. She may give this to the King; some say to the Queen. Either is appropriate.

182 **violets:** symbol of faithfulness. It has been suggested that she might be speaking to Horatio, if, instead of the Gentleman, he is watching over her. Otherwise, she may speak to Laertes.

Laertes - loud, boastful, ambitious, colourful
- opposite of Hamlet

As day does to your eye.
Danes (*within*).   Let her come in.   **150**
Laertes.   How now, what noise is that?
        Re-enter Ophelia.

Laertes is sad when seeing Ophelia

O heat, dry up my brains! tears seven times salt,
Burn out the sense and virtue of mine eye!
By heaven, thy madness shall be paid with weight,
Till our scale turn the beam. O rose of May,   **155**
Dear maid, kind sister, sweet Ophelia!
O heavens! is't possible a young maid's wits
Should be as mortal as an old man's life?
Nature is fine in love, and where 'tis fine
It sends some precious instance of itself   **160**
After the thing it loves.
Ophelia (*sings*).   They bore him barefac'd on the bier:
                Hey non nonny, nonny, hey nonny:
                And in his grave rain'd many a tear,—
Fare you well, my dove!   **165**
Laertes.   Hadst thou thy wits, and didst persuade revenge,
It could not move thus.
Ophelia (*sings*).   You must sing a-down a-down,
                An you call him a-down-a.
O, how the wheel becomes it! It is the false   **170**
steward that stole his master's daughter.
Laertes.   This nothing's more than matter.
Ophelia.   There's rosemary, that's for remembrance; pray
you, love, remember; and there is pansies, that's
for thoughts.   **175**
Laertes.   A document in madness, thoughts and remembrance fitted.
Ophelia.   There's fennel for you, and columbines; there's
rue for you, and here's some for me, we may call
it herb of grace o' Sundays: O, you must wear your   **180**
rue with a difference, there's a daisy: I would give
you some violets, but they wither'd all when my
father died, they say a' made a good end,—

184 **For bonnie . . . joy:** a lost ballad that may refer to Robin Hood.

185 **thought:** melancholy; **passion:** suffering.

186 **favour:** beauty.

187-96 an early ballad, sung to an old tune called "The Milkmaid's Dumps".

193 **flaxen:** pale yellowish-brown, coloured like dressed flax; **poll:** part of head on which hair grows.

197 **of:** on; **and of . . . souls:** an ending common to inscriptions on monuments. These are Ophelia's last words in the play and as such have a singular poignancy.

199 **commune with your grief:** share your sorrow.

203 **collateral:** indirect.

204 **us touch'd:** me guilty.

210 **his means of death:** how he died; **obscure:** lowly, mean.

211 **trophy:** emblem or memorial placed over a grave or on a tomb; **hatchment:** a square or diamond-shaped tablet displaying the armorial bearings of a deceased person.

212 **ostentation:** funeral pomp or ceremonious rites.

214 **call't in question:** ask for an explanation.

215 **And where . . . fall:** The King little realizes that he himself will be called to account. The great axe would be that wielded by the executioner.

See also p. 270.

(*sings*) For bonnie sweet Robin is all my joy.
Laertes.   Thought and afflictions, passion, hell itself,   185
    She turns to favour and to prettiness.
Ophelia (*sings*).   And will a' not come again?
                    And will a' not come again?
                    No, no, he is dead,
                        Go to thy death-bed,   190
                    He never will come again.
                    His beard was as white as snow,
                    All flaxen was his poll:
                        He is gone, he is gone,
                        And we cast away moan,   195
                    God ha' mercy on his soul!
    And of all Christian souls, I pray God. God be
        wi' you.   *Exit.*
Laertes.   Do you see this, O God?
King.   Laertes, I must commune with your grief,
    Or you deny me right. Go but apart,   200
    Make choice of whom your wisest friends you will,
    And they shall hear and judge 'twixt you and me;
    If by direct or by collateral hand
    They find us touch'd, we will our kingdom give,
    Our crown, our life, and all that we call ours,   205
    To you in satisfaction; but if not,
    Be you content to lend your patience to us,
    And we shall jointly labour with your soul
    To give it due content.
Laertes.   Let this be so.
    His means of death, his obscure funeral,   210
    No trophy, sword, nor hatchment o'er his bones,
    No noble rite, nor formal ostentation,
    Cry to be heard, as 'twere from heaven to earth,
    That I must call't in question.
King.   So you shall;
    And where the offence is, let the great axe fall. 215
    I pray you, go with me.   *Exeunt.*

If any hint that king was guilty, king will give up crown.

irony — king's actually guilty.

1   **what:** What sort of people?

8   **He shall . . . him:** The line suggests a sceptical stoicism. It recalls the prayer of an old sailor mentioned by Montaigne: "O God, Thou wilt save me, if it be Thy will, and if Thou choosest, Thou wilt destroy me; but however it be, I will always hold my rudder straight."

9   **ambassador:** Hamlet.

11   **let to know:** made to know, informed.

12   **overlook'd:** looked over, perused.

13   **means:** introduction.

14-15 **ere we . . . sea:** before we had been at sea two days; **appointment:** equipment.

17   **compell'd:** enforced.

20-21 **thieves of mercy:** merciful thieves; **they knew . . . did:** This statement refers to the fact that Hamlet would repay them. Some editors have interpreted it as meaning that Hamlet arranged the capture. See III. iv. 206-10. It is more likely that the earlier reference did not refer to any specific plan.

23   **fly death:** Add *with*. The image suggests the utmost swiftness.

24-25 **yet are . . . matter:** My words will be unable to express the seriousness of the affair, just as small shot cannot fill the barrel of a cannon of large calibre.

Scene 6

ANOTHER ROOM IN THE CASTLE.

Enter Horatio and a Servant.

Horatio.   What are they that would speak with me?
Servant.   Sea-faring men, sir: they say they have letters for you.
Horatio.   Let them come in.   *Exit Servant.*
   I do not know from what part of the world
   I should be greeted; if not from Lord Hamlet.   5
            Enter Sailors.
First Sailor.   God bless you, sir.
Horatio.   Let him bless thee too.
First Sailor.   He shall, sir, an please him. There's a letter
   for you, sir, it came from the ambassador that was
   bound for England, if your name be Horatio, as I am   10
   let to know it is.
Horatio.
   (*reads*) "Horatio, when thou shalt have overlook'd
   this, give these fellows some means to the king: they
   have letters for him. Ere we were two days old
   at sea, a pirate of very warlike appointment gave us   15
   chase; finding ourselves too slow of sail, we put on
   a compell'd valour, and in the grapple I boarded
   them; on the instant they got clear of our ship, so I
   alone became their prisoner. They have dealt with
   me like thieves of mercy, but they knew what they   20
   did; I am to do a turn for them. Let the king have
   the letters I have sent, and repair thou to me with as
   much speed as thou wouldest fly death; I have words
   to speak in thine ear will make thee dumb, yet are
   they much too light for the bore of the matter. These   25
   good fellows will bring thee where I am. Rosencrantz and Guildenstern hold their course for
   England: of them I have much to tell thee. Farewell.   "He that thou knowest thine HAMLET."

On way to England, pirates attacked and Hamlet is free.

30 **give you way:** allow you free scope, permit you to gain access to the King.

See also p. 271.

1 **conscience:** awareness of the facts; **acquittance:** acquittal, discharge; **seal:** confirm.
3 **sith:** since; **knowing:** intelligent.
5 **pursued my life:** Claudius is aware of Hamlet's designs. (Lucianus was the *nephew* of the King.)
6 **feats:** deeds.
7 **capital:** punishable by death.
9 **mainly:** very greatly; **two special reasons:** How valid are the reasons Claudius gives?
10 **unsinew'd:** weak.
13 **be it either which:** whichever it be.
14 **conjunctive:** closely connected with.
15 **as the . . . sphere:** According to the Ptolemaic theory, the planets were set in crystal spheres; as the latter revolved, the former were carried around. The King implies that he and Gertrude were inseparable.
17 **count:** trial.
18 **general gender:** common people. This reference to the people's devotion is a point in Hamlet's favour.
20 **the spring . . . stone:** The baths at King's Newnham, Warwickshire, were said to have this property (perhaps through a coating of limestone).
21-24 **convert his . . . graces:** make his chains an ornament, so that he would win sympathy as a martyr; **my arrows . . . them:** Light arrows would be blown back by a rough wind; similarly, the King's plans would have reacted on his own head in the face of public clamour. With his customary nimbleness of thought, Shakespeare moves from one image to another (ll. 18-25).

Come, I will give you way for these your letters   **30**
And do't the speedier, that you may direct me
To him from whom you brought them.   *Exeunt.*

Scene 7

ANOTHER ROOM IN THE CASTLE.

Enter King and Laertes.

King.   Now must your conscience my acquittance seal,
   And you must put me in your heart for friend,
   Sith you have heard, and with a knowing ear,
   That he which hath your noble father slain
   Pursued my life.
Laertes.   It well appears: but tell me   **5**
   Why you proceeded not against these feats,
   So criminal and so capital in nature,
   As by your safety, wisdom, all things else,
   You mainly were stirr'd up.
King.   O, for two special reasons,
   Which may to you perhaps seem much unsinew'd,   **10**
   But yet to me they're strong. The queen his mother
   Lives almost by his looks; and for myself—
   My virtue or my plague, be it either which—
   She's so conjunctive to my life and soul,
   That, as the star moves not but in his sphere,   **15**
   I could not but by her. The other motive,
   Why to a public count I might not go,
   Is the great love the general gender bear him;
   Who, dipping all his faults in their affection,
   Would, like the spring that turneth wood to stone,   **20**
   Convert his gyves to graces, so that my arrows,
   Too slightly timber'd for so loud a wind,
   Would have reverted to my bow again
   But not where I have aim'd them.

[Handwritten margin notes:
"Hamlet wanted to kill me"
"Why didn't you kill Hamlet"
the reasons Gertrude loves him so he would not want to kill Hamlet Also Hamlet is liked.]

27 **if praises . . . again:** if I may praise her as she once was.

28-29 **stood challenger . . . perfections:** was unequalled in her perfection. The picture is that of a heroic figure (her worth) in a conspicuous place (on mount), uttering a challenge to all the age, daring it to deny her perfection. The traditional challenge by the King's Champion was observed for the last time at the Coronation Banquet of King George IV in 1821. The custom was for the Champion to ride, fully armed, on a charger into Westminster Hall; he would throw down his gauntlet and challenge any man who denied the monarch's right to succeed to the throne.

32 **shook:** customarily used by Shakespeare as the past participle, although *shaked* and *shaken* are both found.

44 **naked:** destitute, devoid of resources.

45 **kingly eyes:** satirical, like the tone of the letter in general.

49 **abuse:** deception.

50 **the hand:** the writing.

51 **character:** handwriting; **naked:** destitute, unprovided.

53 **advise:** So in F; Q2 has *devise*.

Laertes.   And so have I a noble father lost;   25
   A sister driven into desperate terms,
   Whose worth, if praises may go back again,
   Stood challenger on mount of all the age
   For her perfections: but my revenge will come.
King.   Break not your sleeps for that: you must not think   30
   That we are made of stuff so flat and dull
   That we can let our beard be shook with danger,
   And think it pastime. You shortly shall hear more:
   I lov'd your father, and we love ourself;
   And that, I hope, will teach you to imagine —   35
      Enter a Messenger, with letters.
   How now! what news?
Messenger.   Letters, my lord, from Hamlet:
   These to your majesty; this to the queen.
King.   From Hamlet? who brought them?
Messenger.   Sailors, my lord, they say; I saw them not:
   They were given me by Claudio; he receiv'd them   40
   Of him that brought them.
King.   Laertes, you shall hear them.
   Leave us.   *Exit Messenger.*
   (*reads*) "High and mighty, you shall know I am set
   naked on your kingdom. To-morrow shall I beg
   leave to see your kingly eyes, when I shall, first asking   45
   you pardon, thereunto recount the occasion of my
   sudden and more strange return.
                  "HAMLET."
   What should this mean? Are all the rest come back?
   Or is it some abuse, and no such thing?
Laertes.   Know you the hand?   50
King.   'Tis Hamlet's character. "Naked!"
   And in a postscript here, he says "alone:"
   Can you advise me?
Laertes.   I am lost in it, my lord. But let him come;
   It warms the very sickness in my heart,   55
   That I shall live and tell him to his teeth,

58 **how otherwise:** How can it be otherwise (when I have his letter in my hand)?

62 **checking at:** abandoning. The metaphor is drawn from falconry, the favourite sport of the Elizabethans. "To check at" meant *to swerve aside from;* a hawk sometimes veered from its proper victim and pursued another that crossed its flight.

63 **work:** move.

64 **in my device:** in my contrivance.

67 **uncharge the practice:** not suspect the plot, make no accusation of treachery.

70 **organ:** instrument; **falls:** happens.

73 **your sum of parts:** all your talents.

76 **of the unworthiest siege:** least deserving of high rank. A "siege" is literally a *seat,* the metaphor being drawn from guests *seated* at a banquet. The King dislikes the fashionable rapier-play introduced from the Continent.

77 **riband:** ribbon, in the sense of ornament.

78-81 **for youth . . . graveness:** The informal dress of youth is just as appropriate to it as are the furs and garments of middle age, which are worn to indicate prosperity (perhaps, care for health) and solemnity. (Shakespeare may have been nearing forty when he wrote *Hamlet.*)

84 **can well:** are experts. Norman horsemen at this time were famous.

"Thus didst thou."

King.   If it be so, Laertes,—
    As how should it be so? how otherwise?—
    Will you be ruled by me?

Laertes.   Ay, my lord;
    So you will not o'errule me to a peace.   60

King.   To thine own peace. If he be now return'd,
    As checking at his voyage, and that he means
    No more to undertake it, I will work him
    To an exploit now ripe in my device,
    Under the which he shall not choose but fall: 65
    And for his death no wind of blame shall breathe,
    But even his mother shall uncharge the practice,
    And call it accident.

Laertes.   My lord, I will be ruled;
    The rather, if you could devise it so
    That I might be the organ.

King.   It falls right.
    You have been talk'd of since your travel much,   70
    And that in Hamlet's hearing, for a quality
    Wherein they say you shine: your sum of parts
    Did not together pluck such envy from him,
    As did that one, and that in my regard   75
    Of the unworthiest siege.

Laertes.   What part is that, my lord?

King.   A very riband in the cap of youth,
    Yet needful too; for youth no less becomes
    The light and careless livery that it wears
    Than settled age his sables and his weeds,   80
    Importing health and graveness. Two months since,
    Here was a gentleman of Normandy:—
    I've seen myself, and serv'd against, the French,
    And they can well on horseback: but this gallant
    Had witchcraft in't; he grew unto his seat,   85
    And to such wondrous doing brought his horse
    As had he been incorps'd, and demi-natur'd

87-88 **as had . . . beast:** as if he had been physically part of that excellent animal and even shared its nature. The image is that of a centaur; **topp'd:** surpassed.

89-90 **forgery:** invention; **that I . . . did:** that his exploits exceeded all I could imagine.

92 **Lamond:** The passage is probably introduced in allusion to some specific person, perhaps Shakespeare's patron, the Earl of Southampton.

93 **brooch:** a jewel-ornament, specially one worn about the neck.

95 **made confession:** unwillingly (as a Frenchman) acknowledged your superiority (as a Dane).

96 **a masterly report:** a report of your masterly skill.

97 **art and . . . defence:** skilful exercise in the science of defence.

100 **scrimers:** fencers.

101 **motion:** in fencing, movement of the body acquired by drill and training.

105 **to play with you:** to engage in a fencing match with you.

111 **begun by time:** created by circumstance (Dover Wilson).

112 **passages of proof:** incidents that prove it.

113 **qualifies:** moderates.

114-15 **There lives . . . it:** Love contains the seeds of its own destruction.

116 **nothing is . . . still:** Nothing remains at the same level of goodness forever.

117 **plurisy:** excess, surfeit; with a play on *pleurisy,* an inflammation of the membrane enveloping the lungs.

118-19 **that we . . . would:** What we intend to do, we should do when we are minded to. (Otherwise, innumerable obstacles will thwart our good intentions.)

There will be a duel set up -Laertes and Hamlet.
Claudius will probably want to ensure Laertes wins.

With the brave beast: so far he topp'd my thought
That I, in forgery of shapes and tricks,
Come short of what he did.
Laertes.   A Norman was't?   90
King. A Norman.
Laertes. Upon my life, Lamond.
King.   The very same.
Laertes. I know him well: he is the brooch indeed
And gem of all the nation.
King. He made confession of you,   95
And gave you such a masterly report
For art and exercise in your defence,
And for your rapier most especial,
That he cried out, 'twould be a sight indeed
If one could match you: the scrimers of their nation,   100
He swore, had neither motion, guard, nor eye,
If you oppos'd them. Sir, this report of his
Did Hamlet so envenom with his envy
That he could nothing do but wish and beg
Your sudden coming o'er, to play with you.   105
Now, out of this—

Hamlet was envious that he heard the Laertes was good. These are lies! Hamlet would not do that.

Laertes.   What out of this, my lord?
King. Laertes, was your father dear to you?
Or are you like the painting of a sorrow,
A face without a heart?

are you really a man?

Laertes.   Why ask you this?
King. Not that I think you did not love your father,   110
But that I know love is begun by time,
And that I see, in passages of proof,
Time qualifies the spark and fire of it.
There lives within the very flame of love
A kind of wick or snuff that will abate it;   115
And nothing is at a like goodness still,
For goodness, growing to a plurisy,
Dies in his own too much: that we would do
We should do when we would; for this "would"

Whatever we decide now, we should right away, not wait.

120   **abatements:** diminutions.

110-21 These lines recall the speech of the Player King, III. ii. 184-213.

122-3 **spendthrift's sigh:** Every sigh was thought to cost the individual a drop of blood; "spendthrift" suggests a person who is draining his life away; **And then . . . easing:** A sigh may relieve our feelings but at great physical cost; similarly, saying "I ought to act" may ease one's conscience, but does not conduce to action and thus places a still heavier burden on that same conscience; **quick:** the heart, the tender or sensitive part.

118-23 **that we . . . easing:** These lines are a pertinent comment on the character of Hamlet and the moral of the play. Claudius' irony is unintentional.

126   Laertes' quick, blunt reply reminds us of Hamlet's failure to kill Claudius at prayer.

127   **sanctuarize:** afford a place of refuge for a murderer. Certain mediaeval churches provided a sanctuary for a murderer until he could be brought to trial.

129   **keep close . . . chamber:** The King is most anxious to prevent Hamlet and Laertes from meeting.

131   **put on:** set to work, instigate.

132   **varnish:** gloss; **fame:** reputation.

133   **in fine:** finally.   134 **remiss:** careless.

135   **contriving:** plotting. Hamlet's idealism is illustrated here.

136   **peruse:** examine closely.

138   **sword:** probably the Italian or French rapier, a weapon longer than the English broadsword. The rapier was intended for thrusting; **unbated:** not blunted at the edge and point; **a pass of practice:** a treacherous thrust. Some editors suggest that there is a double meaning, the other being *a bout for practice.*

139   **requite:** repay; **I will do't:** Laertes shows no hesitation at the thought of such treachery. Indeed, he is ready to go the King one better.   140 **anoint:** smear.

141   **unction:** salve, soft ointment used for medical purposes or as a religious rite, sometimes as preparation for death; **mountebank:** travelling quack, one who pretends to have skill in medicine or surgery.   142 **mortal:** deadly.   143 **cataplasm:** poultice.

144-5 **simples that . . . moon:** Herbs collected by moonlight were believed to have special powers.

147   **contagion:** poison; **gall:** graze. Laertes shows no compunction in making this dastardly plan.

150   **may fit . . . shape:** may enable us to carry out our scheme.

151   **our drift . . . performance:** our intentions appear through faulty execution of our design.

    changes
    And hath abatements and delays as many   120
    As there are tongues, are hands, are accidents,
    And then this "should" is like a spendthrift's sigh,
    That hurts by easing. But, to the quick o' the ulcer:
    Hamlet comes back: what would you undertake,
    To show yourself in deed your father's son   125
    More than in words?
Laertes.   To cut his throat i' the church. — *Hamlet didn't even do +*
King.   No place indeed should murder sanctuarize;
    Revenge should have no bounds. But, good Laertes,
    Will you do this, keep close within your chamber.
    Hamlet return'd shall know you are come home: 130
    We'll put on those shall praise your excellence
    And set a double varnish on the fame
    The Frenchman gave you; bring you in fine together
    And wager o'er your heads: he, being remiss,
    Most generous, and free from all contriving,   135
    Will not peruse the foils, so that with ease,
    Or with a little shuffling, you may choose   *Hamlet will get sword*
    A sword <u>unbated</u>, and in a pass of practice   *that is dull; Laertes*
    Requite him for your father.   *will have sharp.*
Laertes.   I will do't;
    And for that purpose I'll <u>anoint my sword</u>. ← *poison* 140
    I bought an unction of a mountebank,   *on sword.*
    So mortal, that but dip a knife in it,
    Where it draws blood, no cataplasm so rare,
    Collected from all simples that have virtue
    Under the moon, can save the thing from death   145
    That is but scratch'd withal: I'll touch my point
    With this contagion, that, if I gall him slightly,
    It may be death.
King.   Let's further think of this;
    Weigh what convenience both of time and means
    May fit us to our shape: if this should fail,   150
    And that our drift look through our bad performance,

152 **assay'd:** attempted.
154 **did blast in proof:** exploded in trial just as a gun bursts.
155 **your cunnings:** your respective skills.
158 **bouts:** rounds.
160 **chalice:** goblet. Several years later, in *Macbeth*, Shakespeare wrote (I. vii. 10-12): "This even-handed justice/Commends the ingredients of our poison'd chalice/To our own lips"; **for the nonce:** for the occasion.
161 **venom'd stuck:** poisoned thrust.
162 **may hold:** may be carried out.
164 **One woe . . . heel:** The image is one of haste and urgency. One can almost see a file of men, each stumbling over the man ahead.
167 **ascaunt:** So in Q2; F has *aslant,* which is the meaning.
168 **hoar:** The underside of a willow leaf is whitish in appearance.
169 **therewith:** with the willow, a symbol of love forsaken. This recalls poor Barbara's willow song, sung by Desdemona in *Othello,* IV. iii. 41-57.
170 **crow-flowers:** buttercups; others say, *ragged robin;* **long purples:** a kind of orchis found in woods and meadows.
171 **liberal:** free in speech, licentious.
172 **cold:** chaste.
173 **pendent:** Willow branches droop down towards the water; **crownet:** So in Q2; in the form of a coronet; F has *coronet.*
174 **envious:** spiteful; **sliver:** a small branch.
176 **weeping brook:** pathetic fallacy.
178 **lauds:** hymns (Q2). F and Q1 have *tunes.* Snatches of old hymns in praise of God would have a sad appropriateness.
179 **incapable of:** insensible to.
180 **indued:** suited.
167-84 Gertrude's account of Ophelia's death was no doubt reported by an eye-witness who reconstructed the scene. The passage has a quiet beauty and a moving pathos. Gertrude speaks with sincere grief. It has been suggested that Shakespeare in this account is thinking of the death of a certain Katharine Hamlet who was drowned in the Avon near Stratford. (This occurred when he was a boy of fifteen.) The river is lined with willows, and wild flowers grow on its banks.

'Twere better not assay'd: therefore this project
Should have a back or second, that might hold
If this did blast in proof. Soft! let me see:
We'll make a solemn wager on your cunnings: 155
I ha't:
When in your motion you are hot and dry—
As make your bouts more violent to that end—
And that he calls for drink, I'll have prepar'd him
A chalice for the nonce, whereon but sipping,   160
If he by chance escape your venom'd stuck,
Our purpose may hold there. But stay, what noise?
          Enter Queen.
    How now, sweet queen?
Queen.   One woe doth tread upon another's heel,
    So fast they follow: your sister's drown'd, Laertes.   165
Laertes.   Drown'd! O, where?
Queen.   There is a willow grows ascaunt the brook,
    That shows his hoar leaves in the glassy stream;
    Therewith fantastic garlands did she make
    Of crow-flowers, nettles, daisies, and long purples,   170
    That liberal shepherds give a grosser name,
    But our cold maids do dead men's fingers call them:
    There, on the pendent boughs her crownet weeds
    Clambering to hang, an envious sliver broke,
    When down her weedy trophies and herself   175
    Fell in the weeping brook, her clothes spread wide,
    And mermaid-like a while they bore her up:
    Which time she chanted snatches of old lauds,
    As one incapable of her own distress,
    Or like a creature native and indued   180
    Unto that element: but long it could not be
    Till that her garments, heavy with their drink,
    Pull'd the poor wretch from her melodious lay
    To muddy death.
Laertes.   Alas, then she is drown'd!
Queen.   Drown'd, drown'd.   185

188 **trick:** habit, wont. Laertes cannot restrain his tears.
190 **The woman . . . out:** My gentle feelings will have expressed themselves. On hearing of the murder of his wife and family, Macduff says in *Macbeth* (IV. iii. 230): "Oh, I could play the woman with mine eyes."
192 **douts:** extinguishes.

See also p. 271.

S.D. **Enter two Clowns:** The grave-diggers are rustics, and the lines they exchange serve to emphasize the daring of Shakespeare, who knew that the tragedy of Ophelia's death would be heightened by their argument. At the same time, paradoxically, the tension of the audience is released so that it may mount again as the scene progresses.
  4 **straight:** immediately; **the crowner . . . her:** The coroner has dealt with the case; **finds it:** brings in a verdict for.
  9 **se offendendo:** The grave-digger means *se defendendo,* in self defence; Q2 has *so offended.*
 10 **wittingly:** knowingly.
 12 **to act . . . perform:** The earnest ignorance adds to the humour. It is possibly a corruption of phrases found in the famous case of the suicide of Sir James Hales, who walked into a river at Canterbury and was drowned. As a result of this case, the law of the period recognized suicide as homicide. One statement made by the defence lawyer was that *"The act* of destruction *consists of three parts";* **argal:** ergo, therefore.

Laertes.   Too much of water hast thou, poor Ophelia,
  And therefore I forbid my tears: but yet
  It is our trick: nature her custom holds,
  Let shame say what it will: when these are gone,
  The woman will be out. Adieu, my lord: 190
  I have a speech of fire that fain would blaze,
  But that this folly douts it.   *Exit.*
King.   Let's follow, Gertrude: *Ironic*
  How much I had to do to calm his rage!   *to Gertrude*
  Now fear I this will give it start again;
  Therefore let's follow.   *Exeunt.*   195

ACT V

Scene 1

THE NEXT DAY.
A CHURCHYARD.

Peasants

Enter two Clowns, with spades, &c.

First Clown.   Is she to be buried in Christian burial when
  she wilfully seeks her own salvation?
Second Clown. I tell thee she is; therefore make her grave
  straight: the crowner hath sat on her, and finds it
  Christian burial.   5
First Clown. How can that be, unless she drown'd herself
  in her own defence?
Second Clown.   Why, 'tis found so.
First Clown. It must be "se offendendo;" it cannot be else.
  For here lies the point: if I drown myself wittingly,   10
  it argues an act: and an act hath three branches; it
  is, to act, to do, to perform; argal, she drown'd
  herself wittingly.

17 **will he, nill he:** willy-nilly, whether he likes it or not.

19-21 **he that . . . life:** He that is not a suicide is not a suicide. The logic is irrefutable and a *reductio ad absurdum*.

15-21 The First Clown's lines are a somewhat garbled version of the discussion that raged over whether Sir James Hales had gone to the water or whether the water had come to him. If it had been proved that Sir James had committed suicide and therefore felony, his property would have been forfeit to the Crown (Dover Wilson).

23 **crowner's quest law:** coroner's inquest law.

26 **out o' Christian burial:** without the rites of the Church and in unsanctified ground.

27 **thou say'st:** You speak the truth.

28 **countenance:** permission, sanction.

30 **even:** fellow.

32 **hold up:** follow; **Adam's profession:** possibly an allusion to the old couplet: "When Adam delved and Eve span,/Who was then the gentleman?"

38 **arms:** Note the pun.

40 **confess thyself:** The old saying ran: "Confess thyself and be hanged."

41 **Go to:** an expression used to express protest, incredulity, etc.

43 **mason:** worker in stone; **shipwright:** ship-builder.

These clowns use big words for things they don't understand.

Second Clown. Nay, but hear you, goodman delver.

First Clown. Give me leave. Here lies the water; good: 15
here stands the man; good: if the man go to this
water and drown himself, it is, will he, nill he, he
goes, mark you that; but if the water come to him
and drown him, he drowns not himself: argal, he
that is not guilty of his own death shortens not his 20
own life.

Second Clown. But is this law? *should be coroners*

First Clown. Ay, marry, is't; crowner's quest law.

Second Clown. Will you ha' the truth on't? If this had not *If she hadn't*
been a gentlewoman, she should have been buried 25 *been*
out o' Christian burial. *a somebody*

First Clown. Why, there thou say'st: and the more pity
that great folk should have countenance in this
world to drown or hang themselves, more than
their even Christian. Come, my spade; there is 30
no ancient gentlemen but gardeners, ditchers, and
grave-makers: they hold up Adam's profession.

Second Clown. Was he a gentleman?

First Clown. A' was the first that ever bore arms.

Second Clown. Why, he had none. 35

First Clown. What, art a heathen? How dost thou understand the Scripture? The Scripture says Adam
digg'd: could he dig without arms? I'll put
another question to thee: if thou answerest me not
to the purpose, confess thyself— 40

Second Clown. Go to.

First Clown.
What is he that builds stronger than either the
mason, the shipwright, or the carpenter?

Second Clown.
The gallows-maker; for that frame outlives a thousand
tenants. 45

First Clown. I like thy wit well, in good faith: the gallows
does well; but how does it well? it does well to

53 **unyoke:** give your brains a rest (after a mighty effort); oxen are unyoked from the plough at the end of the day's work.

56 **Mass:** by the Mass.

57-58 **Cudgel thy . . . beating:** a reflection on the mental powers of the Second Clown; there is no use in his racking his little brain.

61 **Yaughan:** So in F; possibly a tavern-keeper in the neighbourhood of the Globe. Q2 reads *Get thee in;* **stoup:** a measure for liquor, holding two quarts; S.D. **He digs, and sings:** The following song is a mutilated version of Lord Vaux's "The Aged Lover Renounceth Love", published in *Tottel's Miscellany*, 1558. The audience, familiar with the original, would be amused by the Clown's rendition, which is punctuated by grunts: "for-a", "there-a". Since Hamlet and Horatio hear the song, they must enter before line 66.

68 **Custom hath . . . easiness:** Habit has made it a matter of indifference to him.

69-70 **the hand . . . sense:** One who is not used to it would be more sensitive.

76 **knave:** fellow; **jowls:** dashes, knocks.

77 **jaw-bone:** According to an ancient tradition, Cain murdered his brother with this weapon.

those that do ill: now, thou dost ill to say the
gallows is built stronger than the church: argal, the
gallows may do well to thee. To't again, come.

Second Clown.
"Who builds stronger than a mason, a shipwright, or a carpenter?"

First Clown. Ay, tell me that, and unyoke.

Second Clown. Marry, now I can tell.

First Clown. To't. 55

Second Clown. Mass, I cannot tell.

First Clown. Cudgel thy brains no more about it, for your
dull ass will not mend his pace with beating, and
when you are ask'd this question next, say "a grave-
maker: the houses he makes lasts till doomsday." 60
Go, get thee to Yaughan, and fetch me a stoup of liquor.
Exit Second Clown.

He digs, and sings.
In youth, when I did love, did love,
    Methought it was very sweet
To contract, O, the time, for-a my behove,
    O, methought, there-a was nothing-a meet. 65
Enter Hamlet and Horatio.

Hamlet. Has this fellow no feeling of his business that he
sings in grave-making?

Horatio.
Custom hath made it in him a property of easiness.

Hamlet. 'Tis e'en so: the hand of little employment hath
the daintier sense. 70

First Clown (sings).   But age, with his stealing steps
                Hath clawed me in his clutch,
            And hath shipped me into the land,
                As if I had never been such.
Throws up a skull.

Hamlet. That skull had a tongue in it, and could sing once: 75
how the knave jowls it to the ground, as if 'twere
Cain's jaw-bone, that did the first murder! This

78-79 **pate of a politician:** skull of a crafty schemer; **this ass now o'er-reaches:** this grave-digger now gets the better of. According to Dover Wilson, "It is the ass's turn to get the better of Cain" (New Shakespeare *Hamlet*); **circumvent God:** try to outwit God. Perhaps this is a reference to the fact that Cain quibbled when asked where Abel was.

82 **courtier:** The courtier was associated with flattery, as the politician was with scheming.

88-89 **my Lady Worm's:** The parody of the court is carried on ironically; **chopless:** jawless; **mazzard:** head, used contemptuously to imply the littleness of life.

90 **revolution:** change brought about by the turn of Fortune's wheel; **trick:** art, skill.

91 **breeding:** to breed, to bring into the world.

92 **loggits:** or *loggats,* a game in which thick sticks are thrown to lie as near as possible to a stake fixed in the ground or a block of wood on the floor (Onions).

99 **quiddities:** quibbles; **quillets:** subtleties.

100 **tenures:** rights or titles by which property is held; **tricks:** trickery. **102** **sconce:** head.

103 **action of battery:** a pun on the idea of a legal action for assault and battery. **104** **statutes:** bonds.

105 **recognizances:** obligations, bonds testifying that A owes B a sum of money; **fines:** conveyances, documents by which transfer of property is effected; **vouchers:** guarantors, witnesses called to warrant a tenant's title. **106** **recoveries:** transfers.

99-106 These legal terms have to do with a lawyer's attempt to gain control of a piece of land. Along with what follows (ll. 107-18), they illustrate Hamlet's virtuosity and cause the reader to speculate about whether Shakespeare had had some training in law.

106-8 **is this . . . dirt:** Is this the end of his conveyances, to have his superior head full of pure earth? The word play is evidence of Hamlet's nimble wit.

109-10 **doubles:** sharp turns; **a pair of indentures:** Agreements between mutually contracting parties were written in duplicate on a single sheet; the two copies were then cut with a wavy line. In case of trouble, the two parts could be fitted together; **will his . . . indentures:** Will all his documents be reduced to a single piece of parchment?

111 **this box:** the coffin. It is ironic that the lawyer's documents, now useless to him, once took up more room than he himself (the inheritor) at this point requires. Some editors prefer to interpret "box" as *skull.*

might be the pate of a politician, which this ass now o'er-reaches; one that would circumvent God, might it not? 80

Horatio. It might, my lord.

Hamlet. Or of a courtier, which could say "Good morrow, sweet lord? How dost thou, sweet lord?" This might be my lord such-a-one, that prais'd my lord such-a-one's horse, when he went to beg it, might it not? 85

Horatio. Ay, my lord.

Hamlet. Why, e'en so: and now my Lady Worm's, chopless, and knocked about the mazzard with a sexton's spade: here's fine revolution, an we had the trick to see't; did these bones cost no more the breeding, but to play at loggits with them? mine ache to think on't. 90

First Clown (*sings*).   A pick-axe, and a spade, a spade,
                For and a shrouding sheet:
            O, a pit of clay for to be made 95
                For such a guest is meet.

Throws up another skull.

Hamlet. There's another: why may not that be the skull of a lawyer? Where be his quiddities now, his quillets, his cases, his tenures, and his tricks? why does he suffer this mad knave now to knock him about the 100 sconce with a dirty shovel, and will not tell him of his action of battery? Hum! This fellow might be in's time a great buyer of land, with his statutes, his recognizances, his fines, his double vouchers, his 105 recoveries: is this the fine of his fines and the recovery of his recoveries, to have his fine pate full of fine dirt? will his vouchers vouch him no more of his purchases, and doubles, than the length and breadth of a pair of indentures? The very convey- 110 ances of his lands will scarcely lie in this box, and must the inheritor himself have no more, ha?

113 **jot:** whit, from the Greek *iota,* the letter *i.*

114-17 **Is not . . . that:** Hamlet implies that only fools will put their trust in paper, particularly legal documents. (Shakespeare himself, like many of his contemporaries, went to law frequently.)

122, 128 **liest:** *Lie* is used in a double sense: a) reside, b) prevaricate.

127, 129 **quick:** a) living, b) swift.

122-30 The First Clown is more than a match even for the quick-witted Hamlet as they fence with words.

138-9 **absolute:** positive; **by the card:** originally, *by the sailor's compass;* hence, *precisely;* **equivocation:** ambiguity; a reference to the Jesuit doctrine of equivocation, which was much discussed at this period.

141-3 **pick'd:** fastidious; **the toe . . . kibe:** perhaps a reference to the fact that yeomen farmers, enriched by recent wars, were seeking to join the ranks of the upper classes. The image is that of one person treading so closely on another's heels that he chafes or grazes the chilblain of the man ahead.

Horatio.   Not a jot more, my lord.

Hamlet.   Is not parchment made of sheep-skins?

Horatio.   Ay, my lord, and of calves-skins too.   115

Hamlet.

They are sheep and calves which seek out assurance in that. I will speak to this fellow. Whose grave's this, sirrah?

First Clown.   Mine, sir.

(*sings*) O, a pit of clay for to be made   120
            For such a guest is meet.

Hamlet.   I think it be thine indeed, for thou liest in't.

First Clown.   You lie out on't, sir, and therefore 'tis not yours: for my part, I do not lie in't, and yet it is mine.   125

Hamlet.   Thou dost lie in't, to be in't and say it is thine: 'tis for the dead, not for the quick; therefore thou liest.

First Clown.   'Tis a quick lie, sir; 'twill away again from me to you.   130

Hamlet.   What man dost thou dig it for?

First Clown.   For no man, sir.

Hamlet.   What woman then?

First Clown.   For none neither.

Hamlet.   Who is to be buried in't?   135

First Clown. One that was a woman, sir; but, rest her soul, she's dead.

Hamlet. How absolute the knave is! we must speak by the card, or equivocation will undo us. By the Lord, Horatio, this three years I have took note of it, the   140 age is grown so pick'd, that the toe of the peasant comes so near the heel of the courtier, he galls his kibe. How long hast thou been grave-maker?

First Clown. Of all the days i' the year I came to't that day that our last king Hamlet overcame Fortinbras.   145

Hamlet.   How long is that since?

First Clown. Cannot you tell that? every fool can tell that:

147-9 The grave-digger's failure to recognize Hamlet **creates** dramatic irony. Why might the grave-digger fail to **recognize** Hamlet?

151 **a':** he. The reference to the mad English by a Danish sexton (who is as English as roast beef) is also ironic and cheerfully satirical.

160-3 The Clown's literal answers again create humour through his deliberate misunderstanding; **I have . . . years:** Along with the preceding reference to Hamlet's birth, these lines appear to establish Hamlet's age. They tie in with the reference **made** by the Player King (III. ii. 153ff.). Most readers get **the** impression that Hamlet was much nearer twenty than thirty; his behaviour at the beginning of the play seems that of a much younger man. Perhaps this speech is a concession to the age of Burbage, who, born in 1567, would be approximately 34 if we take 1601 as the date when the play was written.

164 **How long . . . rot:** Hamlet's intellectual curiosity is one of his distinguishing traits.

166 **pocky:** infected with the pox.

167 **the laying in:** burial.

172 **whoreson:** an epithet of contempt, used almost casually by the Clown.

173-4 **three and twenty years:** It has been suggested that there **may** be a reference here to Richard Tarlton, a famous stage-clown who had died in 1588. The precise date seems to imply **a** specific allusion.

180 **flagon of Rhenish:** a large bottle of Rhine wine (hock).

181 **Yorick:** posssibly the Danish name *Georg*.

it was that very day that young Hamlet was born:
he that is mad, and sent into England.

Hamlet. Ay, marry, why was he sent into England? 150

First Clown. Why, because a' was mad; a' shall recover his
wits there; or, if a' do not, 'tis no great matter
there.

Hamlet. Why?

First Clown. 'Twill not be seen in him there; there the men 155
are as mad as he.

Hamlet. How came he mad?

First Clown. Very strangely, they say.

Hamlet. How "strangely"?

First Clown. Faith, e'en with losing his wits. 160

Hamlet. Upon what ground?

First Clown. Why, here in Denmark: I have been sexton
here, man and boy, thirty years.

Hamlet. How long will a man lie i' the earth ere he rot?

First Clown. I' faith, if a' be not rotten before a' die—as we 165
have many pocky corses now-a-days, that will
scarce hold the laying in—a' will last you some eight
year or nine year: a tanner will last you nine year.

Hamlet. Why he more than another?

First Clown. Why, sir, his hide is so tann'd with his trade 170
that a' will keep out water a great while; and your
water is a sore decayer of your whoreson dead body.
Here's a skull now hath lien you i' the earth three
and twenty years.

Hamlet. Whose was it? 175

First Clown. A whoreson mad fellow's it was; whose do
you think it was?

Hamlet. Nay, I know not.

First Clown. A pestilence on him for a mad rogue! a'
pour'd a flagon of Rhenish on my head once. This 180
same skull, sir, was, sir, Yorick's skull, the king's
jester.

Hamlet. This?

185   **Alas, poor Yorick:** a phrase that has captured the imagination of generations of theatre-goers; as he holds the skull of the jester in his hand, Hamlet succinctly sums up the irony of human life.

188-9   **it:** the skull; **how abhorred . . . is:** My mind is filled with disgust to think of the contrast between the Yorick I knew and the skull I hold in my hand; **my gorge rises at it:** It turns my stomach.

191   **gibes:** jests; **gambols:** capers.

192-3   **that were . . . roar:** that used to make everyone at the table roar with laughter.

194   **chop-fallen:** with jaw hanging down; hence, dejected.

196   **favour:** appearance.

199   **Alexander:** The conqueror of the world could not conquer death. It is recorded by Plutarch that Alexander's corpse resisted decay for some time.

206   **bung-hole:** an opening used to fill a cask.

207   **curiously:** minutely. Horatio does not approve of Hamlet's morbid train of thought.

209   **modesty:** moderation; that is, it is not an exaggeration; **likelihood:** probability; that is, without stretching the truth.

212   **loam:** paste of clay and sand.

214   **imperious:** imperial; **Cæsar:** another symbol of the earthly conqueror.

217   **flaw:** sudden gust of wind, squall.

208-17   These lines are further evidence of Hamlet's lively and fertile imagination. The quatrain expresses a wry irony.

Famous speech

First Clown. E'en that.

Hamlet. Let me see. (*takes the skull.*) Alas, poor Yorick! 185
I knew him, Horatio, a fellow of infinite jest, of most
excellent fancy: he hath borne me on his back a
thousand times, and now how abhorred in my
imagination it is! my gorge rises at it. Here hung
those lips that I have kiss'd I know not how oft; 190
where be your gibes now? your gambols, your
songs, your flashes of merriment, that were wont to
set the table on a roar? Not one now to mock your
own grinning, quite chop-fallen. Now get you to
my lady's table, and tell her, let her paint an inch 195
thick, to this favour she must come; make her laugh
at that. Prithee, Horatio, tell me one thing. *your all going to look like this.*

Horatio. What's that, my lord?

Hamlet. Dost thou think Alexander looked o' this fashion
i' the earth? *The Great* 200

Horatio. E'en so.

Hamlet. And smelt so? pah! *Puts down the skull.*

Horatio. E'en so, my lord.

Hamlet. To what base uses we may return, Horatio! Why
may not imagination trace the noble dust of Alex- 205
ander, till he find it stopping a bung-hole? *too weird.*

Horatio. 'Twere to consider too curiously, to consider so.

Hamlet. No, faith, not a jot; but to follow him thither
with modesty enough, and likelihood to lead it: as
thus: Alexander died, Alexander was buried, Alex- 210
ander returneth to dust, the dust is earth, of earth we
make loam, and why of that loam, whereto he was
converted, might they not stop a beer-barrel?

Imperious Cæsar, dead and turn'd to clay,
Might stop a hole, to keep the wind away. 215
O, that that earth, which kept the world in awe,
Should patch a wall to expel the winter's flaw!

220 **maimed rites:** imperfect or mutilated ceremony; **betoken:** suggest.

222 **fordo:** destroy; **it:** its; **estate:** rank.

223 **couch we:** Let us hide.

225 **a very noble youth:** The dramatic irony adds an element of pathos to Hamlet's position.

227-8 **Her obsequies . . . warranty:** Her funeral rites have been made as elaborate as authority permits; **doubtful:** It is uncertain whether or not she committed suicide.

229 **but that . . . order:** were it not that the King's command overrules the regular procedure.

230 **ground unsanctified:** A suicide was buried beneath a pile of stones at a cross-roads, and a stake was driven through his heart. The ecclesiastical authorities were not bound to accept a coroner's verdict.

231 **for:** instead of.

232 **shards:** bits of pottery.

233 **virgin crants:** maiden garlands. These wreaths were often hung in the church after a burial.

234-5 **strewments:** flowers strewn on the grave; **bringing home . . . burial:** Ophelia is to be laid to rest in sanctified ground to the accompaniment of the passing bell.

238 **requiem:** a dirge or solemn chant for the repose of the dead.

239 **peace-parted souls:** souls that have departed in peace.

241 **violets:** Ophelia is inevitably associated with flowers. Note the previous references and comment on their significance; **churlish:** rude, rough.

242 **ministering angel:** with reference to Mark 1: 13; **ministering:** rendering aid or service. The picture of Ophelia is an appropriate one.

243 **liest howling:** in hell; **What, the fair Ophelia:** Hamlet realizes for the first time whose funeral is taking place.

[handwritten: Funeral procession]

But soft! but soft, awhile: here comes the king.
>   *Enter the Corpse of Ophelia, a Priest, King, Queen,*
>   *Laertes, Courtiers.*
The queen, the courtiers: who is this they follow?
And with such maimed rites? This doth betoken   220
The corse they follow did with desperate hand
Fordo it own life: 'twas of some estate.
Couch we awhile, and mark.   *Retiring with Horatio.*

[handwritten: They will hide]

Laertes.   What ceremony else?
Hamlet.   That is Laertes, a very noble youth: mark.   225
Laertes.   What ceremony else?
Priest.   Her obsequies have been as far enlarg'd
>   As we have warranty: her death was doubtful,
>   And, but that great command o'ersways the order,
>   She should in ground unsanctified have lodg'd   230
>   Till the last trumpet; for charitable prayers,
>   Shards, flints and pebbles should be thrown on her:
>   Yet here she is allow'd her virgin crants,
>   Her maiden strewments, and the bringing home
>   Of bell and burial.   235

[handwritten: suicide]
[handwritten: if the king hadn't ordered me, she'll be buried in a unsanctified grave.]

Laertes.   Must there no more be done?
Priest.   No more be done:
>   We should profane the service of the dead
>   To sing a requiem and such rest to her
>   As to peace-parted souls.
Laertes.   Lay her i' the earth,
>   And from her fair and unpolluted flesh   240
>   May violets spring! I tell thee, churlish priest,
>   A ministering angel shall my sister be,
>   When thou liest howling.

[handwritten: you'll be screaming in hell while my sister is an angel]

Hamlet.   What, the fair Ophelia!
Queen (*scattering flowers*). Sweets to the sweet: farewell!
>   I hop'd thou shouldst have been my Hamlet's wife,   245
>   I thought thy bride-bed to have deck'd, sweet maid,
>   And not have strew'd thy grave.
Laertes.   O, treble woe

249 **ingenious sense:** powers of quick apprehension (object of the preposition "of").

247-51 Laertes expresses himself in elaborate fashion, though his grief is sincere. He blames Hamlet for Ophelia's madness, which in turn caused her death.

251 S.D. **Leaps into the grave:** The Elizabethan graves were evidently wider and shallower than modern ones are. On stage, the trapdoor would be utilized.

253 **flat:** plain, level ground.

254 **Pelion:** a high mountain in Thessaly (northern Greece). In the war against the gods of Olympus, the giants piled Mount Pelion on top of Mount Ossa in order to reach their enemies in heaven; **skyish:** reaching to the sky.

255 **blue:** because seen at a distance; **Olympus:** On this mountain, the highest in Greece, lived the gods.

256 **bears such an emphasis:** expresses itself with such force.

257 **conjures the wandering stars:** charms the planets.

258 **wonder-wounded:** struck with astonishment.

259 **Hamlet the Dane:** Hamlet here uses a royal title to identify himself; S.D. **Leaps into the grave:** Of this passage, Sir John Gielgud writes: "Hamlet and Laertes should surely not fight in the grave, for the moment they disappear from view it is impossible to see clearly what is happening and the effect on the stage is bound to be ridiculous when they are separated and have to climb sheepishly out again" (Gilder).

262 **splenitive:** hot-headed, liable to fits of anger.

268 **wag:** move.

270 **I lov'd Ophelia:** This statement should be taken into consideration when the nunnery scene is analysed. It has been suggested that Hamlet is carried away here by the excitement of the situation.

273 **O, he is mad:** It suits Claudius' purpose to have Laertes believe this. Why?

274 **forbear:** leave him alone.

Fall ten times double on that cursed head
Whose wicked deed thy most ingenious sense
Depriv'd thee of! Hold off the earth a while,   250
Till I have caught her once more in mine arms:
    Leaps into the grave.
Now pile your dust upon the quick and dead,
Till of this flat a mountain you have made
To o'ertop old Pelion, or the skyish head
Of blue Olympus.
Hamlet (*advancing*).   What is he whose grief   255
  Bears such an emphasis? whose phrase of sorrow
  Conjures the wandering stars, and makes them stand
  Like wonder-wounded hearers? This is I,
  Hamlet the Dane.   *Leaps into the grave.*
Laertes.   The devil take thy soul!   *Grappling with him.*
Hamlet.   Thou pray'st not well.   260
  I prithee take thy fingers from my throat;
  For, though I am not splenitive and rash,
  Yet have I in me something dangerous,
  Which let thy wisdom fear. Hold off thy hand.
King.   Pluck them asunder.
Queen.   Hamlet, Hamlet!
All.   Gentlemen!   265
Horatio.   Good my lord, be quiet.
    The Attendants part them, and they come out
    of the grave.
Hamlet.   Why, I will fight with him upon this theme
  Until my eyelids will no longer wag.
Queen.   O my son, what theme?
Hamlet.   I lov'd Ophelia: forty thousand brothers   270
  Could not, with all their quantity of love,
  Make up my sum. What wilt thou do for her?
King.   O, he is mad, Laertes.
Queen.   For love of God, forbear him.
Hamlet.   'Swounds, show me what thou'lt do: 275

276 **woo't:** wilt thou; **tear thyself:** rend thy clothing.

277 **eisel:** vinegar (Theobald). The drinking of vinegar was believed to induce melancholy. It may be a contemptuous reference to suggest that Laertes' grief is not genuine. Q2 has *esill;* **eat a crocodile:** and thereby be enabled to shed crocodile tears; used of a show of insincere grief.

279 **outface:** stare down and thus get the better of.

280 **quick:** alive. 281 **prate:** rant.

283 **singeing his . . . zone:** burning its head against the sun's path (the belt between the Tropics of Cancer and Capricorn).

284 **make Ossa . . . wart:** By contrast, Mount Ossa will appear as a small knoll; **mouth:** brag. Hamlet is suddenly aware that he is outdoing Laertes and despises himself.

285 **mere:** sheer. Gertrude is trying to shield Hamlet, though not for the same reason as Claudius.

287 **anon:** soon.

288 **when that . . . disclos'd:** when the twin fledgelings covered with yellow down are hatched.

289 **His silence . . . drooping:** in contrast with his previous excited behaviour.

290 **What is . . . thus:** It would seem that Hamlet, because he did not deliberately murder Polonius, does not understand Laertes' fury. Hamlet had left Denmark before Ophelia's madness and death.

291 **but it . . . matter:** Hamlet is suddenly apathetic. It is as if he were an actor in some great design over which he has no control.

292-3 **Let Hercules . . . day:** Even though Laertes (Hercules) has been raving, Hamlet's hour will come. There are said to be thirty-six references to Hercules in the plays of Shakespeare.

294 **I pray . . . him:** The King appears most considerate, but he has his own reasons for wanting Hamlet kept under surveillance.

295 **Strengthen your . . . speech:** Let your thoughts about our talk last night increase your patience. The time reference suggests that much has happened in a short space of time.

296 **the present push:** an immediate test.

297 **your:** Claudius is careful to dissociate himself from such a creature as Hamlet.

298 **a living monument:** Several interpretations are suggested: *a life-like statue, an enduring one;* there is perhaps an oblique reference to Hamlet as a sacrifice.

299 **an hour of quiet:** Claudius little thinks that his own death is also imminent.

See also p. 274.

Woo't weep? woo't fight? woo't fast? woo't
   tear thyself?
Woo't drink up eisel? eat a crocodile?
I'll do't. Dost come here to whine?
To outface me with leaping in her grave?
Be buried quick with her, and so will I: 280
And, if thou prate of mountains, let them throw
Millions of acres on us, till our ground,
Singeing his pate against the burning zone,
Make Ossa like a wart! Nay, an thou'lt mouth,
I'll rant as well as thou.
Queen.   This is mere madness: 285
   And thus a while the fit will work on him;
   Anon, as patient as the female dove
   When that her golden couplets are disclos'd,
   His silence will sit drooping.
Hamlet.   Hear you, sir;
   What is the reason that you use me thus? 290
   I lov'd you ever: but it is no matter;
   Let Hercules himself do what he may,
   The cat will mew, and dog will have his day.   *Exit.*
King.   I pray thee, good Horatio, wait upon him.
                        Exit Horatio.
   (*to Laertes*) Strengthen your patience in our last
     night's speech; 295
   We'll put the matter to the present push.
   Good Gertrude, set some watch over your son.
   This grave shall have a living monument:
   An hour of quiet shortly shall we see;
   Till then in patience our proceeding be.   *Exeunt.* 300

1   This is evidently an interrupted scene.

6   **mutines in the bilboes:** mutineers in irons; "bilboes" are shackles sliding along an iron bar that is locked to the floor; **rashly:** hastily, impulsively.

7   **know:** acknowledge.

9   **pall:** fail; **learn:** teach.

10-11   **There's a . . . will:** This famous passage implies a belief in an overruling providence that seems to direct our limited free will. Hamlet senses that ultimately fate controls our destiny; **rough-hew:** give a rough or crude form to; for example, shaping timber with an axe.

13   **sea-gown:** a short-sleeved, high-collared, coarse gown reaching down to the mid-leg and much used by sailors; **scarf'd:** gathered loosely.

14   **them:** Rosencrantz and Guildenstern.

15   **finger'd:** filched; a colloquial word meaning *pinched;* **in fine:** in conclusion.

18   **grand commission:** possibly spoken ironically.

20   **larded:** garnished; **several:** separate.

21   **importing Denmark's . . . too:** concerning the health of the respective kings; polite inquiries and good wishes.

22   **bugs:** bugbears (goblins in the shape of bears); **with, ho . . life:** threatening dire terrors if Hamlet is allowed to live.

23   **on the . . . bated:** immediately on looking it over, with not a moment wasted.

18-25   These lines recall the story of Bellerophon.

Scene 2

A HALL IN THE CASTLE.

Enter Hamlet and Horatio.

Hamlet. So much for this, sir: now shall you see the other;
    You do remember all the circumstance?
Horatio.   Remember it, my lord!
Hamlet.   Sir, in my heart there was a kind of fighting,
    That would not let me sleep: methought I lay   5
    Worse than the mutines in the bilboes. Rashly,
    And prais'd be rashness for it, let us know,
    Our indiscretion sometime serves us well
    When our deep plots do pall, and that should learn us
    There's a divinity that shapes our ends,   10
    Rough-hew them how we will.
Horatio.   That is most certain.
Hamlet.   Up from my cabin,
    My sea-gown scarf'd about me, in the dark
    Grop'd I to find out them, had my desire,
    Finger'd their packet, and in fine withdrew   15
    To mine own room again; making so bold,
    My fears forgetting manners, to unseal
    Their grand commission; where I found, Horatio,
    A royal knavery, an exact command,
    Larded with many several sorts of reasons,   20
    Importing Denmark's health, and England's too,
    With, ho! such bugs and goblins in my life,
    That, on the supervise, no leisure bated,
    No, not to stay the grinding of the axe,
    My head should be struck off.
Horatio.   Is't possible?   25
Hamlet.   Here's the commission, read it at more leisure.
    But wilt thou hear now how I did proceed?
Horatio.   I beseech you.

29 be-netted: ensnared.

30-31 or: ere, before; **Or I . . . play:** Before I could consciously begin to think, my brain(s) had involuntarily begun to work out a solution.

32 wrote it fair: in the equivalent of our copper-plate script.

33-34 statists: statesmen; **I once . . . fair:** It is said that Elizabethan noblemen were taught in youth to write well, but (as is frequently the case today) their writing degenerated as they grew older. Queen Elizabeth I is herself a case in point. Some scholars believe that a manuscript in the British Museum, part of a play about Sir Thomas More, is in Shakespeare's own hand. The surviving specimens of his signature are hardly models of calligraphy.

36 yeoman's service: good and faithful service; the ancient yeomen of England were famous for military valour.

37 effect: drift, tenor.

38 conjuration: appeal.

39-41 as England, as love, as peace: Hamlet parodies the high-flown language of diplomacy; **wheaten garland:** a symbol of peace and prosperity.

42 and stand . . . amities: and remain a connecting link in their friendship.

43 as'es: may also be a pun on *asses*, the repetition suggesting a string of laden donkeys (of great charge); **of great charge:** of great weight or significance.

47 shriving-time: time to hear a person's confession and grant him absolution; hence, a short interval.

44-47 Many readers find it hard to justify this heartless action. What excuse did Hamlet have?

48 ordinant: guiding, providential.

50 model: counterpart in miniature.

51 writ: commission.

52 subscrib'd it . . . impression: signed it (with Claudius' name) and sealed it.

53 changeling: a reference to the child left by the fairy-people when they steal a human infant.

54 what to . . . sequent: the sequel.

56 go to't: go to their deaths, a euphemism. Horatio is shocked.

57 they did . . . employment: They sought to have the King make use of them.

58-59 near: on; **their defeat . . . grow:** Their destruction was caused by their own meddling. Hamlet suspects that they know of the plot against him.

60 baser: less noble, of more humble origin.

Hamlet.   Being thus be-netted round with villanies,—
Or I could make a prologue to my brains,   30
They had begun the play,—I sat me down,
Devis'd a new commission, wrote it fair:
I once did hold it, as our statists do,
A baseness to write fair, and labour'd much
How to forget that learning, but, sir, now   35
It did me yeoman's service: wilt thou know
The effect of what I wrote?
Horatio.   Ay, good my lord.
Hamlet.   An earnest conjuration from the king,
As England was his faithful tributary,
As love between them like the palm might flourish,   40
As peace should still her wheaten garland wear
And stand a comma 'tween their amities,
And many such-like "as'es" of great charge,
That, on the view and knowing of these contents,
Without debatement further, more or less,   45
He should those bearers put to sudden death,
Not shriving-time allow'd.
Horatio.   How was this seal'd?
Hamlet.   Why, even in that was heaven ordinant.
I had my father's signet in my purse,
Which was the model of that Danish seal: 50
Folded the writ up in the form of the other,
Subscrib'd it, gave't the impression, plac'd it
    safely,
The changeling never known. Now, the next day
Was our sea-fight; and what to this was sequent
Thou know'st already.   55
Horatio.   So Guildenstern and Rosencrantz go to't.
Hamlet.   Why, man, they did make love to this employ-
    ment;
They are not near my conscience; their defeat
Does by their own insinuation grow:
'Tis dangerous when the baser nature comes   60

[Handwritten marginal notes:]
he sealed the bag and found letters 35
to hell 45
Kill Rose & Guild 50
Hamlet changed letter to kill bearer of letter, and Hamlet had seal 55 of Denmark, so letter was believed
"hoisted by own petor"

61 **pass:** thrust; **fell incensed:** fiercely angered. The metaphor of the duel is aptly ironic.

62 **Why, what a king is this:** Horatio bluntly indicates that such cynical cruelty ill befits a sovereign.

63 **does it . . . upon:** Is it not my duty?

65 **popp'd in:** Hamlet thinks of Claudius as a usurper; **election:** The great jurist Blackstone has stated that the throne of Denmark was elective.

66 **thrown out . . . life:** sought to take my very life. The metaphor is drawn from the sport of fishing; **angle:** fishing hook or line.

67 **cozenage:** deception; **is't not perfect conscience:** Is it not consistent with a clear conscience?

68 **quit:** requite.

69-70 **to let . . . evil:** to permit this cancerous ulcer to continue in its evil course.

73 **it:** the time; **the interim is mine:** Hamlet speaks as one who has foreknowledge.

74 **one:** the reference may be to the single thrust of a rapier. Hamlet's fatalism is marked.

75-76 **But I . . . myself:** Hamlet's contrition is appealing; it is all the more poignant in the light of the plans.

77-78 **by the . . . his:** Hamlet sees the similarity in their situations.

79 **bravery:** bravado, showy display.

80 **S.D. Enter Osric:** a satire on the elegant Elizabethan courtier whose dress and language are alike affected and high-flown.

83 **water-fly:** gnat; this small creature is aimlessly busy. It has been suggested that the term is used in reference to the winged doublet with its projections from the shoulders. Osric is sure to have picked up fashion's latest fads.

86-88 **crib:** bin; **mess:** a group of persons into which the company at a banquet was divided; **let a . . . mess:** a satirical reference to the idea that a man can gain entry to the court as long as he has wealth (land and cattle), no matter what his personal attributes. At the court of Claudius, such a person could flourish; **chough:** jackdaw.

92 **diligence of spirit:** Hamlet is mocking.

Between the pass and fell incensed points
Of mighty opposites.
Horatio.   Why, what a king is this!
Hamlet. Does it not, think'st thee, stand me now upon—
　He that hath kill'd my king, and whor'd my mother,
　Popp'd in between the election and my hopes,   65
　Thrown out his angle for my proper life,
　And with such cozenage—is't not perfect conscience,
　To quit him with this arm? and is't not to be
　　damn'd,
　To let this canker of our nature come
　In further evil?   70
Horatio. It must be shortly known to him from England
　What is the issue of the business there.
Hamlet. It will be short: the interim is mine;
　And a man's life's no more than to say "One".
　But I am very sorry, good Horatio,   75
　That to Laertes I forgot myself;
　For, by the image of my cause, I see
　The portraiture of his: I'll court his favours:
　But, sure, the bravery of his grief did put me
　Into a towering passion.
Horatio.   Peace! who comes here?   80
　　　Enter Osric.
Osric. Your lordship is right welcome back to Denmark.
Hamlet. I humbly thank you, sir. (*to Horatio*) Dost know
　this water-fly?
Horatio. No, my good lord.
Hamlet. Thy state is the more gracious, for 'tis a vice to   85
　know him. He hath much land, and fertile: let a
　beast be lord of beasts, and his crib shall stand at the
　king's mess: 'tis a chough, but, as I say, spacious in
　the possession of dirt.
Osric. Sweet lord, if your lordship were at leisure, I should   90
　impart a thing to you from his majesty.
Hamlet. I will receive it, sir, with all diligence of spirit.

[Handwritten margin notes: He sees similarities in situation with Laertes — both fathers killed; pretentious; overtalk; If you've got time, I want to talk to you]

93 **bonnet:** hat; no doubt an elaborate and plumed piece of head-gear flourished by Osric, whose gestures and manner of speaking Hamlet imitates. One of low degree could not remain *covered* in the presence of his superiors; hence, Osric's excuses and embarrassment; **his:** its.

97-98 **or my complexion:** Perhaps Hamlet intended to add *deceives me.*

94-100 Osric, like Polonius on an earlier occasion, is made ridiculous by his fear of disagreeing with Hamlet who, he fears, may be mad.

104 **nay, good . . . faith:** Osric's objections are overruled; he puts on his hat.

107 **differences:** distinguishing qualities; **soft society:** a grossly inappropriate remark. Laertes was far from gentle.

108-10 **feelingly:** perceptively, with an understanding of his merits; **card or . . . gentry:** picture or pattern of courtesy and refined elegance; **card:** chart (mariner's compass); **calendar:** register; **the continent:** the sum total; **parts:** attributes.

111 **his definement . . . you:** The list of his perfections loses nothing through your description.

112-15 **divide him inventorially:** make a catalogue of his qualities; **would dizzy . . . memory:** would be a mathematical feat that would make the memory reel; **and yet . . . sail:** and yet any attempt to describe him would be slow and awkward, since his attributes outdistance the account given of them, as a vessel of quick sail speeds ahead of one that is yawing or falling off course; **in the verity of extolment:** to praise him truly; **article:** importance.

116-17 **his infusion . . . rareness:** qualities of such high value and rarity; **to make . . . him:** to speak of him truly; **his semblable . . . mirror:** Nothing is like him but his reflection.

118-19 **who else . . . more:** Anyone who tries to imitate him is no better than a shadow.

111-19 Hamlet outdoes Osric in affectation, mixing metaphors that are maritime and mercantile.

121 **the concernancy:** What are we driving at?

122 **more rawer:** crude (a double comparative); an affected way of asking why Laertes is being discussed.

123 **sir:** Osric is bewildered.

124 **in another tongue:** in more reasonable language.

125 **You will . . . really:** You will be able to speak plain English if you really try.

126 **What imports . . . gentleman:** Why is Laertes' name mentioned?

Your bonnet to his right use, 'tis for the head.

Osric. I thank your lordship, it is very hot.

Hamlet.

No, believe me, 'tis very cold, the wind is northerly. 95

Osric. It is indifferent cold, my lord, indeed.

Hamlet. But yet methinks it is very sultry and hot, or my
complexion—

Osric. Exceedingly, my lord; it is very sultry, as 'twere
I cannot tell how: my lord, his majesty bade me 100
signify to you that he has laid a great wager on your
head: sir, this is the matter—

Hamlet. I beseech you, remember—

Hamlet moves him to put on his hat.

Osric. Nay, good my lord, for my ease, in good faith.
Sir, here is newly come to court Laertes; believe 105
me, an absolute gentleman, full of most excellent
differences, of very soft society, and great showing:
indeed, to speak feelingly of him, he is the card or
calendar of gentry; for you shall find in him the
continent of what parts a gentleman would see. 110

Hamlet. Sir, his definement suffers no perdition in you,
though, I know, to divide him inventorially would
dizzy the arithmetic of memory, and yet but yaw
neither, in respect of his quick sail. But in the verity
of extolment, I take him to be a soul of great article, 115
and his infusion of such dearth and rareness, as, to
make true diction of him, his semblable is his mirror,
and who else would trace him, his umbrage, nothing
more.

Osric. Your lordship speaks most infallibly of him. 120

Hamlet. The concernancy, sir? why do we wrap the gentleman in our more rawer breath?

Osric. Sir?

Horatio. Is't not possible to understand in another tongue?
You will to't, sir, really. 125

Hamlet. What imports the nomination of this gentleman?

128-9 **His purse . . . spent:** His supply of fancy words is exhausted.

132-3 **it would . . . me:** Hamlet implies that Osric's testimonial would not do him (Hamlet) much credit.

136 **compare with:** vie with.

137-8 **to know . . . himself:** It is presumptuous for a man to judge another, for he does not know himself.

139-40 **but in . . . unfellow'd:** But according to those in his retinue, he has a reputation for being unequalled.

141 **weapon:** style of fencing.

144 **Barbary:** from North Africa.

145 **impawn'd:** wagered.

146 **poniards:** daggers; **assigns:** accessories, fittings.

147 **girdle:** sword belt; **hanger:** triangular buckled sling by which the rapier hung from the belt, often richly ornamented; **carriages:** another term for "hangers"; Hamlet understands it to mean "gun carriages for transporting cannon".

148 **dear to fancy:** pleasingly ornamented; **responsive:** corresponding.

149-50 **of very liberal conceit:** tastefully designed.

144-50 Six horses against six rapiers and daggers would suggest that the beast and the weapons (a rapier and a dagger) were of equal value.

152 **edified by the margent:** instructed by the notes in the margin, as in Coleridge's "The Ancient Mariner".

155 **germane:** appropriate.

161 **laid:** wagered; **passes:** rounds, bouts.

Osric. Of Laertes?

Horatio. His purse is empty already; all's golden words are
spent.

Hamlet. Of him, sir.   130

Osric. I know you are not ignorant—

Hamlet. I would you did, sir; yet, in faith, if you did, it
would not much approve me. Well, sir?

Osric. You are not ignorant of what excellence Laertes
is—   135

Hamlet. I dare not confess that, lest I should compare with
him in excellence; but to know a man well were to
know himself.

Osric. I mean, sir, for his weapon; but in the imputation
laid on him, by them in his meed, he's unfellow'd.   140

Hamlet. What's his weapon?

Osric. Rapier and dagger.

Hamlet. That's two of his weapons: but, well.

Osric. The king, sir, hath wager'd with him six Barbary
horses, against the which he has impawn'd, as I take   145
it, six French rapiers and poniards, with their assigns,
as girdle, hanger, and so: three of the carriages, in
faith, are very dear to fancy, very responsive to the
hilts, most delicate carriages, and of very liberal
conceit.   150

Hamlet. What call you the carriages?

Horatio. I knew you must be edified by the margent ere you
had done.

Osric. The carriages, sir, are the hangers.

Hamlet. The phrase would be more germane to the matter   155
if we could carry a cannon by our sides: I would it
be hangers till then. But on: six Barbary horses
against six French swords, their assigns, and three
liberal-conceited carriages; that's the French bet against
the Danish. Why is this all "impawned" as you call it?   160

Osric. The king, sir, hath laid, sir, that in a dozen passes
between yourself and him, he shall not exceed you

163   **twelve for nine:** Dr. Johnson, the eminent eighteenth-century critic, wrote: "This wager I do not understand. In a dozen passes, the one must exceed the other more or less than three hits. Nor can I comprehend how in a dozen there can be twelve for nine." Dover Wilson suggests the following explanation: "He" refers to Laertes who has "laid down *conditions*" that a) he (Laertes) must win by at least three up and that b) the match must be of twelve bouts instead of the customary nine. Hamlet would thus have to win at least *four* to Laertes' *eight,* since winning *seven* would give Laertes only *two* over Hamlet's *five.* (It is also conceivable that Shakespeare's mathematics were at fault!)

165   **vouchsafe the answer:** accept the challenge.

166   Hamlet pretends not to understand Osric's use of the word "answer", which normally means *reply.*

169   **breathing time:** time for taking exercise.

170   **foils:** bated or blunted rapiers for fencing.

175-7   **I commend . . . lordship:** Osric departs with an elaborate flourish, imitated and exaggerated by Hamlet; **commend:** a) as used by Osric, *present my respects,* b) as interpreted by Hamlet, *praise his own politeness* (since no one else would).

178   **This lapwing . . . head:** Osric is compared to a forward fledgeling; young lapwings run as soon as they are hatched. The shell is the elaborate hat. Osric's youth is referred to in line 187.

179   **comply . . . it:** use elaborate politeness before being suckled.

181-5   **drossy:** frivolous. Hamlet criticizes the standards of his time. (Nowadays public opinion sets great store by professional hockey players and film stars); **tune of the time:** the outer forms of fashion; **habit of encounter:** style of address and exchange of compliments; **a kind . . . out:** This passage is a sustained metaphor drawn from the fermenting of barley for brewing purposes. These frothy courtiers (a "yesty collection") think they are getting the better of the tested wisdom of experienced courtiers (the malted barley beneath the foam); but if you really test them, they collapse, "the bubbles are out".

81-185   The Osric episode, in prose as is the grave-diggers' scene, serves to release the dramatic tension. The humour of the Clown may be contrasted with that generated by Osric.

185   S.D. **Enter a Lord:** Claudius' anxious desire to get the matter settled is suggested by the sending of a second messenger.

186   **commended:** sent his respects.

187-8   **attend:** await.   189   **play:** fence.   192   **fitness:** inclination.

195   **in happy time:** It is an appropriate moment.

196-7   **to use . . . Laertes:** to receive Laertes politely.

three hits: he hath laid on twelve for nine; and
it would come to immediate trial if your lordship
would vouchsafe the answer.   165

Hamlet.   How if I answer "no"?

Osric.   I mean, my lord, the opposition of your person in trial.

Hamlet.   Sir, I will walk here in the hall: if it please his
majesty (it is the breathing time of day with me) let
the foils be brought, the gentleman willing, and the   170
king hold his purpose, I will win for him an I can: if
not, I will gain nothing but my shame, and the odd hits.

Osric.   Shall I deliver you so?

Hamlet.   To this effect, sir, after what flourish your nature will.

Osric.   I commend my duty to your lordship.   175

Hamlet. Yours, yours. (*exit Osric.*) He does well to commend it himself; there are no tongues else for's turn.

Horatio. This lapwing runs away with the shell on his head.

Hamlet. He did comply with his dug before he sucked it.
Thus has he—and many more of the same breed that   180
I know the drossy age dotes on—only got the tune
of the time and outward habit of encounter; a kind
of yesty collection, which carries them through and
through the most profound and winnowed opinions; and
do but blow them to their trial, the bubbles are out.   185

   Enter a Lord.

Lord.   My lord, his majesty commended him to you by
young Osric, who brings back to him, that you attend him in the hall: he sends to know if your
pleasure hold to play with Laertes, or that you will
take longer time?   190

Hamlet.   I am constant to my purposes; they follow the
king's pleasure: if his fitness speaks, mine is ready;
now or whensoever, provided I be so able as now.

Lord.   The king and queen and all are coming down.

Hamlet.   In happy time.   195

Lord. The queen desires you to use some gentle entertainment to Laertes before you fall to play.

200 **since he . . . France:** a reminder of the passage of time.

202-3 **how ill . . . heart:** According to Coleridge, Shakespeare had a "fondness for presentiment". Note the first lines of *The Merchant of Venice* and the forebodings of Brutus and Cassius before the battle at Philippi.

205 **gain-giving:** misgiving.

207-8 **forestal their repair:** prevent their coming; **fit:** ready.

209-14 **whit:** particle; **we defy augury:** I pay no heed to superstitious omens; **there is . . . sparrow:** Matthew 10: 29; Hamlet seems here to express a belief in fate and predestination; it ties in with "There's a divinity that shapes our ends" (V. ii. 10); **if it . . . all:** Hamlet here sums up ideas that Shakespeare absorbed from his reading of Montaigne's essay "That to philosophize is to learn how to die". The essay begins with a quotation from Cicero: "To philosophize is no other thing than for a man to prepare himself to death." A pertinent sentence in the essay states: "It is uncertain where death looks for us; let us expect her everywhere." **since no . . . betimes:** Since no man knows what the future may hold, what does it matter if he leaves early? S.D. The F stage direction omits the daggers, since by 1623, a change of fashion in fencing had occurred.

216 **Give me your pardon:** Hamlet is carrying out his mother's request.

218 **this presence:** those present.

221-2 **that might . . . awake:** that might arouse your duty as a son, your sense of honour, your personal disapproval; **I here . . . madness:** Only by assuming that at times Hamlet really was mad (though at other times he was feigning madness) can we accept this statement. At this critical juncture, Shakespeare would hardly wish to destroy sympathy for the protagonist by having him tell a deliberate falsehood. Hamlet's display at the grave of Ophelia suggests that he was beside himself.

Hamlet.   She well instructs me.   *Exit Lord.*
Horatio.   You will lose, my lord.
Hamlet.

   I do not think so; since he went into France, I have   **200**
   been in continual practice; I shall win at the odds;
   but thou wouldst not think how ill all's here about my
   heart, but it is no matter.

Horatio.   Nay, good my lord,—

Hamlet. It is but foolery; but it is such a kind of gain-giving **205**
   as would perhaps trouble a woman.

Horatio.   If your mind dislike any thing, obey it. I will forestal their repair hither, and say you are not fit.

Hamlet.   Not a whit; we defy augury: there is special
   providence in the fall of a sparrow. If it be now,   **210**
   'tis not to come; if it be not to come, it will be now;
   if it be not now, yet it will come: the readiness is
   all; since no man knows aught of what he leaves, what
   is't to leave betimes? Let be.

A table prepared; trumpets, drums, and Officers with cushions:
   King, Queen, and all the State; foils, daggers, and
   Laertes.

King.   Come, Hamlet, come, and take this hand from me.   **215**
             The King puts Laertes' hand into Hamlet's.

Hamlet.   Give me your pardon, sir: I have done you wrong;
   But pardon't, as you are a gentleman.
   This presence knows,
   And you must needs have heard, how I am punish'd
   With a sore distraction. What I have done,   **220**
   That might your nature, honour, and exception
   Roughly awake, I here proclaim was madness.
   Was't Hamlet wrong'd Laertes? Never Hamlet.
   If Hamlet from himself be ta'en away,
   And when he's not himself does wrong Laertes,   **225**
   Then Hamlet does it not, Hamlet denies it.
   Who does it then? His madness. If't be so,
   Hamlet is of the faction that is wrong'd;

231 let my . . . evil: Hamlet asserts that the murder of Polonius was not deliberate.

233-4 that I . . . brother: In my ignorance, I have unwittingly injured one dear to me. (Perhaps there is an indirect reference to what the future might have held for Ophelia and Hamlet.) On the other hand, F reads *mother;* Gertrude had indeed been shocked and distressed by the murder; **in nature:** Laertes replies that he is satisfied with regard to his duty as a son.

236-40 but in . . . ungor'd: A man's honour was of great consequence, and he was obliged to defend it unless (as was the custom) men of wisdom and experience (experts) ruled that it was unnecessary. Laertes wishes to keep his reputation unsullied.

241-2 I do . . . it: Laertes' hypocrisy creates dramatic irony.

243 brother's wager: Hamlet has been generous in his apology and is completely unsuspicious.

244 foils: a pun on "blunted sword" and "setting of a jewel", which sets it off to advantage.

247 stick fiery off: stand out brilliantly.

249 Give them the foils: Dover Wilson asserts that Osric was an accomplice in the plot and that he laid the unbated, poisoned rapier on a side table with the others. Laertes, after complaining that the one he had chosen from those that Osric was holding was too heavy, went over to the table and picked up the right rapier. If Osric had been holding all the foils, Hamlet might by chance have selected the one Laertes intended to use. In Sir John Gielgud's production, Osric held the foils and Laertes selected one; but, at a signal from the King, put it back and took another. Hamlet meanwhile had his back to them.

251 Your grace . . . side: Claudius has stipulated that the weaker should have odds. Hamlet implies that the King was wise in giving him a good handicap.

255 This likes me well: This pleases me well. Hamlet's only anxiety is that the foils be of the same length. The length of a rapier might vary from 3 feet 3 inches to 5 feet 5 inches. In a match where the thrust rather than the slash was used, length was an important factor. Hamlet, as Claudius had forecast, does not "peruse the foils".

257 stoups: vessels for holding wine to the amount of two quarts.

His madness is poor Hamlet's enemy.
Sir, in this audience,   230
Let my disclaiming from a purpos'd evil
Free me so far in your most generous thoughts,
That I have shot my arrow o'er the house,
And hurt my brother.
Laertes.   I am satisfied in nature,
Whose motive, in this case, should stir me most   235
To my revenge: but in my terms of honour
I stand aloof, and will no reconcilement,
Till by some elder masters of known honour
I have a voice and precedent of peace,
To keep my name ungor'd. But till that time   240
I do receive your offer'd love like love
And will not wrong it.
Hamlet.   I embrace it freely,
And will this brother's wager frankly play.
Give us the foils. Come on.
Laertes.   Come, one for me.
Hamlet. I'll be your foil, Laertes: in mine ignorance 245
Your skill shall, like a star i' the darkest night,
Stick fiery off indeed.
Laertes.   You mock me, sir.
Hamlet. No, by this hand.
King. Give them the foils, young Osric. Cousin Hamlet,
You know the wager?
Hamlet.   Very well, my lord;   250
Your grace has laid the odds o' the weaker side.
King. I do not fear it; I have seen you both:
But since he is better, we have therefore odds.
Laertes. This is too heavy; let me see another.
Hamlet. This likes me well. These foils have all a length? 255
            They prepare to play.
Osric. Ay, my good lord.
King. Set me the stoups of wine upon that table.
If Hamlet give the first or second hit,

259 **quit in . . . exchange:** if he and Laertes exchange simultaneous hits in the third round.

260 **ordnance:** cannon.

262 **union:** a large, valuable pearl.

265 **kettle:** kettle-drum.

265-7 These lines have a fine, resounding ring.

271 **palpable:** unmistakable.

272 **this pearl is thine:** Claudius draws the pearl ring from his finger, releases the poison catch, and drops it (the ring) into the cup.

277 **He's fat:** The statement has been much discussed. Some critics see in it a reference to a rather portly Burbage. Others have emended the word "fat" to *faint*. Still others believe that it implies *sweaty*. The idea of a stout Hamlet is repugnant to most people.

278 **napkin:** handkerchief. Perspiration running down a fencer's forehead might conceivably get into his eyes and momentarily blind him.

280 **Good madam:** Hamlet gives the fencer's salute as his mother drinks his health; **Gertrude, do not drink:** a harrowing moment for Claudius.

281 **I will:** How likely is it that Gertrude knows the drink is poisoned?

Or quit in answer of the third exchange,
Let all the battlements their ordnance fire;   260
The king shall drink to Hamlet's better breath,
And in the cup an union shall he throw,
Richer than that which four successive kings
In Denmark's crown have worn. Give me the cups;
And let the kettle to the trumpet speak,   265
The trumpet to the cannoneer without,
The cannons to the heavens, the heaven to earth,
"Now the king drinks to Hamlet." Come, begin;
And you, the judges, bear a wary eye.

> *drinks to prove nothing wrong*

       Trumpets the while.

Hamlet. Come on, sir.
Laertes.   Come, my lord.   *They play.*
Hamlet.   One.
Laertes.   No.
Hamlet.   Judgement. 270
Osric. A hit, a very palpable hit.
       Drum, trumpets, and shot.
       Flourish, a piece goes off.
Laertes.   Well, again.
King. Stay, give me drink. Hamlet, this pearl is thine;
  Here's to thy health; give him the cup.
Hamlet. I'll play this bout first, set it by a while.
  Come. (*They play.*) Another hit; what say you?   275
Laertes. A touch, a touch, I do confess't.
King. Our son shall win.
Queen.   He's fat and scant of breath.
  Here, Hamlet, take my napkin, rub thy brows:
  The queen carouses to thy fortune, Hamlet.
Hamlet. Good madam!
King.   Gertrude, do not drink.   280
Queen. I will, my lord; I pray you, pardon me.
King (aside). It is the poison'd cup; it is too late.
Hamlet. I dare not drink yet, madam; by and by.
Queen. Come, let me wipe thy face.

285 **I do not think't:** Claudius' craft in preparing the poisoned cup is now explained. Laertes may not win.

286 **And yet . . . conscience:** Lines like this give Shakespeare's villains a touch of humanity. Possibly Laertes has not been extending himself, owing to a feeling of guilt.

289 **make a . . . me:** trifle with me. Hamlet senses that Laertes is not fencing with his normal verve.

292 **Have at you now:** Laertes lunges quickly and unexpectedly, drawing blood from Hamlet's right arm. Hamlet, enraged at this treachery, throws down his sword and wrests Laertes' weapon from him. He steps back and with ironical politeness allows Laertes to pick up the blunt rapier. In Sir John Gielgud's production, Hamlet used his sword to disarm Laertes, whose weapon fell to the floor. As he stooped to pick it up, Hamlet put his foot on it, and in exchange offered Laertes the capped rapier. Hamlet then picked up the poisoned weapon. In the exchange that follows, Hamlet, now furious, wounds Laertes with the fateful weapon, despite the King's cry. The fight ends as the Queen collapses.

294 **They bleed on both sides:** The audience knows at once that both young men are doomed.

296 **as a . . . springe:** The woodcock is easily trapped in a snare; Laertes implies that he was a fool to be thus caught in his own trap.

296-7 Some editors believe that this speech of Laertes shows Osric to have been an accomplice.

298 **she swounds:** Claudius selfishly tries to protect himself; his self-control is remarkable.

299-300 Gertrude's last words are a warning, too late, to her son.

301 **let the . . . lock'd:** Claudius is trapped.

307 **the foul practice:** the treacherous plot.

311 **The point envenom'd too:** Hamlet is still more infuriated at the treachery.

312 **Then, venom, to thy work:** a line of infinite power as Hamlet secures his revenge. The word "venom" suggests *vengeance* and *virulence*.

314 **but hurt:** only wounded. The King deceives himself.

Laertes. My lord, I'll hit him now.
King.   I do not think't.   285
Laertes (*aside*). And yet it is almost against my conscience.
Hamlet. Come for the third, Laertes: you do but dally;
  I pray you, pass with your best violence;
  I am afeard you make a wanton of me.
Laertes. Say you so? come on.   *They play.*   290
Osric. Nothing neither way.
Laertes. Have at you now!
      Laertes wounds Hamlet; then, in scuffling, they
      change rapiers, and Hamlet wounds Laertes.
King.   Part them; they are incens'd.
Hamlet. Nay, come, again.   *The Queen falls.*
Osric.   Look to the queen there, ho!
Horatio. They bleed on both sides. How is it, my lord?
Osric. How is't, Laertes?   295
Laertes. Why, as a woodcock to mine own springe, Osric;
  I am justly kill'd with mine own treachery.
Hamlet. How does the queen?
King.   She swounds to see them bleed.
Queen. No, no, the drink, the drink,—O my dear Hamlet,—
  The drink, the drink! I am poison'd.   *Dies.*   300
Hamlet. O villainy! Ho! let the door be lock'd:
  Treachery! seek it out.   *Laertes falls.*
Laertes. It is here, Hamlet: Hamlet, thou art slain;
  No medicine in the world can do thee good,
  In thee there is not half an hour's life;   305
  The treacherous instrument is in thy hand,
  Unbated and envenom'd: the foul practice
  Hath turn'd itself on me; lo, here I lie,
  Never to rise again: thy mother's poison'd:
  I can no more: the king, the king's to blame.   310
Hamlet. The point envenom'd too!
  Then, venom, to thy work.   *Stabs the King.*
All. Treason! treason!
King. O, yet defend me, friends; I am but hurt.

315-17 Hamlet, the agent of nemesis, puns on the word "union" as he forces Claudius to drink of the cup the King had prepared for another purpose and thus be *united* with Gertrude; **serv'd:** paid back.

318 **temper'd by himself:** Claudius is seemingly an expert.

321 Laertes dies of the wound rather than the poison; this would explain why Hamlet survives him.

323 **I am dead:** Hamlet realizes that he is virtually dead, since he is aware of the poison coursing through his veins; **wretched:** unhappy.

324 **this chance:** what has happened.

325 **mutes:** silent witnesses; the imagery is drawn from the theatre.

326 **fell:** cruel; **sergeant:** an officer whose duty it is to summon persons to appear in court. Death, like a sheriff's officer, presents the final summons, a grim metaphor.

329-30 **report me . . . unsatisfied:** Hamlet wants his name cleared.

331 **an antique Roman:** Brutus and Cassius committed suicide when their cause was lost. Macbeth exclaims (V. viii. 1-2): "Why should I play the Roman fool, and die/On mine own sword?" Horatio's gesture seems strangely unlike him, but indicates how deeply he is moved.

333 Hamlet wrests the cup from him and makes an urgent appeal.

337-9 **absent thee . . . story:** The familiar lines are deeply moving and charged with vowel and consonant melody. The contrast in sound is summed up in the words "felicity" and "harsh". The monosyllables of line 338 emphasize the difficulty of the task laid on Horatio; it will be a painful one emotionally, if not physically.

340-2 **Young Fortinbras . . . volley:** The approach of the conqueror is heralded triumphantly.

343 **potent poison:** The alliteration suggests that breathing is becoming difficult; **o'er-crows:** triumphs over, as a victorious cock crows over its defeated opponent.

344 **news from England:** Is Hamlet thinking of the deaths he has ordered?

Hamlet.   Here, thou incestuous, murderous, damned Dane, 315
   Drink off this potion: is thy union here?
   Follow my mother.   *King dies.*
Laertes.   He is justly serv'd;
   It is a poison temper'd by himself.
   Exchange forgiveness with me, noble Hamlet:
   Mine and my father's death come not upon thee,   320
   Nor thine on me!   *Dies.*
Hamlet.   Heaven make thee free of it! I follow thee.
   I am dead, Horatio. Wretched queen, adieu!
   You that look pale, and tremble at this chance,
   That are but mutes or audience to this act,   325
   Had I but time—as this fell sergeant death
   Is strict in his arrest—O, I could tell you—
   But let it be. Horatio, I am dead;
   Thou livest; report me and my cause aright
   To the unsatisfied.
Horatio.   Never believe it: *Horcho*   330
   I am more an antique Roman than a Dane,   *can't stand it.*
   Here's yet some liquor left.
Hamlet.   As thou'rt a man,
   Give me the cup: let go, by heaven I'll have't.
   O God, Horatio, what a wounded name,
   Things standing thus unknown, shall live behind me!   335
   If thou didst ever hold me in thy heart,
   Absent thee from felicity a while,
   And in this harsh world draw thy breath in pain,
   To tell my story.   *March afar off.*
          What warlike noise is this?
Osric.   Young Fortinbras, with conquest come from Poland, 340
   To the ambassadors of England gives
   This warlike volley.
Hamlet.   O, I die, Horatio;
   The potent poison quite o'er-crows my spirit:
   I cannot live to hear the news from England,
   But I do prophesy the election lights   345

Hamlet gives his kingdom
to Fortinbras
Everythin righet.

345-6 **the election . . . voice:** With the death of Claudius, Hamlet is in fact King, unless we accept the idea that the throne was elective. In any case, his vote would be influential in the choice of a new monarch.

347 **occurrents, more and less:** events great and small.

348 **which have solicited:** which have influenced (me to act as I have done); **The rest is silence:** The sibilants suggest a whisper as Hamlet's troubled soul finds peace at last.

349 **cracks:** breaks.

350 **flights of angels:** Horatio's scepticism is forgotten in this bright image of a heavenly host.

349-50 A noble and eloquent farewell, profound in its simplicity. We recall Hamlet's earlier longing for sleep.

354 **This quarry . . . havoc:** This heap of dead betokens indiscriminate slaughter.

355 **toward:** in preparation; **eternal cell:** the grave.

354-7 Death, the huntsman, will devour the slain (the quarry).

357 **dismal:** calamitous.

362 **his mouth:** Horatio points to Claudius.

365 **jump:** exactly, pat.

368 **stage:** platform.

371 **of carnal . . . acts:** the deeds of Claudius—adultery, murder, incest.

372 **accidental judgements:** the death of Ophelia (and of Gertrude?); **casual slaughters:** the unintentional murder of Polonius.

373 **of deaths . . . cause:** the execution of Rosencrantz and Guildenstern. (Hamlet's own death?)

On Fortinbras: he has my dying voice;
So tell him, with the occurrents, more and less,
Which have solicited. The rest is silence.
> *Dies.*

    ✗ Death

Horatio.   Now cracks a noble heart. Good night, sweet
    prince,
  And flights of angels sing thee to thy rest!   350
> *March within.*

  Why does the drum come hither?
> *Enter Fortinbras, and the English Ambassadors,*
> *with drum, colours, and Attendants.*

Fortinbras.   Where is this sight?
Horatio.   What is it you would see?
  If aught of woe, or wonder, cease your search.
Fortinbras.   This quarry cries on havoc. O proud death,
  What feast is toward in thine eternal cell,   355
  That thou so many princes at a shot
  So bloodily hast struck?
First Ambassador.   The sight is dismal;
  And our affairs from England come too late:
  The ears are senseless that should give us hearing,
  To tell him his commandment is fulfill'd,   360
  That Rosencrantz and Guildenstern are dead:
  Where should we have our thanks?
Horatio.   Not from his mouth
  Had it the ability of life to thank you:
  He never gave commandment for their death.
  But since, so jump upon this bloody question,   365
  You from the Polack wars, and you from England,
  Are here arriv'd, give order that these bodies
  High on a stage be placed to the view,
  And let me speak to the yet unknowing world
  How these things came about: so shall you hear   370
  Of carnal, bloody and unnatural acts,
  Of accidental judgements, casual slaughters,
  Of deaths put on by cunning and for no cause,

374-5 **and, in . . . heads:** the deaths of Claudius and Laertes; **upshot:** conclusion, the final deciding shot in an archery contest.

376 **deliver:** report.

378 **embrace:** accept.

379 **of memory:** which are not forgotten.

380 **vantage:** opportunity.

382 **and from . . . more:** Hamlet's dying words will have great influence.

383 **presently:** immediately.

381-5 Horatio's counsel implies that he has become his stable self again.

386 **soldier:** Ophelia had referred to Hamlet's soldierly qualities (III. i. 153). Fortinbras' comment is significant.

387 **put on:** put to the test.

388 **to have . . . royal:** a tribute to Hamlet's kingly qualities; **passage:** death.

See also p. 275.

And, in this upshot, purposes mistook
Fall'n on the inventors' heads: all this can I   375
Truly deliver.
Fortinbras.   Let us haste to hear it,
   And call the noblest to the audience.
   For me, with sorrow I embrace my fortune:
   I have some rights of memory in this kingdom,
   Which now to claim my vantage doth invite me.   380
Horatio.   Of that I shall have also cause to speak,
   And from his mouth whose voice will draw on more:
   But let this same be presently perform'd,
   Even while men's minds are wild, lest more mischance
   On plots and errors happen.
Fortinbras.   Let four captains   385
   Bear Hamlet like a soldier to the stage,
   For he was likely, had he been put on,
   To have proved most royal: and, for his passage,
   The soldiers' music and the rite of war
   Speak loudly for him.   390
   Take up the bodies: such a sight as this
   Becomes the field, but here shows much amiss.
   Go, bid the soldiers shoot.
                                        Exeunt.

ACT I, SCENE 1

Dramatic Importance

The opening scene in a Shakespearian play is of the greatest dramatic importance. It must provide enough information to enable the audience to understand the situation. This information must include the introduction of some of the main characters. Notice how skilfully Shakespeare, through the text, makes the audience aware of the names of the speakers. Often the leading character is merely mentioned or perhaps described so that the way is paved for his appearance in a subsequent scene.

The opening scene must also create interest; interest may be created by means of atmosphere. Opening scenes in Shakespeare provide us with lively arguments, or a shipwreck, or supernatural beings, all of which tend to create suspense. In brief, the opening scene should make us want to hear or read the rest of the play.

The opening scene of *Hamlet* is one of the most impressive in the whole Shakespearian canon. The setting, "Elsinore. A platform before the castle", with its dark battlements and nervous sentries, catches our interest immediately. At once the notes of mystery and strangeness are struck as the bell tolls twelve on a frosty night. The two appearances of the silent Ghost of the late King provide the high points of the scene, but Shakespeare also manages to present us with information regarding the military preparations in Denmark. We also get a vivid picture of the scholar Horatio. The end of the scene with its mention of young Hamlet makes us wonder how he will respond to the news of his dead father's mysterious appearance on the castle ramparts.

Questions

1. a) Describe the prevailing atmosphere in this scene.
   b) Explain how this atmosphere is created.

2. Horatio is represented as being a scholar. How does Shakespeare reveal this characteristic?
3. What reasons are suggested by Horatio for the appearance of the late King's ghost?
4. How is the Ghost made impressive and awe-inspiring?
5. Dover Wilson[1] refers to a tradition that Shakespeare "writ the scene of the Ghost in *Hamlet* at his House which bordered on the Charnel House and Church-yard". What might have given rise to such a tradition?

ACT I, SCENE 2

Dramatic Importance

Scene 2 provides a distinct contrast with Scene 1 in that it deals with the actual world, with a considerable number of characters, and with a variety of incidents. Nevertheless it is like the first scene in that it provides us with information and with suspense.

The scene is divided into three main sections, the first of which centres around Claudius. It may be, as Sir John Gielgud suggests, that this is the first meeting of the Privy Council since Claudius' accession. Introduced here, the new King shows that he is capable and resourceful; he refers tactfully to his marriage and then dispatches ambassadors to Norway to cope with the Fortinbras situation. He deals skilfully with Laertes and compliments Polonius; he also manages to get his way with regard to Hamlet, although that young man is far from being

[1] J. Dover Wilson, *What Happens in 'Hamlet'*, 3rd ed. (Cambridge, Cambridge University Press, 1951), p. 56.

won over. Thus, by means of a single council, Shakespeare has introduced Claudius, Gertrude, Polonius, Laertes, and Hamlet, and the strands of the plot begin to take shape on the loom of the play.

The second main division of this major scene is Hamlet's soliloquy. (See notes on the soliloquies, p. xxxii.) The first soliloquy reveals Hamlet's melancholy and its apparent causes. We see him as a supremely sensitive, highly imaginative and intellectual prince, much given to introspection and capable of true and deep emotion. The picture we get of him is an intensely dramatic and powerful one; his figure is etched forever on our minds.

The third division of the scene links us with Scene 1, as Horatio makes his promised report to Hamlet. Tension mounts in the rapid-fire exchange as Hamlet excitedly questions the three about the apparition. Suspense is created when Hamlet promises to join them on the ramparts that night, but the shadow of doom seems to be already present: "I doubt some foul play."

Questions

1. How does Claudius reveal himself as a capable monarch in this scene?
2. What qualities of Hamlet's character are brought out a) by his first words in the play? b) in his soliloquy? c) in his conversation with Horatio and the sentries?
3. What contrasts are brought out between the characters of Hamlet and Laertes?
4. Outline the Norwegian situation as presented in this scene.
5. How is Scene 2 related to Scene 1?
6. There are four items on the agenda of the Privy Council: an explanation of the situation in Denmark, the Norway affair, Laertes' request, Hamlet's request. Why is each important?

ACT I, SCENE 3

Dramatic Importance

A family scene, filled with brotherly and fatherly advice, creates an atmosphere quite different from that of the appearance of the Ghost and the problems of Hamlet and his relatives. Laertes, like his father, is fond of laying down the law and tends to patronize his sister. His warnings against Hamlet acquaint us with the romantic plot and serve to establish Laertes as a sophisticated man-about-town.

Polonius' advice to Laertes stamps the old man as wily and worldly; Shakespeare's problem was to portray a bore without boring his audience. His portrait of "senility encroaching upon wisdom" (Johnson) is masterly.

Ophelia's conversation with Laertes and with Polonius establishes her as affectionate, fond of her brother and father, and docile; under the circumstances, she has no choice but to obey her father's harsh commands. We sympathize with her, caught up as she is in a world too cruel and complicated for one so fragile and wistful.

Questions

1. The word "Advice" provides a suitable title for the scene. How does Laertes' advice to Ophelia resemble a) Polonius' advice to Laertes? b) Polonius' advice to Ophelia?
2. How is sympathy created in this scene a) for Ophelia? b) for Hamlet?
3. What sources of humour are to be found in this scene?

ACT I, SCENE 4

Dramatic Importance

The contrast, on the one hand between Hamlet and his friends tensely awaiting the appearance of the Ghost and, on the other hand the roistering of Claudius, is very sharp and dramatic. Suspense is also created by the opening speeches.

The Ghost's appearance, though expected, seems sudden and startles Hamlet, whose speech as he addresses it is intense and yet musical. Hamlet's determination is shown by the way he thrusts off those who would hinder him; here is no weakling. Once again the silence of the Ghost adds to the atmosphere of awe that surrounds it.

Questions

1. Show that this scene contains examples of contrast, surprise, and suspense.
2. What differences are brought out between the characters of Hamlet and Claudius?
3. How is Horatio's concern for Hamlet brought out?

ACT I, SCENE 5

Dramatic Importance

This scene is of primary importance in the development of the plot, for it is here that Hamlet is made aware for the first time that his Uncle Claudius is the murderer of the late King, his father. It is here that he swears to avenge his father's death. He also learns of his mother's adultery, and his disillusionment becomes all the greater. As Horatio protests against his "wild and whirling words", Hamlet, in a flash, decides to play the madman and thereby confuse his enemy. His last words in the scene illustrate, his despair with his lot, though he is also determined to avenge his father's death.

Questions

1. a) State the substance of the Ghost's revelation to Hamlet.
   b) How does Hamlet receive this news?
2. What reasons would Hamlet have for feigning madness?

ACT I

Dramatic Importance

In five skilfully informative and exciting scenes, Shakespeare has introduced seven important characters including the Ghost. He has made us aware of the domestic situation in the royal family, and through the Ghost's revelation he has caused us to realize that this is to be a play of revenge. Hamlet's plan to feign madness also creates suspense. In addition, Shakespeare has established the Fortinbras plot on the international scene with the dispatch of the ambassadors to Norway. We have also met Polonius and his family; Laertes departs for Paris but will return at a later date to play an important part. Hints are presented with regard to Ophelia and the romantic plot.

Questions

1. Of what importance is the Ghost in the triangular relationship of Claudius, Gertrude, and Hamlet?

2. Of what importance is Hamlet in the triangular relationship of Ophelia, Laertes, and Polonius?

3. Of what importance in Act I are a) Cornelius and Voltimand? b) Horatio?

4. a) On what occasions does the Ghost appear in Act I?
   b) Why is the Ghost dramatically effective?
   c) How does its last appearance differ from the others?
   d) Why do we assume that it would be visible to the audience?

5. By reference to the main characters and various plots and episodes in it, show that Act I provides a sound introduction to the play.

6. "At the end of the first act, the Elizabethan audience could no more be certain of the honesty of the Ghost and of the truth of the story it had related, than the perplexed hero himself."[1] Comment on the importance of this statement.

7. "At the end of the first act, the back upon which the tragic load rests begins to show signs of breaking . . . because of the sheer weight of the load."[2] What is "the load" that is referred to? What are the "signs of breaking"?

8. "The Ghost and his message form the main theme of Act I."[3] Comment on this statement.

9. "In a word, Shakespeare wishes us to feel that Hamlet assumes madness because he cannot help it: that is to say, the mood comes unsought but is welcomed as affording relief when it does come and is accordingly purposely elaborated and prolonged."[4] Illustrate.

[1] J. Dover Wilson, *What Happens in 'Hamlet'*, 3rd ed. (Cambridge, Cambridge University Press, 1951), p. 84.
[2] *Ibid.*, p. 50.
[3] *Ibid.*, p. 88.
[4] *Ibid.*, p. 92.

ACT II, SCENE 1

Dramatic Importance

The scene falls into two parts, which are unified by the presence of Polonius. The first part deals with his instructions to
Reynaldo for the purpose of spying on Laertes. It is clear from
this conversation that a month or more must have passed,
since Laertes is now in Paris, and Polonius has evidently received word of this. The second part deals with Ophelia's revelation of Hamlet's strange behaviour; Polonius leaps to the conclusion that Hamlet's madness is caused by Ophelia's rejection
of the Prince's love.

The scene gives us a clear picture of Polonius the busybody
who, now, full of his own importance is about to seek an audience with Claudius. Suspense is created by Hamlet's behaviour,
but there is an element of dramatic irony here, since we heard
him tell of his plan to put on an "antic disposition".

Questions

1.   And thus do we of wisdom and of reach,
       With windlasses and with assays of bias,
       By indirections find directions out.

   By means of specific references, show how Polonius prac-
   tises the philosophy referred to here.

2. a) Describe and b) account for Hamlet's behaviour to
   Ophelia as she reports it to Polonius.

3. a) What does Ophelia's account reveal about her character?
   b) What does Polonius' reaction reveal about his character?

4. It has been suggested that Hamlet sought out Ophelia in
   the hope that she would give him support and strength.
   What evidence is there of this in Ophelia's description?
   If this is true, what decision did he come to? Illustrate
   from the text.

ACT II, SCENE 2

Dramatic Importance

This scene, the longest in the play, develops with masterly skill to its climax in Hamlet's second soliloquy. Disturbed by Hamlet's "madness", the King and Queen have invited two old schoolfellows of Hamlet, Rosencrantz and Guildenstern, to find out what is troubling him. No sooner have they been introduced than Polonius announces that he has discovered the cause of Hamlet's strange behaviour, but keeps Claudius and Gertrude in suspense until the ambassadors to Norway have given their report. The upshot of this is that young Fortinbras requests permission to cross Denmark on his way to fight against Poland. His name, which has been so skilfully introduced, will not be heard again until Act IV.

Polonius, shamelessly reading Hamlet's letter to Ophelia, is sure of the reason for Hamlet's madness; namely, thwarted love; he develops a plan to have the two supposed lovers meet while he and Claudius spy upon them. Following encounters first with Polonius and then with Rosencantz and Guildenstern, Hamlet welcomes the Players, requesting "a passionate speech". After this highly dramatic account of the slaughter of Priam and the anguish of Hecuba, Hamlet delivers his second soliloquy. Here he excoriates himself for his failure to act, but all his energies are caught up in a plan to present before the King a play that will reproduce the circumstances of the elder Hamlet's murder.

The complications of the plot are now more sharply defined, and suspense mounts as we wonder what will be the outcome of Hamlet's meeting with Ophelia and whether Claudius will reveal his guilt at the play within the play.

Apart from the Players, the only new characters are Rosencrantz and Guildenstern, insipid nonentities whom Hamlet despises for their subservience to the King. The facets of Hamlet's own character appear in still more complicated brilliance: his wit, his imagination, his cynicism (which is a kind of inverted idealism), and his introspective, intellectual nature. He is truly Shakespeare's portrait of a genius who is also an enigma.

Questions

1. a) Explain the reason for the arrival of Rosencrantz and Guildenstern at the Danish court.

   b) Summarize Hamlet's attitude towards them, giving the reason for it.

2. a) What report is brought to Claudius by the ambassadors to Norway?

   b) Why is this introduced into the play?

3. a) How does Polonius proceed to prove his theory about the cause of Hamlet's madness?

   b) What plan does he suggest in order to test it?

4. a) How does Hamlet react to the arrival of the Players?

   b) What does his attitude towards them reveal about him?

   c) What use does he propose to make of them?

5. a) Show that the First Player's speech, spoken by Æneas to Dido, presents pictures of three persons.

   b) What is the difference between Polonius' attitude towards it and Hamlet's?

6. a) Show that Hamlet's soliloquy "O, what a rogue" contributes to the plot, characterization, and atmosphere of the play.

   b) Into what two main divisions does it fall?

   c) Compare the soliloquies "O that this too too sullied flesh" and "O, what a rogue and peasant slave" under the following headings: subject matter, characteristics of Hamlet revealed, and imaginative qualities of the style.

7. a) What references are made in this scene to Hamlet's madness?

   b) On what occasions is it illustrated?

   c) What is its dramatic purpose?

ACT II

Dramatic Importance

As Act II ends, the conflict between Hamlet and the King is becoming more sharply defined. Hamlet's madness has aroused the suspicion of Claudius, but he does not seem as yet unduly alarmed. His spies, Rosencrantz, Guildenstern, and Polonius, are active, the last with his eavesdropping scheme. Hamlet, knowing what he knows about the Ghost and his "antic disposition", is in a more favourable position than Claudius in this act. He too has his scheme, which he hopes will establish his uncle's guilt. Thus Act II hinges on Hamlet's madness and the designs of the two antagonists.

Questions

1. Show that Hamlet's supposed madness dominates Act II.
2. What evidence is there of his sanity?
3. Laertes, Fortinbras, and Hamlet make an interesting triangle. What are the main points of difference among the three so far in the play?
4. What two schemes referred to in this act will be put into effect in Act III?
5. If the main conflict is between Claudius and Hamlet, who has the advantage as Act II ends? Why?
6. Show that Polonius' garrulity and Hamlet's biting wit provide humour in this act.
7. "The second act of *Hamlet* is comedy; a comedy of masks."[1] Comment on this statement.

[1]J. Dover Wilson, *What Happens in 'Hamlet'*, 3rd ed. (Cambridge, Cambridge University Press. 1951), p. 89.

8. "The attitude of Hamlet towards Ophelia is without doubt the greatest of all puzzles in the play, greater even than that of the delay itself."[1] Describe the attitude referred to and state why it is a puzzle.

ACT III, SCENE 1

Dramatic Importance

Rosencrantz and Guildenstern report to the King and Queen; the revenge plot is advanced in their reference to the production of the play within the play, which is to be presented that night. Hamlet's soliloquy suggests that despite his plan, he has lost the initiative. Although Polonius' scheme to explain Hamlet's madness has failed, it does show the King that he himself stands in some danger. He reacts with characteristic resourcefulness in his plan to send Hamlet to England. Polonius too has another scheme, typical of his devious mind; this entails spying on Hamlet; the old man proposes to listen in on the Prince's conversation with Gertrude. The forces opposing Hamlet seem at this point to be in the ascendant.

Questions

1. a) With regard to Hamlet's soliloquy "To be, or not to be", state the theme and summarize the content.

   b) If the soliloquy were omitted, what difference would it make to the play?

   c) Account for the fame of the passage.

   d) Which of the major preceding soliloquies does it resemble? How?

[1]*Ibid.*, p. 101.

2. a) Of what dramatic importance (to plot, characterization, and atmosphere) is Hamlet's interview with Ophelia?
   b) Why is it almost essential to assume either that Hamlet had overheard Polonius' plans, or that he became aware of the presence of both men?

3. Show how the forces opposed to Hamlet have gained the ascendancy in this scene.

4. Of the "To be, or not to be" soliloquy, Dover Wilson[1] says: "No one but Shakespeare could have interrupted an exciting dramatic intrigue with a passage like this. The surprise and the audacity of it take our breath away, and render the pity of it the more overwhelming." Explain and comment on this passage.

5. It has been suggested that the principal purpose of the "To be, or not to be" soliloquy is to give us the one picture in the play of Hamlet, the scholar, the intellectual, pondering a problem of moral philosophy. Discuss this statement.

6. "Here (in the 'To be, or not to be' soliloquy) is a purely philosophical or speculative statement of the general tragedy of man."[2] Discuss.

---

[1] J. Dover Wilson, *What Happens in 'Hamlet'*, 3rd ed. (Cambridge, Cambridge University Press, 1951), p. 128.

[2] H. B. Charlton, *Shakespearian Tragedy* (Cambridge, Cambridge University Press, 1948), p. 97.

ACT III, SCENE 2

Dramatic Importance

In this scene, Hamlet scores a decisive victory in that he establishes Claudius' guilt. The climax of the play within the play is considered by some to be the crisis in the revenge plot. Other critics prefer a different turning point; namely, Hamlet's failure to kill the King at prayer.

Hamlet's character is more fully revealed in this scene. In his advice to the Players we see him at ease, sparkling with ideas, imaginative, intelligent. His conversation with Horatio reveals his admiration of stability and good judgement, and by contrast his own impulsive, high-strung nature. With Polonius, Rosencrantz and Guildenstern, he shows his sharpness of wit and satirical sense of humour, since he knows them to be tools of the King. With Ophelia he is brutal. After the play within the play, his excitement reaches a feverish pitch of intensity, but as yet there is no plan of action.

Suspense and variety are evident in the scene from the advice to the Players to the episode with the recorders, and we are led forward in the play by Hamlet's promise to visit his mother.

Questions

1. On the assumption that Shakespeare is voicing his ideas on acting in the advice to the Players, give a synopsis of his views on the subject.
2. Outline the qualities in Horatio that Hamlet admires, explaining why he admires them.
3. a) What is the dramatic importance of the play within the play?
   b) To what extent does it fulfil Hamlet's purpose?
4. Select the passage (or passages) that Hamlet might have

written for the play within the play. Give reasons for your choice.

5. What is added to the play by the recorder episode?
6. Show how Poionius adds unconsciously to the humour oi the scene.
7. Give the dramatic importance in this scene of a) Rosencrantz and Guildenstern, b) Horatio.
8. a) If the revenge plot is considered as a game of chess between Hamlet and his uncle, which of the contestants is in the more favourable position?
   b) What will the next move be?
9. Why may the establishment of Claudius' guilt be considered the crisis of the revenge plot?

ACT III, SCENE 3

Dramatic Importance

Acting with speed and decision, unlike Hamlet, Claudius takes steps to get rid of the Prince by sending him out of the country. Polonius' scheme creates suspense and will provide dramatic irony. Claudius' character is revealed as he vainly searches his conscience.

The most absorbing aspect of the scene, however, is Hamlet's failure to take advantage of his opportunity. The complexity of his character fascinates us, though a simpler man might have achieved his revenge and ended the matter. The interview with the Queen is now imminent.

Questions

1. *Resolved,* That Hamlet should have killed the King at prayer. Debate this issue.

2. Which may be regarded as the more logical crisis of the play: the King's revelation of his guilt in the preceding scene, or Hamlet's failure to kill him in this scene?

3. a) Explain how Shakespeare creates sympathy for Claudius in this scene.
   b) Of what dramatic importance is this attempt to create sympathy?

4. How is Polonius' behaviour in this scene consistent with his previous actions?

5. a) Of what significance is Claudius' plan to send Hamlet to England?
   b) What qualities of Claudius are revealed?

6. Analyse Hamlet's reasons for not killing the King as presented in his speech ll. 73-96.

ACT III, SCENE 4

Dramatic Importance

The murder of Polonius is considered by some critics to be the turning point of the play: it obviously gives Claudius additional plausible reasons for sending Hamlet to England; it leads to the return of Laertes and the madness of Ophelia. Hamlet's interview with the Queen supports the fact that she was not a party to the murder of her first husband and also brings out, for those who are prepared to accept it, the Oedipus complex. The appearance of the Ghost serves to emphasize the existence of Hamlet's delay and to remind the Prince of his plain duty.

Hamlet's ability to act impulsively is underlined in this scene; his failure to kill the King cannot be blamed merely on his habit "of thinking too precisely on the event". Gertrude's affection for her son is brought out here; she promises to keep his secret and appears much moved by his accusations.

Questions

1. a) What effect will the murder of Polonius have on the revenge plot?
   b) What does it reveal about Hamlet?
2. a) What purpose is served by the interview between Hamlet and Gertrude?
   b) What is the substance of his accusations?
3. Why does the Ghost reappear in this scene?
4. What are the reasons for considering that the murder of Polonius is the turning point of the play?
5. In what respects is the murder of Polonius a mistake on Hamlet's part?
6. What reason does the Queen have a) for thinking Hamlet mad? b) for believing him to be sane?

ACT III

Dramatic Importance

Five episodes of the utmost significance in the play are found in Act III. Professor Levin[1] refers to these as the Nunnery Scene, the Play Scene, the Prayer Scene, the Closet Scene, and the Portrait Scene.

Hamlet's brutal rejection of Ophelia brings out the misogyny that is poisoning his nature. (This hatred of women is caused

[1] H. Levin, *The Question of Hamlet* (London, Oxford University Press, 1959), p. xi.

by his revulsion at his mother's incestuous marriage.) His behaviour towards Ophelia prompts Polonius to arrange for
Hamlet's interview with Gertrude, an interview that will be
fraught with dire consequences for the eavesdropper. Hamlet's
behaviour, certainly not that of an irresponsible madman, results
in Claudius' decision to send this dangerous young man to England. The play within the play, preceded by Hamlet's brilliant
advice to the Players, succeeds in establishing, to Hamlet's
delighted satisfaction, the guilt of Claudius. As the Prince goes to
meet his mother, he meets the King, who is ostensibly praying.
Hamlet loses a perfect opportunity to kill Claudius and thus to
execute the Ghost's command. His failure here and his murder
of Polonius give the King the advantage in their conflict. Hamlet,
however, does make clear to Gertrude the enormity of her
behaviour, but her sympathy cannot save him from his uncle and
from himself. As the act ends, the initiative has passed to the
enemy.

Hamlet's character continues to absorb and puzzle the reader.
The "To be, or not to be" soliloquy is arresting; the advice to
the Players is masterly; the coarse treatment of Ophelia is
inexcusable; the praise of Horatio is winning; the denunciation
of Gertrude shocks us; the wit and satire fascinate us. Because
of this complexity, he seems "to spectators in the theatre to be
more life-like than any other character in literature."[1]

Suspense is marked at various points in the act, as the tension
rises and falls and rises. As the act ends, we wonder what will
be the consequences of the murder of Polonius, whether the
King will succeed in banishing Hamlet, and what Hamlet means
by his reference to the "enginer hoist with his own petar".

Questions

1. "To decide whether or not life is worth living is to answer
   the most fundamental question of philosophy."

[1]J. Dover Wilson, *What Happens in 'Hamlet'*, 3rd ed. (Cambridge, Cambridge University Press, 1951), p. 219.

    a) What arguments does Hamlet give i) for committing suicide? ii) for not committing suicide?

    b) What is his final decision? Why?

    c) Why is this the most famous of all the soliloquies?

    d) What dramatic purpose does it serve?

2. What similarities and differences are there between Hamlet's treatment of Ophelia in the Nunnery Scene and his treatment of his mother in the Portrait Scene?

3. What part is played in Act III a) by Claudius? b) by Polonius?

4. State concisely the importance of each of the following episodes:

    a) the Nunnery Scene (III. i. 90-151),

    b) the Play Scene (III. ii. 94-291),

    c) the Prayer Scene (III. iii. 36-98),

    d) the Closet Scene (III. iv. 1-33),

    e) the Portrait Scene (III. iv. 34-217).

5. Show how the following add to our conception of Hamlet's character:

    a) the "To be, or not to be" soliloquy,

    b) his advice to the Players,

    c) his speech to Horatio (III. ii. 58-76),

    d) the recorder episode,

    e) the lines spoken while Claudius is praying,

    f) the murder of Polonius,

    g) his interview with his mother.

7. What developments have taken place a) in the revenge plot? b) in the romantic plot?

8. Of the three possible crises in Act III, which do you regard as the turning point of the play?

ACT IV, SCENE 1

Dramatic Importance

Gertrude reports the murder of Polonius to Claudius, who is more than ever determined to get rid of Hamlet at once.

Questions
1. How does Gertrude seek to shield Hamlet in this scene?
2. What are Claudius' chief concerns with regard to the murder?

ACT IV, SCENE 2

Dramatic Importance

This brief scene shows Hamlet's attitude towards the King's spies and reveals once more his "antic disposition", adopted here to distract his former schoolfellows.

Question
1. If this scene were omitted, what difference would it make to the play?

ACT IV, SCENE 3

Dramatic Importance

The King is now desperately eager to get rid of Hamlet,

whose life is a threat to Claudius' own. His plan for having Hamlet murdered on arrival in England is a clever device.

Questions

1. a) What reason does Claudius give for not proceeding with legal action against Hamlet?
   b) Give other reasons.
2. a) What are the details of the King's plan?
   b) Why is he confident that it will be carried out?

ACT IV, SCENE 4

Dramatic Importance

The introduction of Fortinbras is one of the important elements in this scene, for it links up the beginning and the ending of the play. It also provides a dramatic contrast between a man of action and a man tormented by thought. Finally, although Hamlet, ironically, does not see Fortinbras, the latter provides, with his men and his cause, the inspiration for Hamlet's final soliloquy. The omission of this soliloquy from F implies that it is of more significance in its character revelation than in its contribution to the plot. In it, we see a Hamlet quieter, but bitter in his detachment. One of the insoluble problems of the play is underlined by his anguished cry: "I do not know/Why yet I live to say 'this thing's to do,'/Sith I have cause, and will, and strength, and means/To do't."

Questions

1. Of what importance is the first appearance of Fortinbras?
2. What points of comparison and contrast are suggested between him and Hamlet?

3. a) Which of the preceding soliloquies ("O that this too too sullied flesh", "O, what a rogue and peasant slave", "To be, or not to be") does this one most resemble? b) Explain why.
4. What would be lost if this soliloquy were omitted from the play?
5. "Some craven scruple/Of thinking too precisely on the event." Comment on this phrase as providing the reason for Hamlet's delay.

ACT IV, SCENE 5

Dramatic Importance

The death of Polonius is bringing grim results. The madness of Ophelia springs in large part from the murder of her father, and Laertes' return is caused by the death of Polonius. The reader inevitably contrasts this scene with the last meeting of the brother and sister at the time of the departure of Laertes for France. When he warned his sister against Hamlet, nothing could have been further from his mind than that the Prince would murder Polonius. The contrast between Hamlet and Laertes is sharply marked. Claudius' behaviour is that of a brave, bold man. Nevertheless, the outstanding feature of the scene is the pathos created by Ophelia's madness.

Questions

1. What dramatic purpose is served by the madness of Ophelia?
2. What are the causes of Ophelia's madness?
3. How does her behaviour win the sympathy of the audience?

4. How does this scene bring out the contrast between Hamlet and Laertes?
5. How does Claudius in this scene show a) courage? b) resourcefulness?

ACT IV, SCENE 6

Dramatic Importance

The letter from Hamlet to Horatio provides surprise and creates suspense. The fact that the Prince has returned without the King's permission will certainly create trouble. Hamlet's account of his behaviour suggests that when occasion demanded, he could act with resolution.

Questions

1. What qualities of Hamlet are shown in the letter he has written?
2. How will Hamlet's return affect the plot?
3. How does this scene allow for the passage of time?

ACT IV, SCENE 7

Dramatic Importance

Laertes is no sooner convinced that Claudius is not responsible for Polonius' death than the King receives letters announcing

Hamlet's return. With his usual supple skill, he flatters Laertes and presents him with a plan to get rid of Hamlet. In a fencing match, Laertes will use an unbated weapon; to make assurance doubly sure, Laertes suggests that he anoint his rapier with a deadly poison. There is no hesitation in Laertes, and his determination to secure revenge, even by foul means, provides a sharp contrast to Hamlet's procrastination. Claudius adds to the plot by suggesting that a poisoned drink be held in readiness, and at this moment, Gertrude brings the sad tale of Ophelia's death by drowning. Laertes, overcome with grief, has even more reason to take vengeance on Hamlet.

The scene advances the plot in that Hamlet will shortly be brought to bay; his enemies are closing in. We wonder if, in view of the counter-plot against him, he will ever achieve his revenge. Claudius shows his devious, crafty nature, and Laertes appears unscrupulous, though his desire for justice is understandable. Ophelia's untimely end shows how Hamlet's failure to act is responsible for yet another death.

Questions

1. How does coincidence help to advance the plot in this scene?
2. Summarize the results of Polonius' death as they appear in this scene.
3. Show that the forces in opposition to Hamlet appear to have gained the upper hand.
4. a) What reasons are given by Claudius for not bringing Hamlet to a public trial?
   b) What further reason may there be?
5. a) Show how Laertes' cause parallels that of Hamlet.
   b) How do their reactions provide a contrast between them?
   c) How do you account for the difference in their reactions?
6. What qualities a) of Claudius, b) of Laertes, c) of Gertrude, are brought out in this scene?

ACT IV

Dramatic Importance

The first five scenes of Act IV present the consequences of the murder of Polonius: Hamlet's banishment, Ophelia's madness, and Laertes' return. The remaining two scenes show the results of Hamlet's unexpected return. Claudius, the opportunist, very neatly makes use of Laertes, who, in securing his own revenge, will rid the King of a mortal enemy. The report of Ophelia's death at the end of the scene adds a note of pathos and reminds us that the House of Polonius dominates this act.

Two speeches of significance are to be found. Hamlet's soliloquy brings out the contrast between his inaction on the one hand and the energy and initiative of Fortinbras on the other. This contrast is further sharpened by the behaviour of Laertes. The second important speech is Gertrude's report, which is almost like an operatic aria in its musical and lyrical quality.

Now that the forces opposed to Hamlet are once more in the ascendant, we wonder whether their schemes will be carried out successfully and whether Hamlet can in any way circumvent his enemies and achieve his purpose.

Questions

1. How does Ophelia's madness compare with that of Hamlet?
2. Show that Act IV deals largely with the consequences of Polonius' death.
3. a) How does Hamlet differ i) from Fortinbras? ii) from Laertes?
   b) How does he resemble them in cause and/or in character up to this point in the play?
4. Show that Claudius is courageous, resourceful, and unscrupulous in his behaviour during Act IV.

5. In Act IV, how has Hamlet a) outmanoeuvred Claudius? b) once more apparently fallen into his clutches?
6. Although Hamlet himself does not appear in the last three scenes of this act, show that we are not permitted to forget him.
7. One critic[1] refers to Ophelia's "apparently half-sought death". Explain and comment.

ACT V, SCENE 1

Dramatic Importance

The macabre humour of the grave-diggers' scene provides a grotesque setting for Hamlet's return. His quick mind plays with the idea of death, and the dramatic irony of the situation adds to the power of the scene. The unexpected encounter with Laertes acts as a preliminary to their later duel and reveals, in Hamlet's short-lived fury, his love for Ophelia.

Questions

1. Show how Ophelia dominates this scene.
2. How does the scene bring out Hamlet's intellectual curiosity and his speculative powers?
3. Why did Hamlet attack Laertes?
4. Analyse the humour of the grave-diggers' episode and state the importance of the interlude in the play (V. i. 1-61).
5. Assess the dramatic importance of Ophelia's funeral.

[1] L. C. Knights, *An Approach to Hamlet* (London, Chatto & Windus, Ltd., 1960).

ACT V, SCENE 2

Dramatic Importance

This scene presents the climax and the catastrophe, as well as the outcome, of the tragedy. As it begins, Hamlet explains his stratagem for the execution of Rosencrantz and Guildenstern, a scheme that suggests a certain cold-blooded cruelty. It is followed by the Osric episode with its exaggerated banter and description of the King's wager. Claudius' anxiety is shown by his sending of another messenger, and Hamlet in a mood of fatalism agrees to take part in the duel. Hamlet's apology to Laertes suggests that at times he really was troubled with madness; the line between the actual and the feigned is hard to draw. Excitement and tension mount as the duel begins; the King's plan goes awry as Gertrude drinks the poison, but Laertes in a treacherous move achieves his purpose, only to be served with the same medicine. It is his confession that reveals Claudius' guilt, and Hamlet in a final burst of fury achieves his long-sought revenge. Thwarting Horatio's desire to die, Hamlet insists that his friend tell the story behind these murderous deeds and clear the Prince's name. As Hamlet dies, Fortinbras makes his entrance and takes command of the situation. By his order, Hamlet is borne, "like a soldier, to the stage". Life has returned, as always in Shakespearian tragedy, to a C major chord.

Questions

1. a) What fate has Hamlet contrived for Rosencrantz and Guildenstern?
   b) Why?
   c) To what extent is his action justified?
   d) What is Horatio's opinion?
2. a) Of what importance to the plot and atmosphere is the Osric episode?
   b) What does it add to our picture of Hamlet?

3. How likely is it that Osric was an accomplice in the plot against Hamlet?

4. "His madness is poor Hamlet's enemy".
   a) Explain this remark.
   b) What does it imply about the "antic disposition"?

5. Gertrude may have committed suicide. What is the evidence for and against this conception?

6. Explain how Hamlet got possession of Laertes' sword.

7. Show how nemesis overtook a) Claudius, b) Laertes, c) Gertrude, d) Hamlet.

8. Of what importance is Horatio in the last scene?

9. What dramatic purpose is served by the arrival of Fortinbras as the play ends?

10. How did Hamlet finally fulfil the Ghost's injunction?

11. To what extent is the end of the play dramatically satisfying?

12. In what respect are Horatio's lines "so shall you hear . . . inventors' heads" a fair summary of the play?

13. To what extent does the conclusion of the play satisfy the demands of justice?

ACT V

Dramatic Importance

The final act of the play deals with Hamlet's return to Denmark and its consequences. It begins with preparations for Ophelia's funeral and ends with preparations for Hamlet's. Although death is the dominant factor, the act is punctuated with two humorous sections: the grave-diggers' scene and the Osric episode, which by contrast tend to deepen the tragedies they precede. Hamlet achieves his long-sought revenge almost by accident, since the death of Claudius is not the result of any specific plan on his part. With the burial of Ophelia, and the deaths of Gertrude and Laertes, we are reminded of the cost of the fulfilment of Hamlet's vow to the Ghost. It is, however, his own death that seems to give this tragedy its peculiar poignancy. Evil has been exorcised, and the survival of Horatio, along with the arrival of Fortinbras, indicates that stability and strength have been re-established in Denmark. Good people have perished in the convulsion, but the moral order has prevailed.

Questions
1. Show that death dominates the last act.
2. a) Compare the humour of the grave-diggers' scene with that of the Osric episode.
   b) How does each serve to bring out the character of Hamlet?
   c) What purpose does each serve in this act?
3. What part is played by Horatio in the last act?
4. How does the moral order triumph as the play ends?
5. *Hamlet* is a revenge play. How is this aspect illustrated in the last act?

GENERAL QUESTIONS ON THE WHOLE PLAY

PART A   The elements of tragedy, based on Bradley's *Shakespearean Tragedy*.[1]

1. "A Shakespearean tragedy is a story of human actions

[1]A. C. Bradley, *Shakespearean Tragedy* (London, Macmillan & Co., Ltd., 1904), *passim*.

producing exceptional calamity and ending in the death of a man in high estate."[1] To what extent does Bradley's definition apply to *Hamlet*?

2. Conflict is indispensable to drama. Show that *Hamlet* presents both an outward and an inward conflict.

3. The central feeling in a great tragedy is, according to Bradley, one of waste. How is this illustrated in *Hamlet*?

4. "The ultimate power in the tragic world is a moral order."[2] To what extent does good overcome evil as the play ends?

5. "The hero in a Shakespearean play always contributes in some measure to the disaster in which he perishes."[3] How true is this of Hamlet?

6. "Character is destiny." To what extent does this statement explain Hamlet's fate?

7. Show that Shakespeare makes use in *Hamlet* of a) abnormal conditions of mind, b) the supernatural, c) chance.

PART B

8. Hamlet's madness is "less than madness and more than feigned."[4] Explain and discuss.

9. Comment on the following statement of T. S. Eliot[5]: "So far from being Shakespeare's masterpiece, the play is most certainly an artistic failure. . . . Shakespeare tackled a problem that was too much for him."

10. How do Hamlet's seven soliloquies a) reveal character? b) create atmosphere? c) advance the plot?

11. Discuss the importance of spying in the play.

[1] *Ibid.*
[2] *Ibid.*
[3] *Ibid.*
[4] T. S. Eliot, *The Sacred Wood* (London, Methuen & Co., Ltd., 1920).
[5] *Ibid.*, p. 98.

12. "It is a coarse and barbarous piece that would not be tolerated by the lowest riff-raff of France or Italy. Such a work seems the product of a drunken savage" (Voltaire). What aspects of the play might justify this scathing comment?

13. By referring to the speeches of Hamlet, Ophelia, and the grave-diggers, show that there is a preoccupation with death in the play.

14. What factors in *Hamlet* would contribute to its effectiveness as a film?

Structure

1. Harley Granville-Barker[1] sees in the structure three movements: the first, Act I; the second, Act II to the end of Act IV, Scene 4; the third, Act IV, Scene 5 to the end. Comment on the validity of this division.

2. Apply the terms exposition, complication, crisis, falling action (sometimes called resolution), catastrophe (climax), and outcome to the play.

3. Select the crisis or turning point of the action and give reasons for your choice.

4. It has been said that the only incidents which occur by chance in the play are a) the arrival of the Players, b) Hamlet's escape with the pirates. Comment.

5. Professor G. B. Harrison[2] also suggests that the play falls into three divisions: how Hamlet learnt of the murder in the orchard, how Hamlet proved his uncle guilty, how Hamlet and Laertes simultaneously took their vengeance. Compare these divisions with those suggested by Granville-Barker.

6. What do letters add to the play?

[1]H. Granville-Barker, *Prefaces to Hamlet* (Princeton, Princeton University Press).

[2]G. B. Harrison, *Shakespeare's Tragedies* (London, Routledge & Kegan Paul, Ltd., 1952), p. 98, 106.

7. a) What fate overtakes each member of the Polonius family?

   b) To what extent was Hamlet responsible in each case?

Theme

1. In all versions of the Hamlet story, the theme is the same: revenge. Justify the idea that *Hamlet* is a tragedy of revenge.

2. "The centre of attention within the play lies in the hero's efforts to do his duty."[1] Illustrate this statement.

3. "The theme is evil, its contagion, and its inevitable self-destruction,—'evil breeding evil, and leading to ruin'."[2] Explain and illustrate this argument.

Setting

1. Although most of the scenes take place in "a room (a hall) in the castle", show that the following settings are also used: a platform before the castle, a room in Polonius' house, the Queen's closet, a plain in Denmark, a churchyard.

2. a) Of what importance is the general setting, Denmark?

   b) How does Shakespeare ignore it?

Time

1. In what historical period is the play supposedly set?

2. What evidence is there that Shakespeare thought of the action as taking place in the London of his own day?

3. How much time appears to elapse between the beginning and the end of the play? Refer to incidents that suggest the passage of time.

Atmosphere

1. Show that Act I, Scene 1, sets the atmosphere of the

[1]Bradley, *op. cit.*, p. 82.
[2]L. C. Knights, *An Approach to Hamlet* (London, Chatto & Windus, Ltd., 1960).

play. (Describe the details and sense impressions that contribute to this effect.)

2. Show that the scenes in which Polonius appears add to the humour of the play.

3. How does Hamlet use his "antic disposition" to create humour?

4. a) What two episodes in Act V contribute humour?
   b) What purpose is served by their inclusion?

5. Sir Laurence Olivier's production of *Hamlet* was filmed in black and white. Discuss the reasons for this.

6. How is the principle of nemesis illustrated in the play?

7. Show how dramatic irony adds to the atmosphere of tragedy, as in the duel scene, Act V, Scene 2, and to the atmosphere of comedy, as in Act V, Scene 1, the grave-diggers' episode. Refer to other examples of this device.

8. At what point in *Hamlet* is suspense greatest?

9. Illustrate the following dramatic devices: surprise, contrast, effective timing, foreshadowing of events, coincidence.

10. Find examples of the following: pathos, satire, irony (as distinct from dramatic irony), parallelism.

11. Of what importance is the use of the supernatural in the play?

12. It has been pointed out that in *Hamlet* we are increasingly aware of the presence of a supreme power or providence. What evidence is there of this presence?

13. The Ghost has been referred to as "a messenger of divine justice". Comment on the validity of this statement.

Characters and Characterization

1. Using the three main methods of characterization; that is, what a character says, what a character does, what others say about him, show that Hamlet is idealistic.

2. Of all the characters created by Shakespeare, Hamlet is the only one who could have written the plays. Discuss this statement.

3. Hamlet has been described as an enigma. Explain and justify this comment.

4. "That Hamlet is histrionic is no less clear than that he is high-strung, cerebral, magnanimous and sometimes obscene."[1] What evidence is there of each of these qualities?

5. Hamlet appears to be a lineal descendant of Brutus. What qualities do they have in common?

6. "The whole story turns upon the peculiar character of the hero."[2] Justify this comment.

7. The character of Hamlet "has probably exerted a greater fascination, and certainly has been the subject of more discussion than any other in the whole literature of the world."[3] Why does the character of Hamlet exert this fascination?

8. "The energy of resolve is dissipated in an endless brooding on the deed required."[4] Find examples from Hamlet's own speeches to show that this could be considered the reason for his delay in murdering the King.

9. "Hamlet is, through the whole piece, rather an instrument than an agent" (Samuel Johnson). What evidence is there to support this statement?

10. One of Hamlet's characteristic traits is a trick of repetition. Give at least four examples of this trait.

11. Hamlet's nimbleness of mind often shows itself in his love of word play: "intellectual and verbal gymnastics". Illustrate this quality by means of at least three examples.

12. Describe and illustrate Hamlet's sense of humour.

13. How truly was Hamlet in love with Ophelia? Give evidence to support your answer.

---

[1] Mark Van Doren, *Shakespeare* (Doubleday Anchor Books; Garden City, Doubleday & Company Inc., 1954), p. 170.
[2] Bradley, *op. cit.*, p. 89.
[3] *Ibid.*, p. 90.
[4] *Ibid.*, p. 106.

14. A student of chemistry once described Hamlet as an isotope. Comment.

15. The play *Hamlet* has been described as "the tragedy of the unready will wasting itself". To what extent is this a valid comment on the character of Hamlet and the cause of his delay?

16. Hamlet is frequently referred to in the play as "noble". Find at least three examples of this adjective as applied to Hamlet and show what it adds to our concept of his character.

17. "Psychologically, the delay is the natural struggle of a sensitive, peace-loving soul against violence."[1] What are the weaknesses in this argument?

18. "A sceptic, Hamlet is preoccupied with his own personality" (Turgenev). Illustrate the ideas suggested by this comment.

Questions on Other Characters in the Play

1. "All the persons in *Hamlet* except the hero are minor characters."[2] Discuss the validity of this statement.

2. Show that Claudius is neither white nor black, but grey; in other words, illustrate his good and bad qualities.

3. "Claudius has a predilection for poison." Show how he made use of poison and how it affected his career.

4. How does the character of Macbeth resemble that of Claudius?

5. How likely is it that Gertrude was a party to the murder of her first husband?

6. How do you account for the fact that Gertrude inspired the devotion of Hamlet the Elder, Hamlet her son, and Claudius?

7. How does Gertrude serve to bring out the character of Hamlet?

[1] J. T. Shipley, *Guide to Great Plays* (Washington, Public Affairs Press, 1956).
[2] Bradley, *op cit.*

8. "To awaken Gertrude's sense of guilt is his [Hamlet's] fundamental need."[1] Why? How successful is Hamlet?
9. Give the dramatic importance of Polonius' role in the play.
10. Why does Hamlet find Polonius unbearable?
11. How does Laertes resemble Polonius?
12. How does the character of Laertes differ from that of Hamlet?
13. Show how Hamlet and Laertes differ in the way they secure revenge. How can this difference be explained?
14. a) What are the causes of Ophelia's madness?
    b) What are its results?
15. Discuss the lie told by Ophelia to Hamlet. To what extent was she justified in telling it?
16. Give reasons why the character of Ophelia rouses the pity of the audience.
17. a) What are the main points of contrast between Hamlet and Horatio?
    b) How are they alike?
18. How does Horatio show his friendship for Hamlet during the course of the play?
19. How does Fortinbras a) resemble and differ from Hamlet? b) resemble and differ from Laertes?
20. a) What is sycophancy?
    b) To what characters in the play does it apply?

A MULTIPLE CHOICE QUIZ

1. William Shakespeare was born in a) Bread Street, London; b) Henley Street, Stratford-on-Avon; c) Castle Street, Hereford;
   probably on a) May 18, 1600; b) December 11, 1592; c) April 23, 1564.

[1]E. M. W. Tillyard, *Shakespeare's Problem Plays* (Toronto, University of Toronto Press, 1949).

2. His father a) wrote English fluently; b) knew French and Italian; c) made his mark with a pair of glovers' compasses.

3. Shakespeare received his education at a) Eton; b) Winchester; c) Stratford Grammar School.
   He was familiar with the poetry of a) Horace; b) Vergil; c) Ovid.
   Tradition states that he left school at the age of a) 13; b) 16; c) 21.

4. In 1582, Shakespeare married a) Mary Arden; b) Anne Hathaway; c) Elizabeth Cecil;
   who was a) ten years younger than; b) the same age as; c) eight years older than, he was.

5. The Shakespeares had a) three; b) two; c) no, children and a) four; b) two; c) no, grandchildren.

6. Tradition also states that Shakespeare left Stratford in the late 1580's because he was accused of a) forgery; b) poaching; c) murder.

7. He is also said to have been in his early days a) a wool merchant; b) a fletcher; c) a schoolmaster in the country.

8. Still another legend has it that his first employment in London was a) selling papers; b) acting; c) holding the horses at the playhouse door.

9. In 1599, Shakespeare's father received a coat of arms, the motto of which was a) *Ich dien;* b) *Semper fidelis;* c) *Non sans droit.*

10. In 1597, Shakespeare purchased the largest house in Stratford, which was called a) New Place; b) Holmedon House; c) Sunninghill Park;
    for a) £100; b) £60; c) £500.

11. There is a legend that in the garden of this house Shakespeare a) wrote *Hamlet;* b) walked in the rain; c) planted a mulberry tree.

12. Shakespeare died on a) April 23, 1616; b) March 23, 1603; c) December 9, 1608.

He is buried in a) Westminster Abbey; b) Canterbury Cathedral; c) the chancel of Holy Trinity Church at Stratford.

13. His epitaph is a) Exit Shakespeare; b) Here lies one whose name is writ in water; c) Good friend for Jesus' sake forbear/To dig the dust enclosed here;/Blest be the man that spares these stones/And curs'd be he that moves my bones.

14. In an elaborate will, he left his wife a) his manuscripts; b) a house in Blackfriars; c) the second-best bed with the furniture.

15. Judging by references in his plays, Caroline Spurgeon deduces that Shakespeare's favourite sport was a) archery; b) tennis; c) bowling.

16. The only book we know to have been owned by Shakespeare (for it bears his signature) is a copy of a) North's translation of Plutarch; b) Florio's translation of Montaigne; c) Holinshed's *Chronicle*. (The signature may be a forgery.)

17. Altogether Shakespeare is now credited with a) 25; b) 18; c) 37, plays
and a) 50; b) 73; c) 154, sonnets
as well as a) 2; b) 3; c) 4, long poems.

18. Most of his plays were acted in a) the Globe; b) the Swan; c) the Rose, Theatre,
which was a) torn down; b) burned; c) destroyed by enemy action
in a) 1600; b) 1605; c) 1613.

19. Although a) a few; b) none; c) about half, of the plays appeared in quarto during his lifetime,
the collected edition or First Folio was not published until a) two years before his death; b) the year of his death; c) seven years after his death.

20. The longest of the plays is a) *Romeo and Juliet;* b) *Hamlet;* c) *Henry V.*

The shortest of the tragedies is a) *Othello;* b) *Macbeth;* c) *King Lear.*

21. Some critics believe that his last play was a) *Henry VIII;* b) *The Tempest;* c) *A Winter's Tale.* During a production of this play, the theatre burned down; there were no casualties, although "one man had his breeches set on fire"; however, this minor blaze was doused with a bottle of ale.

22. Some scholars, chiefly American, believe that an Elizabethan lawyer and statesman called a) Lamb; b) Bacon: c) Veau, wrote these plays.

23. The structure of a Shakespearian play is often compared to a) a circle; b) an isosceles triangle; c) a rectangle, and the prevailing metre is a) trochaic tetrameter; b) iambic pentameter; c) anapaestic hexameter.

ACKNOWLEDGEMENTS

The editor is grateful to the publishers who have permitted her to quote from the following works:

An Approach to Hamlet by L. C. Knights. Reprinted by permission of Chatto & Windus Ltd.

Form and Meaning in Drama by H. D. F. Kitto. Reprinted by permission of Methuen & Co. Ltd.

Guide to Great Plays by J. T. Shipley. Reprinted by permission of Public Affairs Press.

Hamlet, the New Shakespeare Edition ed. by J. Dover Wilson. Reprinted by permission of the Syndics of the Cambridge University Press.

Hamlet, the New Temple Edition ed. by M. R. Ridley. Reprinted by permission of J. M. Dent & Sons (Canada) Limited.

Hamlet, the Penguin Shakespeare Edition ed. by G. B. Harrison. Reprinted by permission of Penguin Books Ltd.

Hamlet, the Temple Shakespeare Edition ed. by Sir Israel Gollancz. Reprinted by permission of J. M. Dent & Sons (Canada) Ltd.

Hamlet and Oedipus by Ernest Jones. Reprinted by permission of Victor Gollancz, Ltd.

John Gielgud's Hamlet ed. by Rosamond Gilder. Reprinted by permission of Rosamond Gilder.

Prefaces to Shakespeare by H. Granville-Barker. Reprinted by permission of Princeton University Press.

The Question of Hamlet by Harry Levin. Reprinted by permission of Oxford University Press.

The Sacred Wood by T. S. Eliot. Reprinted by permission of Methuen & Co. Ltd.

Shakespeare by Mark Van Doren. Reprinted by permission of Holt, Rinehart and Winston, Inc.

Shakespeare and the Tragic Pattern by Kenneth Muir. Reprinted by permission of The British Academy.

A Shakespeare Glossary by C. T. Onions. Reprinted by permission of Oxford University Press.

Shakespearean Tragedy by A. C. Bradley. Reprinted by permission of Bedford College, University of London.

289

Shakespearian Tragedy by H. B. Charlton. Reprinted by permission of the Syndics of the Cambridge University Press.

Shakespeare's Problem Plays by E. M. W. Tillyard. Reprinted by permission of University of Toronto Press.

Shakespeare's Tragedies by G. B. Harrison. Reprinted by permission of Routledge & Kegan Paul Ltd.

What Happens in 'Hamlet' by J. Dover Wilson. Reprinted by permission of the Syndics of the Cambridge University Press.

Every step has been taken to make the list of acknowledgements comprehensive, but in one case at least, all efforts to trace the owners of copyright failed. It is hoped that any such omissions will be pardoned.

Richard Burbage
1567?-1619

Thomas Betterton
1635?-1710